Advance Praise for *Head First Data Analysis*

"It's about time a straightforward and comprehensive guide to analyzing data was written that makes learning the concepts simple and fun. It will change the way you think and approach problems using proven techniques and free tools. Concepts are good in theory and even better in practicality."

— **Anthony Rose, President, Support Analytics**

"*Head First Data Analysis* does a fantastic job of giving readers systematic methods to analyze real-world problems. From coffee, to rubber duckies, to asking for a raise, *Head First Data Analysis* shows the reader how to find and unlock the power of data in everyday life. Using everything from graphs and visual aides to computer programs like Excel and R, *Head First Data Analysis* gives readers at all levels accessible ways to understand how systematic data analysis can improve decision making both large and small."

— **Eric Heilman, Statistics teacher, Georgetown Preparatory School**

"Buried under mountains of data? Let Michael Milton be your guide as you fill your toolbox with the analytical skills that give you an edge. In *Head First Data Analysis*, you'll learn how to turn raw numbers into real knowledge. Put away your Ouija board and tarot cards; all you need to make good decisions is some software and a copy of this book."

— **Bill Mietelski, Software engineer**

Praise for other *Head First* books

"Kathy and Bert's *Head First Java* transforms the printed page into the closest thing to a GUI you've ever seen. In a wry, hip manner, the authors make learning Java an engaging 'what're they gonna do next?' experience."

—Warren Keuffel, Software Development Magazine

"Beyond the engaging style that drags you forward from know-nothing into exalted Java warrior status, *Head First Java* covers a huge amount of practical matters that other texts leave as the dreaded "exercise for the reader..." It's clever, wry, hip and practical—there aren't a lot of textbooks that can make that claim and live up to it while also teaching you about object serialization and network launch protocols."

—Dr. Dan Russell, Director of User Sciences and Experience Research
IBM Almaden Research Center (and teacher of Artificial Intelligence at
Stanford University)

"It's fast, irreverent, fun, and engaging. Be careful—you might actually learn something!"

—Ken Arnold, former Senior Engineer at Sun Microsystems
Coauthor (with James Gosling, creator of Java), *The Java Programming*
Language

"I feel like a thousand pounds of books have just been lifted off of my head."

—Ward Cunningham, inventor of the Wiki and founder of the Hillside Group

"Just the right tone for the geeked-out, casual-cool guru coder in all of us. The right reference for practical development strategies— gets my brain going without having to slog through a bunch of tired stale professor-speak."

—Travis Kalanick, Founder of Scour and Red Swoosh
Member of the MIT TR100

"There are books you buy, books you keep, books you keep on your desk, and thanks to O'Reilly and the *Head First* crew, there is the ultimate category, *Head First* books. They're the ones that are dog-eared, mangled, and carried everywhere. *Head First SQL* is at the top of my stack. Heck, even the PDF I have for review is tattered and torn."

— Bill Sawyer, ATG Curriculum Manager, Oracle

"This book's admirable clarity, humor and substantial doses of clever make it the sort of book that helps even non-programmers think well about problem-solving."

— Cory Doctorow, co-editor of BoingBoing
Author, *Down and Out in the Magic Kingdom*
and *Someone Comes to Town, Someone Leaves Town*

"I received the book yesterday and started to read it...and I couldn't stop. This is definitely très 'cool.' It is fun, but they cover a lot of ground and they are right to the point. I'm really impressed."

— **Erich Gamma, IBM Distinguished Engineer, and co-author of *Design Patterns***

"One of the funniest and smartest books on software design I've ever read."

— **Aaron LaBerge, VP Technology, ESPN.com**

"What used to be a long trial and error learning process has now been reduced neatly into an engaging paperback."

— **Mike Davidson, CEO, Newsvine, Inc.**

"Elegant design is at the core of every chapter here, each concept conveyed with equal doses of pragmatism and wit."

— **Ken Goldstein, Executive Vice President, Disney Online**

"I ♥ *Head First HTML with CSS & XHTML*—it teaches you everything you need to learn in a 'fun coated' format."

— **Sally Applin, UI Designer and Artist**

"Usually when reading through a book or article on design patterns, I'd have to occasionally stick myself in the eye with something just to make sure I was paying attention. Not with this book. Odd as it may sound, this book makes learning about design patterns fun.

"While other books on design patterns are saying 'Buehler... Buehler... Buehler...' this book is on the float belting out 'Shake it up, baby!'"

— **Eric Wuehler**

"I literally love this book. In fact, I kissed this book in front of my wife."

— **Satish Kumar**

Other related books from O'Reilly

Analyzing Business Data with Excel

Excel Scientific and Engineering Cookbook

Access Data Analysis Cookbook

Other books in O'Reilly's *Head First* series

Head First Java

Head First Object-Oriented Analysis and Design (OOA&D)

Head First HTML with CSS and XHTML

Head First Design Patterns

Head First Servlets and JSP

Head First EJB

Head First PMP

Head First SQL

Head First Software Development

Head First JavaScript

Head First Ajax

Head First Physics

Head First Statistics

Head First Rails

Head First PHP & MySQL

Head First Algebra

Head First Web Design

Head First Networking

Head First C#

Head First Data Analysis

Wouldn't it be dreamy if there was a book on data analysis that wasn't just a glorified printout of Microsoft Excel help files? But it's probably just a fantasy...

Michael Milton

Beijing · Cambridge · Farnham · Köln · Sebastopol · Tokyo

Head First Data Analysis

by Michael Milton

Printed in the United States of America.

Published by O'Reilly Media, Inc., 1005 Gravenstein Highway North, Sebastopol, CA 95472.

O'Reilly Media books may be purchased for educational, business, or sales promotional use. Online editions are also available for most titles (*safari.oreilly.com*). For more information, contact our corporate/institutional sales department: (800) 998-9938 or *corporate@oreilly.com*.

Series Creators:	Kathy Sierra, Bert Bates
Series Editor:	Brett D. McLaughlin
Editor:	Brian Sawyer
Cover Designers:	Karen Montgomery
Production Editor:	Scott DeLugan
Proofreader:	Nancy Reinhardt
Indexer:	Jay Harward
Page Viewers:	Mandarin, the fam, and Preston

Printing History:

July 2009: First Edition.

Mandarin

The fam

Preston

ISBN: 978-0-596-15393-9

[LSI]

Dedicated to the memory of my grandmother, Jane Reese Gibbs.

Author of Head First Data Analysis

Michael Milton

Michael Milton has spent most of his career helping nonprofit organizations improve their fundraising by interpreting and acting on the data they collect from their donors.

He has a degree in philosophy from New College of Florida and one in religious ethics from Yale University. He found reading *Head First* to be a revelation after spending years reading *boring* books filled with terribly important stuff and is grateful to have the opportunity to write an *exciting* book filled with terribly important stuff.

When he's not in the library or the bookstore, you can find him running, taking pictures, and brewing beer.

Table of Contents (Summary)

Table of Contents (the real thing)

Intro

Your brain on data analysis. Here *you* are trying to *learn* something, while here your *brain* is doing you a favor by making sure the learning doesn't *stick*. Your brain's thinking, "Better leave room for more important things, like which wild animals to avoid and whether naked snowboarding is a bad idea." So how *do* you trick your brain into thinking that your life depends on knowing data analysis?

introduction to data analysis

Break it down

1

Data is everywhere.

Nowadays, everyone has to deal with mounds of data, whether they call themselves "data analysts" or not. But people who possess a toolbox of data analysis skills have a **massive edge** on everyone else, because they understand what to *do* with all that stuff. They know how to translate raw numbers into intelligence that **drives real-world action**. They know how to **break down and structure** complex problems and data sets to get right to the heart of the problems in their business.

Define

Disassemble

Evaluate

Decide

experiments

Test your theories

Can you show what you believe?

In a real **empirical** test? There's nothing like a good experiment to solve your problems and show you the way the world really works. Instead of having to rely exclusively on your **observational data**, a well-executed experiment can often help you make **causal connections**. Strong empirical data will make your analytical judgments all the more powerful.

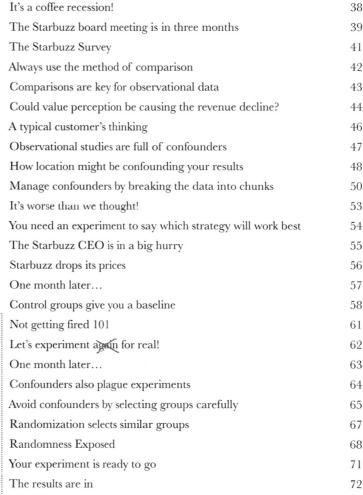

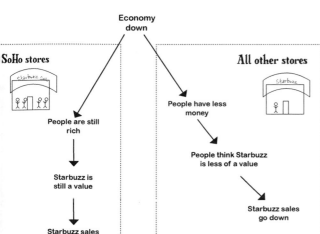

3

optimization

Take it to the max

We all want more of something.

And we're always trying to figure out how to get it. *If* the things we want more of—profit, money, efficiency, speed—can be represented numerically, then chances are, there's an tool of data analysis to help us tweak our *decision variables,* which will help us find the **solution** or *optimal point* where we get the most of what we want. In this chapter, you'll be using one of those tools and the powerful spreadsheet **Solver** package that implements it.

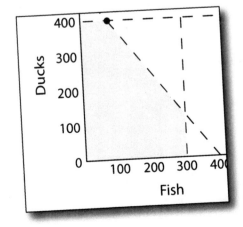

data visualization

Pictures make you smarter

You need more than a table of numbers.

Your data is brilliantly complex, with more variables than you can shake a stick at. Mulling over mounds and mounds of spreadsheets isn't just boring; it can actually be a waste of your time. A clear, highly multivariate visualization can, in a small space, show you the forest that you'd miss for the trees if you were just looking at spreadsheets all the time.

5

hypothesis testing
Say it ain't so

The world can be tricky to explain.

And it can be fiendishly difficult when you have to deal with complex, heterogeneous data to anticipate future events. This is why analysts don't just take the obvious explanations and assume them to be true: the careful reasoning of data analysis enables you to meticulously evaluate a bunch of options so that you can incorporate all the information you have into your models. You're about to learn about **falsification**, an unintuitive but powerful way to do just that.

bayesian statistics

Get past first base

You'll always be collecting new data.

And you need to make sure that every analysis you do incorporates the data you have that's relevant to your problem. You've learned how *falsification* can be used to deal with heterogeneous data sources, but what about **straight up probabilities**? The answer involves an extremely handy analytic tool called **Bayes' rule**, which will help you incorporate your **base rates** to uncover not-so-obvious insights with ever-changing data.

Cough

7

subjective probabilities

Numerical belief

Sometimes, it's a good idea to make up numbers.

Seriously. But only if those numbers describe your own mental states, expressing your beliefs. **Subjective probability** is a straightforward way of injecting some real *rigor* into your hunches, and you're about to see how. Along the way, you are going to learn how to evaluate the spread of data using **standard deviation** and enjoy a special guest appearance from one of the more powerful analytic tools you've learned.

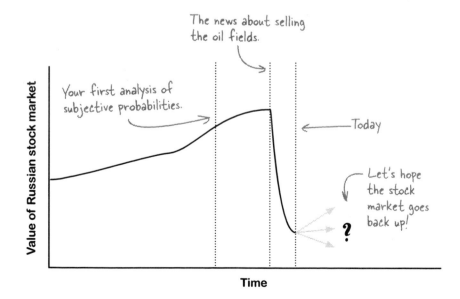

heuristics

8

Analyze like a human

The real world has more variables than you can handle.

There is always going to be data that you can't have. And even when you do have data on most of the things you want to understand, *optimizing* methods are often **elusive** and **time consuming**. Fortunately, most of the actual thinking you do in life is not "rational maximizing"—it's processing incomplete and uncertain information with rules of thumb so that you can make decisions quickly. What is really cool is that these rules can **actually work** and are important (and necessary) tools for data analysts.

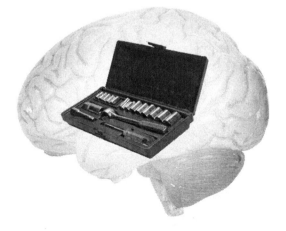

histograms

The shape of numbers

9

How much can a bar graph tell you?

There are about a zillion ways of **showing data with pictures**, but one of them is special. **Histograms**, which are kind of similar to bar graphs, are a super-fast and easy way to summarize data. You're about to use these powerful little charts to measure your data's **spread, variability, central tendency**, and more. No matter how large your data set is, if you draw a histogram with it, you'll be able to "see" what's happening inside of it. And you're about to do it with a new, free, crazy-powerful **software tool**.

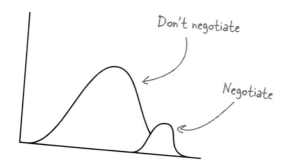

Don't negotiate

Negotiate

regression

Prediction

10

Predict it.

Regression is an incredibly powerful statistical tool that, when used correctly, has the ability to help you predict certain values. When used with a controlled experiment, regression can actually help you predict the future. Businesses use it like crazy to help them build models to explain customer behavior. You're about to see that the judicious use of regression can be very profitable indeed.

Request

THE RAISE RECKONER

What will happen if we request a certain amount of money? Find out with this equation:

$$y=2.3+0.7x$$

Where x is the amount requested, and y is the amount we can expect to receive.

Raise

error

Err well

The world is messy.

So it should be no surprise that your predictions rarely hit the target squarely. But if you offer a prediction with an **error range**, you and your clients will know not only the average predicted value, but also how far you expect typical deviations from that error to be. Every time you express error, you offer a much richer perspective on your predictions and beliefs. And with the tools in this chapter, you'll also learn about how to get error under control, getting it as low as possible to increase confidence.

11

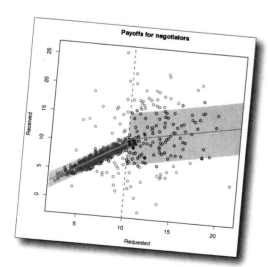

12

relational databases

Can you relate?

How do you structure really, really multivariate data?

A spreadsheet has only *two dimensions*: rows and columns. And if you have a bunch of dimensions of data, the **tabular format** gets old really quickly. In this chapter, you're about to see firsthand where spreadsheets make it really hard to manage multivariate data and learn **how relational database management systems** make it easy to store and retrieve countless permutations of multivariate data.

cleaning data

Impose order

Your data is useless...

...if it has messy structure. And a lot of people who *collect* data do a crummy job of maintaining a neat structure. If your data's not neat, you can't slice it or dice it, run formulas on it, or even really *see* it. You might as well just ignore it completely, right? Actually, you can do better. With a **clear vision** of how you need it to look and a few **text manipulation tools**, you can take the funkiest, craziest mess of data and **whip** it into something useful.

13

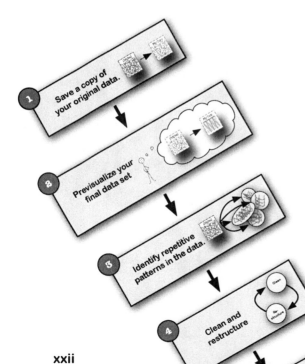

1. Save a copy of your original data.

2. Previsualize your final data set

3. Identify repetitive patterns in the data.

4. Clean and restructure

5. Use your finished data

leftovers

The Top Ten Things (we didn't cover)

You've come a long way.

But data analysis is a vast and constantly evolving field, and there's so much left to learn. In this appendix, we'll go over ten items that there wasn't enough room to cover in this book but should be high on your list of topics to learn about next.

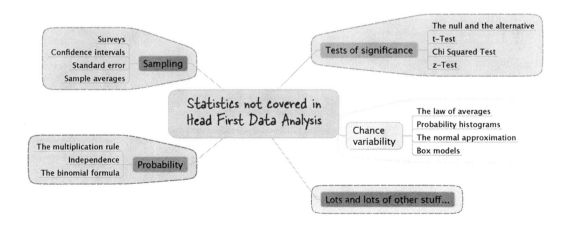

install r

Start R up!

Behind all that data-crunching power is enormous complexity.

But fortunately, getting R installed and *started* is something you can accomplish in just a few minutes, and this appendix is about to show you how to pull off your R install without a hitch.

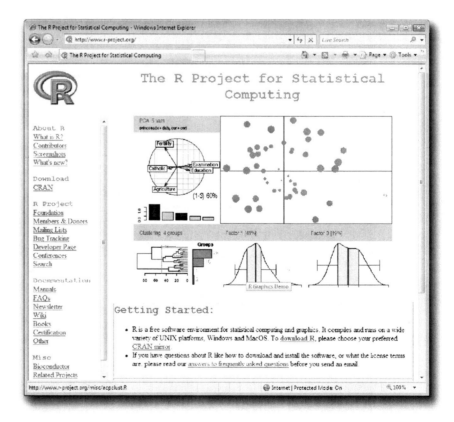

install excel analysis tools

The ToolPak

Some of the best features of Excel aren't installed by default.

That's right, in order to run the optimization from Chapter 3 and the histograms from Chapter 9, you need to activate the **Solver** and the **Analysis ToolPak**, two extensions that are included in Excel by default but not activated without your initiative.

how to use this book

Intro

In this section we answer the burning question:
"So why DID they put that in a data analysis book?"

Who is this book for?

If you can answer "yes" to all of these:

1 Do you feel like there's a world of insights buried in your data that you'd only be able to access if you had the right tools?

2 Do you want to learn, understand, and remember how to create brilliant graphics, test hypotheses, run a regression, or clean up messy data?

3 Do you prefer stimulating dinner party conversation to dry, dull, academic lectures?

this book is for you.

Who should probably back away from this book?

If you can answer "yes" to any of these:

1 Are you a seasoned, brilliant data analyst looking for a survey of bleeding edge data topics?

2 Have you never loaded and used Microsoft Excel or OpenOffice calc?

3 Are you afraid to try something different? Would you rather have a root canal than mix stripes with plaid? Do you believe that a technical book can't be serious if it anthropomorphizes control groups and objective functions?

this book is **not** for you.

[Note from marketing: this book is for anyone with a credit card.]

We know what you're thinking

"How can *this* be a serious data analysis book?"

"What's with all the graphics?"

"Can I actually *learn* it this way?"

We know what your *brain* is thinking

Your brain craves novelty. It's always searching, scanning, *waiting* for something unusual. It was built that way, and it helps you stay alive.

So what does your brain do with all the routine, ordinary, normal things you encounter? Everything it *can* to stop them from interfering with the brain's *real* job—recording things that *matter*. It doesn't bother saving the boring things; they never make it past the "this is obviously not important" filter.

How does your brain *know* what's important? Suppose you're out for a day hike and a tiger jumps in front of you, what happens inside your head and body?

Neurons fire. Emotions crank up. *Chemicals surge.*

And that's how your brain knows...

This must be important! Don't forget it!

But imagine you're at home, or in a library. It's a safe, warm, tiger-free zone. You're studying. Getting ready for an exam. Or trying to learn some tough technical topic your boss thinks will take a week, ten days at the most.

Just one problem. Your brain's trying to do you a big favor. It's trying to make sure that this *obviously* non-important content doesn't clutter up scarce resources. Resources that are better spent storing the really *big* things. Like tigers. Like the danger of fire. Like how you should never have posted those "party" photos on your Facebook page. And there's no simple way to tell your brain, "Hey brain, thank you very much, but no matter how dull this book is, and how little I'm registering on the emotional Richter scale right now, I really *do* want you to keep this stuff around."

Your brain thinks THIS is important.

Great. Only 488 more dull, dry, boring pages.

Your brain thinks THIS isn't worth saving.

We think of a "Head First" reader as a learner.

So what does it take to *learn* something? First, you have to *get* it, then make sure you don't *forget* it. It's not about pushing facts into your head. Based on the latest research in cognitive science, neurobiology, and educational psychology, *learning* takes a lot more than text on a page. We know what turns your brain on.

Some of the *Head First* learning principles:

Make it visual. Images are far more memorable than words alone, and make learning much more effective (up to 89 percent improvement in recall and transfer studies). It also makes things more understandable. **Put the words within or near the graphics** they relate to, rather than on the bottom or on another page, and learners will be up to *twice* as likely to solve problems related to the content.

Use a conversational and personalized style. In recent studies, students performed up to 40 percent better on post-learning tests if the content spoke directly to the reader, using a first-person, conversational style rather than taking a formal tone. Tell stories instead of lecturing. Use casual language. Don't take yourself too seriously. Which would *you* pay more attention to: a stimulating dinner party companion, or a lecture?

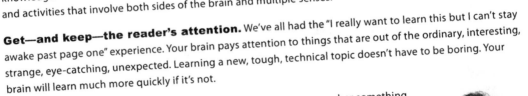

Get the learner to think more deeply. In other words, unless you actively flex your neurons, nothing much happens in your head. A reader has to be motivated, engaged, curious, and inspired to solve problems, draw conclusions, and generate new knowledge. And for that, you need challenges, exercises, and thought-provoking questions, and activities that involve both sides of the brain and multiple senses.

Get—and keep—the reader's attention. We've all had the "I really want to learn this but I can't stay awake past page one" experience. Your brain pays attention to things that are out of the ordinary, interesting, strange, eye-catching, unexpected. Learning a new, tough, technical topic doesn't have to be boring. Your brain will learn much more quickly if it's not.

Touch their emotions. We now know that your ability to remember something is largely dependent on its emotional content. You remember what you care about. You remember when you *feel* something. No, we're not talking heart-wrenching stories about a boy and his dog. We're talking emotions like surprise, curiosity, fun, "what the...?", and the feeling of "I Rule!" that comes when you solve a puzzle, learn something everybody else thinks is hard, or realize you know something that "I'm more technical than thou" Bob from engineering *doesn't*.

Metacognition: thinking about thinking

If you really want to learn, and you want to learn more quickly and more deeply, pay attention to how you pay attention. Think about how you think. Learn how you learn.

Most of us did not take courses on metacognition or learning theory when we were growing up. We were *expected* to learn, but rarely *taught* to learn.

I wonder how I can trick my brain into remembering this stuff...

But we assume that if you're holding this book, you really want to learn data analysis. And you probably don't want to spend a lot of time. If you want to use what you read in this book, you need to *remember* what you read. And for that, you've got to *understand* it. To get the most from this book, or *any* book or learning experience, take responsibility for your brain. Your brain on *this* content.

The trick is to get your brain to see the new material you're learning as Really Important. Crucial to your well-being. As important as a tiger. Otherwise, you're in for a constant battle, with your brain doing its best to keep the new content from sticking.

So just how *DO* you get your brain to treat data analysis like it was a hungry tiger?

There's the slow, tedious way, or the faster, more effective way. The slow way is about sheer repetition. You obviously know that you *are* able to learn and remember even the dullest of topics if you keep pounding the same thing into your brain. With enough repetition, your brain says, "This doesn't *feel* important to him, but he keeps looking at the same thing *over* and *over* and *over*, so I suppose it must be."

The faster way is to do ***anything that increases brain activity,*** especially different *types* of brain activity. The things on the previous page are a big part of the solution, and they're all things that have been proven to help your brain work in your favor. For example, studies show that putting words *within* the pictures they describe (as opposed to somewhere else in the page, like a caption or in the body text) causes your brain to try to makes sense of how the words and picture relate, and this causes more neurons to fire. More neurons firing = more chances for your brain to *get* that this is something worth paying attention to, and possibly recording.

A conversational style helps because people tend to pay more attention when they perceive that they're in a conversation, since they're expected to follow along and hold up their end. The amazing thing is, your brain doesn't necessarily *care* that the "conversation" is between you and a book! On the other hand, if the writing style is formal and dry, your brain perceives it the same way you experience being lectured to while sitting in a roomful of passive attendees. No need to stay awake.

But pictures and conversational style are just the beginning…

Here's what WE did:

We used ***pictures***, because your brain is tuned for visuals, not text. As far as your brain's concerned, a picture really *is* worth a thousand words. And when text and pictures work together, we embedded the text *in* the pictures because your brain works more effectively when the text is *within* the thing the text refers to, as opposed to in a caption or buried in the text somewhere.

We used ***redundancy***, saying the same thing in *different* ways and with different media types, and *multiple senses*, to increase the chance that the content gets coded into more than one area of your brain.

We used concepts and pictures in ***unexpected*** ways because your brain is tuned for novelty, and we used pictures and ideas with at least *some **emotional** content*, because your brain is tuned to pay attention to the biochemistry of emotions. That which causes you to *feel* something is more likely to be remembered, even if that feeling is nothing more than a little ***humor***, ***surprise***, or ***interest.***

We used a personalized, ***conversational style***, because your brain is tuned to pay more attention when it believes you're in a conversation than if it thinks you're passively listening to a presentation. Your brain does this even when you're *reading*.

We included more than 80 ***activities***, because your brain is tuned to learn and remember more when you ***do*** things than when you *read* about things. And we made the exercises challenging-yet-do-able, because that's what most people prefer.

We used ***multiple learning styles***, because *you* might prefer step-by-step procedures, while someone else wants to understand the big picture first, and someone else just wants to see an example. But regardless of your own learning preference, *everyone* benefits from seeing the same content represented in multiple ways.

We include content for ***both sides of your brain***, because the more of your brain you engage, the more likely you are to learn and remember, and the longer you can stay focused. Since working one side of the brain often means giving the other side a chance to rest, you can be more productive at learning for a longer period of time.

And we included ***stories*** and exercises that present ***more than one point of view,*** because your brain is tuned to learn more deeply when it's forced to make evaluations and judgments.

We included ***challenges***, with exercises, and by asking ***questions*** that don't always have a straight answer, because your brain is tuned to learn and remember when it has to *work* at something. Think about it—you can't get your *body* in shape just by *watching* people at the gym. But we did our best to make sure that when you're working hard, it's on the *right* things. That ***you're not spending one extra dendrite*** processing a hard-to-understand example, or parsing difficult, jargon-laden, or overly terse text.

We used ***people***. In stories, examples, pictures, etc., because, well, because *you're* a person. And your brain pays more attention to *people* than it does to *things*.

Cut this out and stick it on your refrigerator.

Here's what YOU can do to bend your brain into submission

So, we did our part. The rest is up to you. These tips are a starting point; listen to your brain and figure out what works for you and what doesn't. Try new things.

① Slow down. The more you understand, the less you have to memorize.

Don't just *read*. Stop and think. When the book asks you a question, don't just skip to the answer. Imagine that someone really *is* asking the question. The more deeply you force your brain to think, the better chance you have of learning and remembering.

② Do the exercises. Write your own notes.

We put them in, but if we did them for you, that would be like having someone else do your workouts for you. And don't just *look* at the exercises. **Use a pencil.** There's plenty of evidence that physical activity *while* learning can increase the learning.

③ Read the "There are No Dumb Questions"

That means all of them. They're not optional sidebars, ***they're part of the core content!*** Don't skip them.

④ Make this the last thing you read before bed. Or at least the last challenging thing.

Part of the learning (especially the transfer to long-term memory) happens *after* you put the book down. Your brain needs time on its own, to do more processing. If you put in something new during that processing time, some of what you just learned will be lost.

⑤ Talk about it. Out loud.

Speaking activates a different part of the brain. If you're trying to understand something, or increase your chance of remembering it later, say it out loud. Better still, try to explain it out loud to someone else. You'll learn more quickly, and you might uncover ideas you hadn't known were there when you were reading about it.

⑥ Drink water. Lots of it.

Your brain works best in a nice bath of fluid. Dehydration (which can happen before you ever feel thirsty) decreases cognitive function.

⑦ Listen to your brain.

Pay attention to whether your brain is getting overloaded. If you find yourself starting to skim the surface or forget what you just read, it's time for a break. Once you go past a certain point, you won't learn faster by trying to shove more in, and you might even hurt the process.

⑧ Feel something.

Your brain needs to know that this *matters*. Get involved with the stories. Make up your own captions for the photos. Groaning over a bad joke is *still* better than feeling nothing at all.

⑨ Get your hands dirty!

There's only one way to learn data analysis: get your hands dirty. And that's what you're going to do throughout this book. Data analysis is a skill, and the only way to get good at it is to practice. We're going to give you a lot of practice: every chapter has exercises that pose a problem for you to solve. Don't just skip over them—a lot of the learning happens when you solve the exercises. We included a solution to each exercise—don't be afraid to peek at the solution if you get stuck! (It's easy to get snagged on something small.) But try to solve the problem before you look at the solution. And definitely get it working before you move on to the next part of the book.

Read Me

This is a learning experience, not a reference book. We deliberately stripped out everything that might get in the way of learning whatever it is we're working on at that point in the book. And the first time through, you need to begin at the beginning, because the book makes assumptions about what you've already seen and learned.

This book is not about software tools.

Many books with "data analysis" in their titles simply go down the list of Excel functions considered to be related to data analysis and show you a few examples of each. *Head First Data Analysis*, on the other hand, is about how to **be a data analyst**. You'll learn quite a bit about software tools in this book, but they are only a means to the end of learning how to do good data analysis.

We expect you to know how to use *basic* spreadsheet formulas.

Have you ever used the SUM formula in a spreadsheet? If not, you may want to bone up on spreadsheets a little before beginning this book. While many chapters do not ask you to use spreadsheets at all, the ones that do assume that you know how to use formulas. If you are familiar with the SUM formula, then you're in good shape.

This book is about more than statistics.

There's plenty of statistics in this book, and as a data analyst you should learn as much statistics as you can. Once you're finished with *Head First Data Analysis*, it'd be a good idea to read *Head First Statistics* as well. But "data analysis" encompasses statistics and a number of other fields, and the many non-statistical topics chosen for this book are focused on the practical, nitty-gritty experience of doing data analysis in the real world.

The activities are NOT optional.

The exercises and activities are not add-ons; they're part of the core content of the book. Some of them are to help with memory, some are for understanding, and some will help you apply what you've learned. ***Don't skip the exercises.***

The redundancy is intentional and important.

One distinct difference in a *Head First* book is that we want you to *really* get it. And we want you to finish the book remembering what you've learned. Most reference books don't have retention and recall as a goal, but this book is about *learning*, so you'll see some of the same concepts come up more than once.

The book doesn't end here.

We love it when you can find fun and useful extra stuff on book companion sites. You'll find extra stuff on data analysis at the following url:
http://www.headfirstlabs.com/books/hfda/.

The Brain Power exercises don't have answers.

For some of them, there is no right answer, and for others, part of the learning experience of the Brain Power activities is for you to decide if and when your answers are right. In some of the Brain Power exercises, you will find hints to point you in the right direction.

The technical review team

Eric Heilman

Tony Rose

Bill Mietelski

Technical Reviewers:

Eric Heilman graduated Phi Beta Kappa from the Walsh School of Foreign Service at Georgetown University with a degree in International Economics. During his time as an undergraduate in DC, he worked at the State Department and at the National Economic Council at the White House. He completed his graduate work in economics at the University of Chicago. He currently teaches statistical analysis and math at Georgetown Preparatory School in Bethesda, MD.

Bill Mietelski is a Software Engineer and a three-time *Head First* technical reviewer. He can't wait to run a data analysis on his golf stats to help him win on the links.

Anthony Rose has been working in the data analysis field for nearly ten years and is currently the president of Support Analytics, a data analysis and visualization consultancy. Anthony has an MBA concentrated in Management and Finance degree, which is where his passion for data and analysis started. When he isn't working, he can normally be found on the golf course in Columbia, Maryland, lost in a good book, savoring a delightful wine, or simply enjoying time with his young girls and amazing wife.

Acknowledgments

My editor:

Brian Sawyer has been an incredible editor. Working with Brian is like dancing with a professional ballroom dancer. All sorts of important stuff is happening that you don't really understand, but you look great, and you're having a blast. Ours has been a exciting collaboration, and his support, feedback, and ideas have been invaluable.

The O'Reilly Team:

Brett McLaughlin saw the vision for this project from the beginning, shepherded it through tough times, and has been a constant support. Brett's implacable focus on *your* experience with the *Head First* books is an inspiration. He is the man with the plan.

Karen Shaner provided logistical support and a good bit of cheer on some cold Cambridge mornings. **Brittany Smith** contributed some cool graphic elements that we used over and over.

Really smart people whose ideas are remixed in this book:

While many of the big ideas taught in this book are unconventional for books with "data analysis" in the title, few of them are uniquely my own. I drew heavily from the writings of these intellectual superstars: Dietrich Doerner, Gerd Gigerenzer, Richards Heuer, and Edward Tufte. Read them all! The idea of the anti-resume comes from Nassim Taleb's *The Black Swan* (if there's a Volume 2, expect to see more of his ideas). **Richards Heuer** kindly corresponded with me about the book and gave me a number of useful ideas.

Friends and colleagues:

Lou Barr's intellectual, moral, logistical, and aesthetic support of this book is much appreciated. **Vezen Wu** taught me the relational model. **Aron Edidin** sponsored an awesome tutorial for me on intelligence analysis when I was an undergraduate. My poker group—**Paul**, **Brewster**, **Matt**, **Jon**, and **Jason**—has given me an expensive education in the balance of heuristic and optimizing decision frameworks.

People I couldn't live without:

The **technical review team** did a brilliant job, caught loads of errors, made a bunch of good suggestions, and were tremendously supportive.

As I wrote this book, I leaned heavily on my friend **Blair Christian**, who is a statistician and deep thinker. His influence can be found on every page. Thank you for everything, Blair.

My family, **Michael Sr.**, **Elizabeth**, **Sara**, **Gary**, and **Marie**, have been tremendously supportive. Above all, I appreciate the steadfast support of my wife **Julia**, who means everything. Thank you all!

Brian Sawyer

Brett McLaughlin

Blair and Niko Christian

Julia Burch

Safari® Books Online

 When you see a Safari® icon on the cover of your favorite technology book that means the book is available online through the O'Reilly Network Safari Bookshelf.

Safari offers a solution that's better than e-books. It's a virtual library that lets you easily search thousands of top tech books, cut and paste code samples, download chapters, and find quick answers when you need the most accurate, current information. Try it for free at *http://my.safaribooksonline.com/?portal=oreilly*.

1 introduction to data analysis

Break it down

I detect ginger, garlic, paprika, and perhaps a hint of fish sauce...

Data is everywhere.

Nowadays, everyone has to deal with mounds of data, whether they call themselves "data analysts" or not. But people who possess a toolbox of data analysis skills have a **massive edge** on everyone else, because they understand what to *do* with all that stuff. They know how to translate raw numbers into intelligence that **drives real-world action**. They know how to **break down and structure** complex problems and data sets to get right to the heart of the problems in their business.

Acme Cosmetics needs your help

It's your first day on the job as a data analyst, and you were just sent this sales data from the CEO to review. The data describes sales of Acme's flagship moisturizer, MoisturePlus.

What has been happening during the last six months with sales?

How do their gross sales figures compare to their target sales figures?

	September	October	November	December	January	February
Gross sales	$5,280,000	$5,501,000	$5,469,000	$5,480,000	$5,533,000	$5,554,000
Target sales	$5,280,000	$5,500,000	$5,729,000	$5,968,000	$6,217,000	$6,476,000
Ad costs	$1,056,000	$950,400	$739,200	$528,000	$316,800	$316,800
Social network costs	$0	$105,600	$316,800	$528,000	$739,200	$739,200
Unit prices (per oz.)	$2.00	$2.00	$2.00	$1.90	$1.90	$1.90

Do you see a pattern in Acme's expenses?

What do you think is going on with these unit prices? Why are they going down?

Take a look at the data. It's fine not to know everything—just **slow down** and take a look.

What do you see? How much does the table tell you about Acme's business? About Acme's MoisturePlus moisturizer?

Good data analysts always want to <u>see</u> the data.

The CEO wants data analysis to help increase sales

He wants you to **"give him an analysis."**

It's kind of a *vague* request, isn't it? It sounds simple, but will your job be that straightforward? Sure, he wants more sales. Sure, he thinks something in the data will help accomplish that goal. But what, and how?

Here's the CEO.

Welcome to the team. Take a look at our data and give me an analysis to help us figure out how to increase sales. Looking forward to your conclusions.

Now what could he mean by this?

BRAIN POWER

Think about what, fundamentally, the CEO is looking for from you with this question. When you analyze data, what are you doing?

Data analysis is careful thinking about evidence

The expression "data analysis" covers a lot of different activities and a lot of different skills. If someone tells you that she's a data analyst, you still won't know much about what *specifically* she knows or does.

You might bet that she knows Excel, but that's about it!

But all good analysts, regardless of their skills or goals, go through this **same basic process** during the course of their work, always using empirical evidence to think carefully about problems.

Define your problem.

Here's the meat of the analysis, where you draw your conclusions about what you've learned in the first two steps.

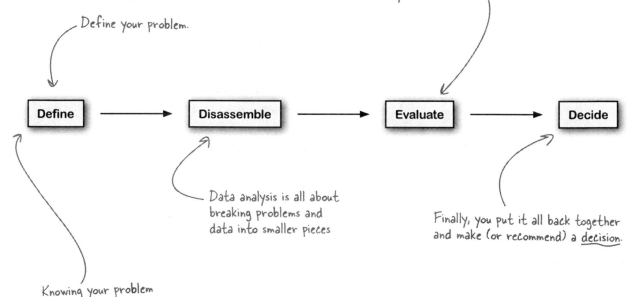

Data analysis is all about breaking problems and data into smaller pieces

Finally, you put it all back together and make (or recommend) a <u>decision</u>.

Knowing your problem is the <u>very first step</u>.

In every chapter of this book, you'll go through these steps over and over again, and they'll become second nature really quickly.

Ultimately, all data analysis is designed to lead to **better decisions**, and you're about to learn how to make better decisions by gleaning insights from a sea of data.

Define the problem

Doing data analysis without **explicitly** defining your problem or goal is like heading out on a road trip without having decided on a destination.

Sure, you might come across some interesting sights, and sometimes you might *want* to wander around in the hopes you'll stumble on something cool, but **who's to say you'll find anything?**

Map

Road trip with a destination.

Map

Road trip without a destination.

Mission accomplished!

Who knows where you'll end up?

Here's a gigantic analytical report.

See the similarity?

Ever seen an "analytical report" that's a **million pages long**, with tons and tons of charts and diagrams?

Every once in a while, an analyst really does need a ream of paper or an hour-long slide show to make a point. But in this sort of case, the analyst often **hasn't focused** enough on his problem and is pelting you with information as a way of ducking his obligation to **solve a problem** and **recommend a decision**.

Sometimes, the situation is even worse: the problem isn't defined at all and the analyst doesn't want you to realize that he's just wandering around in the data.

How do you define your problem?

Your client will help you define your problem

He is the person your analysis is meant to serve. Your client might be your boss, your company's CEO, or even yourself.

Your client is the person who will make decisions on the basis of your analysis. You need to get as much information as you can from him to **define your problem**.

The CEO here wants more sales. But that's only the beginning of an answer. You need to understand more specifically what he means in order to craft an analysis that solves the problem.

> There's a bonus in it for you if you can figure out how to increase MoisturePlus sales.

This is your client, the guy you're working for.

CEO of Acme Cosmetics

It's a really good idea to know your client as well as you can.

 BULLET POINTS

Your client might be:

- well or badly informed about his data
- well or badly informed about his problems or goals

- well or badly informed about his business
- focused or indecisive
- clear or vague
- intuitive or analytic

Keep an eye at the bottom of the page during this chapter for these cues, which show you where you are.

The better you understand your client, the more likely your analysis will be able to help.

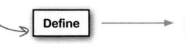
Define → Disassemble → Evaluate → Decide

there are no
Dumb Questions

Q: I always like wandering around in data. Do you mean that I need to have some specific goal in mind before I even look at my data?

A: You don't need to have a problem in mind just to look at data. But keep in mind that *looking* by itself is not yet data analysis. Data analysis is all about identifying problems and then solving them.

Q: I've heard about "exploratory data analysis," where you explore the data for ideas you might want to evaluate further. There's no problem definition in that sort of data analysis!

A: Sure there is. Your problem in exploratory data analysis is to find hypotheses worth testing. That's totally a concrete problem to solve.

Q: Fine. Tell me more about these clients who aren't well informed about their problems. Does that kind of person even need a data analyst?

A: Of course!

Q: Sounds to me like that kind of person needs professional help.

A: Actually, good data analysts help their clients think through their problem; they don't just wait around for their clients to tell them what to do. Your clients will really appreciate it if you can show them that they have problems they didn't even know about.

Q: That sounds silly. Who wants more problems?

A: People who hire data analysts recognize that people with analytical skills have the ability to improve their businesses. Some people see problems as opportunities, and data analysts who show their clients how to exploit opportunity give them a competitive advantage.

Sharpen your pencil

The general problem is that we need to increase sales. What questions would you ask the CEO to understand better what he means specifically? List five.

1. ....

2. ....

3. ....

4. ....

5. ....

Acme's CEO has some feedback for you

Your questions might be different.

This email just came through in response to your questions. Lots of intelligence here...

Here are some sample questions to get the CEO to define your analytical goals.

From: CEO, Acme Cosmetics
To: Head First
Subject: Re: Define the problem

By how much do you want to increase sales?

> I need to get it back in line with our target sales, which you can see on the table. All our budgeting is built around those targets, and we'll be in trouble if we miss them.

How do you think we'll do it?

> Well, that's your job to figure out. But the strategy is going to involve getting people to buy more, and by "people" I mean tween girls (age 11–15). You're going to get sales up with marketing of some sort or another. You're the data person. Figure it out!

Always ask "how much." Make your goals and beliefs quantitative.

How much of a sales increase do you think is feasible? Are the target sales figures reasonable?

> These tween girls have deep pockets. Babysitting money, parents, and so on. I don't think there's any limit to what we can make off of selling them MoisturePlus.

Anticipate what your client thinks about. He's definitely going to be concerned with competitors.

How are our competitors' sales?

> I don't have any hard numbers, but my impression is that they are going to leave us in the dust. I'd say they're 50–100 percent ahead of us in terms of gross moisturizer revenue.

What's the deal with the ads and the social networking marketing budget?

See something curious in the numbers? Ask about it!

> We're trying something new. The total budget is 20 percent of our first month's revenue. All of that used to go to ads, but we're shifting it over to social networking. I shudder to think what'd be happening if we'd kept ads at the same level.

Define → Disassemble → Evaluate → Decide

Break the problem and data into smaller pieces

The next step in data analysis is to take what you've learned about your problem from your client, along with your data, and break that information down into the level of **granularity** that will best serve your analysis.

Divide the problem into smaller problems

You need to divide your problem into **manageable, solvable chunks**. Often, your problem will be **vague**, like this:

"How do we increase sales?"

→ "What do our best customers want from us?"
→ "What promotions are most likely to work?"
→ "How is our advertising doing?"

You can't answer the big problem directly. But by answering the smaller problems, which you've **analyzed** out of the big problem, you can get your answer to the big one.

Answer the smaller problems to solve the bigger one.

Divide the data into smaller chunks

Same deal with the data. People aren't going to present you the precise quantitative answers you need; you'll need to extract important elements on your own.

If the data you receive is a **summary**, like what you've received from Acme, you'll want to know which elements are most important to you.

If your data comes in a **raw** form, you'll want to summarize the elements to make that data more useful.

	September	October	November	December	January	February
Gross sales	$5,280,000	$5,501,000	$5,469,000	$5,480,000	$5,533,000	$5,554,000
Target sales	$5,280,000	$5,500,000	$5,729,000	$5,968,000	$6,217,000	$6,476,000
Ad costs	$1,056,000	$950,400	$739,200	$528,000	$316,800	$316,800
Social network costs	$0	$105,600	$316,800	$528,000	$739,200	$739,200
Unit prices (per oz.)	$2.00	$2.00	$2.00	$1.90	$1.90	$1.90

December Target Sales $5,968,000

November Unit Prices $2.00

These might be the chunks you need to watch.

More on these buzzwords in a moment!

Let's give disassembling a shot...

Now take another look at what you know

Let's start with the data. Here you have a summary of Acme's sales data, and the best way to start trying to isolate the most important elements of it is to find strong **comparisons**.

Break down your summary data by searching for interesting comparisons.

How do January's gross sales compare to February's?

How do the gross and target sales figures compare to each other for October?

	September	October	November	December	January	February
Gross sales	$5,280,000	$5,501,000	$5,469,000	$5,480,000	$5,533,000	$5,554,000
Target sales	$5,280,000	$5,500,000	$5,729,000	$5,968,000	$6,217,000	$6,476,000
Ad costs	$1,056,000	$950,400	$739,200	$528,000	$316,800	$316,800
Social network costs	$0	$105,600	$316,800	$528,000	$739,200	$739,200
Unit prices (per oz.)	$2.00	$2.00	$2.00	$1.90	$1.90	$1.90

How are ad and social network costs changing relative to each other over time?

Does the decrease in unit prices coincide with any change in gross sales?

Making good comparisons is at the core of data analysis, and you'll be doing it throughout this book.

In this case, you want to **build a conception in your mind** of how Acme's MoisturePlus business works by comparing their summary statistics.

Define → **Disassemble** → Evaluate → Decide

You've defined the problem: ***figure out how to increase sales***. But that problem tells you very little about *how* you're expected to do it, so you elicited a lot of useful commentary from the CEO.

Here's the "how" question.

This commentary provides an important **baseline set of assumptions** about how the cosmetics business works. Hopefully, the CEO is right about those assumptions, because they will be the **backbone** of your analysis! What *are* the most important points that the CEO makes?

This commentary is itself a kind of data. Which parts of it are most important?

What's most useful?

> **From: CEO, Acme Cosmetics**
> **To: Head First**
> **Subject: Re: Define the problem**
>
> **By how much do you want to increase sales?**
>
> I need to get it back in line with our target sales, which you can see on the table. All our budgeting is built around those targets, and we'll be in trouble if we miss them.
>
> **How do you think we'll do it?**
>
> Well, that's your job to figure out. But the strategy is going to involve getting people to buy more, and by "people" I mean tween girls (age 11–15). You're going to get sales up with marketing of some sort or another. You're the data person. Figure it out!
>
> **How much of a sales increase do you think is feasible? Are the target sales figures reasonable?**
>
> These tween girls have deep pockets. Babysitting money, parents, and so on. I don't think there's any limit to what we can make off of selling them MoisturePlus.
>
> **How are our competitors' sales?**
>
> I don't have any hard numbers, but my impression is that they are going to leave us in the dust. I'd say they're 50–100 percent ahead of us in terms of gross moisturizer revenue.
>
> **What's the deal with the ads and the social networking marketing budget?**
>
> We're trying something new. The total budget is 20 percent of our first month's revenue. All of that used to go to ads, but we're shifting it over to social networking. I shudder to think what'd be happening if we'd kept ads at the same level.

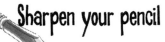

Sharpen your pencil

Summarize what your client believes and your thoughts on the data you've received to do the analysis. ***Analyze*** the above email and your data into smaller pieces that describe your situation.

Your client's beliefs.

1 ....

2 ....

3 ....

4 ....

Your thoughts on the data.

1 ....

2 ....

3 ....

4 ....

Sharpen your pencil
Solution

You just took an inventory of your and your client's beliefs. What did you find?

Your client's beliefs.

Your own answers might be slightly different.

① MoisturePlus customers are tween girls (where tweens are people aged 11–15). They're basically the only customer group.

② Acme is trying out reallocating expenses from advertisements to social networking, but so far, the success of the initiative is unknown.

Good... this is the sort of thing one does nowadays.

③ We see no limit to potential sales growth among tween girls.

④ Acme's competitors are extremely dangerous.

This could be worth remembering.

Your thoughts on the data.

① Sales are slightly up in February compared to September, but kind of flat.

Big problem

② Sales are way off their targets and began diverging in November.

③ Cutting ad expenses may have hurt Acme's ability to keep pace with sales targets.

What should they do next?

④ Cutting the prices does not seem to have helped sales keep pace with targets.

You've successfully broken your problem into smaller, more manageable pieces.

Now it's time to evaluate those pieces in greater detail...

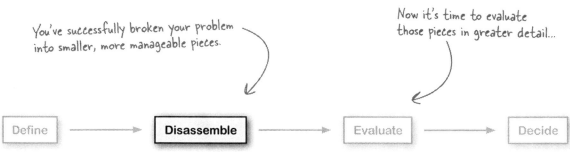

Define → **Disassemble** → Evaluate → Decide

Evaluate the pieces

Here comes the fun part. You know what you need to figure out, and you know what chunks of data will enable you to do it. Now, take a close, focused look at the pieces and form your own judgements about them.

| Define | → | Disassemble | → | **Evaluate** | → | Decide |

Just as it was with disassembly, the key to evaluating the pieces you have isolated is **comparison**.

What do you see when you compare these elements to each other?

Pick any two elements and read them next to each other.

What do you see?

Observations about the problem

> MoisturePlus customers are tween girls (where tweens are people aged 11–15). They're basically the only customer group.

> Acme is trying out reallocating expenses from advertisements to social networking, but so far, the success of the initiative is unknown.

> We see no limit to potential sales growth among tween girls.

> Acme's competitors are extremely dangerous.

Use your imagination!

Observations about the data

> Sales are slightly up in February compared to September, but kind of flat.

> Sales are way off their targets.

> Cutting ad expenses may have hurt Acme's ability to keep pace with sales targets.

> Cutting the prices does not seem to have helped sales keep pace with targets.

You have almost all the right pieces, but one important piece is missing...

Analysis begins when you insert yourself

Inserting yourself into your analysis means **making your own assumptions explicit** and **betting your credibility on your conclusions**.

Whether you're building complex models or making simple decisions, data analysis is all about you: your beliefs, your judgement, your credibility.

Your prospects for success are much better if you are an explicit part of your analysis.

Insert yourself

Good for you

You'll know what to look for in the data.

You'll avoid overreaching in your conclusions.

You'll be responsible for the success of your work.

Good for your clients

Your client will respect your judgments more.

Your client will understand the limitations of your conclusions.

Don't insert yourself

Bad for you

You'll lose track of how your baseline assumptions affect your conclusions.

You'll be a wimp who avoids responsibility!

Bad for your client

Your client won't trust your analysis, because he won't know your motives and incentives.

Your client might get a false sense of "objectivity" or detached rationality.

As you craft your final report, be sure to refer to yourself, so that your client knows where your conclusions are coming from.

Yikes! You don't want to run into these problems.

Define → Disassemble → **Evaluate** → Decide

Make a recommendation

As a data analyst, your job is to empower yourself and your client to make better **decisions**, using insights gleaned from carefully studying your evaluation of the data.

Making that happen means you have to package your ideas and judgments together into a format that can be digested by your client.

That means making your work as simple as it can be, but not simpler! It's your job to **make sure your voice is heard** and that people make good decisions on the basis of what you have to say.

An analysis is useless unless it's assembled into a form that facilitates decisions.

The report you present to your client needs to be focused on making yourself understood and encouraging intelligent, data-based decision making.

Sharpen your pencil

Look at the information you've collected on the previous pages. What do **you** recommend that Acme does to increase sales? Why?

....

....

....

....

....

....

Your report is ready

Acme Cosmetics Analytical Report

Context

MoisturePlus customers are tween girls (where tweens are people aged 11–15). They're basically the only customer group. Acme is trying out reallocating expenses from advertisements to social networking, but so far, the success of the initiative is unknown. We see no limit to potential sales growth among tween girls. Acme's competitors are extremely dangerous.

Interpretation of data

Sales are slightly up in February compared to September, but kind of flat. Sales are way off their targets. Cutting ad expenses may have hurt Acme's ability to keep pace with sales targets. Cutting the prices does not seem to have helped sales keep pace with targets.

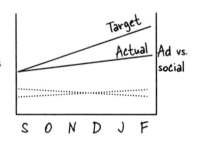

Recommendation

It might be that the decline in sales relative to the target is linked to the decline in advertising relative to past advertising expenses. We have no good evidence to believe that social networking has been as successful as we had hoped. I will return advertising to September levels to see if the tween girls respond. **Advertising to tween girls is the way to get gross sales back in line with targets.**

This is the stuff we got from the CEO at the beginning.

Here's the meat of your analysis.

Your conclusion might be different.

It's a good idea to state your and your clients' assumptions in your report.

A simple graphic to illustrate your conclusion.

What will the CEO think?

Define → Disassemble → Evaluate → **Decide**

The CEO likes your work

Excellent work. I'm totally persuaded. I'll execute the order for more ads at once. I can't wait to see what happens!

Your report is concise, professional, and direct.

It speaks to the CEO's needs in a way that's even clearer than his own way of describing them.

You looked at the data, got greater clarity from the CEO, compared his beliefs to your own interpretation of his data, and recommended a decision.

Nice work!

How will your recommendation affect Acme's business?

Will Acme's sales increase?

An article just came across the wire

Seems like a nice article, on the face of it.

Dataville Business Daily

MoisturePlus achieves complete market saturation among tween girls

Our very own cosmetics industry analysts report that the tween girl moisturizer market is completely dominated by Acme Cosmetics's flagship product, MoisturePlus. According to the DBD's survey, 95 percent of tween girls report "Very Frequent" usage of MoisturePlus, typically twice a day or more.

The Acme CEO was surprised when our reporter told him of our findings. "We are commited to providing our tween customers the most luxurious cosmetic experience possible at just-accessible prices," he said. "I'm delighted to hear that MoisturePlus has achieved so much success with them. Hopefully, our analytical department will be able to deliver this information to me in the future, rather than the press."

Acme's only viable competitor in this market space, Competition Cosmetics, responded to our reporter's inquiry saying, "We have basically given up on marketing to tween girls. The customers that we recruit for viral marketing are made fun of by their friends for allegedly using a cheap, inferior product. The MoisturePlus brand is so powerful that it's a waste of our marketing dollars to compete. With any luck, the MoisturePlus brand will take a hit if something happens like their celebrity endorsement getting caught on video having…

What does this mean for your analysis?

On the face of it, this sounds good for Acme. But if the market's saturated, more ads to tween girls probably won't do much good.

You're lucky I got this call. I canceled the tween girl ad campaign. Now come back to me with a plan that works.

It's hard to imagine the tween girl campaign would have worked. If the overwhelming majority of them are using MoisturePlus two or more times a day, what opportunity is there for increasing sales?

You'll need to find other opportunities for sales growth. But first, you need to get a handle on what just happened to your analysis.

BRAIN BARBELL

Somewhere along the way, you picked up some **bad or incomplete information** that left you blind to these facts about tween girls. What was that information?

You let the CEO's beliefs take you down the wrong path

Here's what the CEO said about how MoisturePlus sales works:

The CEO's beliefs about MoisturePlus

MoisturePlus customers are tween girls (where tweens are people aged 11–15). They're basically the only customer group.

Acme is trying out reallocating expenses from advertisements to social networking, but so far, the success of the initiative is unknown.

We see no limit to potential sales growth among tween girls.

Acme's competitors are extremely dangerous.

This is a mental model...

Take a look at how these beliefs fit with the data. Do the two agree or conflict? Do they describe different things?

	September	October	November	December	January	February
Gross sales	$5,280,000	$5,501,000	$5,469,000	$5,480,000	$5,533,000	$5,554,000
Target sales	$5,280,000	$5,500,000	$5,729,000	$5,968,000	$6,217,000	$6,476,000
Ad costs	$1,056,000	$950,400	$739,200	$528,000	$316,800	$316,800
Social network costs	$0	$105,600	$316,800	$528,000	$739,200	$739,200
Unit prices (per oz.)	$2.00	$2.00	$2.00	$1.90	$1.90	$1.90

The data doesn't say anything about tween girls. He assumes that tween girls are the only buyers and that tween girls have the ability to purchase more MoisturePlus.

In light of the news article, you might want to reassess these beliefs.

We're back to the beginning!

Define → Disassemble → Evaluate → Decide

Your assumptions and beliefs about the world are your mental model

And in this case, it's problematic. If the newspaper report is true, the CEO's beliefs about tween girls are wrong. Those beliefs are the model you've been using to interpret the data.

The world is complicated, so we use **mental models** to make sense of it. Your brain is like a toolbox, and any time your brain gets new information, it picks a tool to help interpret that information.

Mental models can be hard-wired, innate cognitive abilities, or they can be theories that you learn. Either way, they have a **big impact** on how you interpret data.

Your brain is a toolbox.

Mental models are the tools.

Any time you're faced with new information, your brain pulls out a tool to make sense of it.

Sometimes mental models are a big help, and sometimes they cause problems. In this book, you'll get a crash course on how to use them to your advantage.

What's most important for now is that you always make them explicit and give them **the same serious and careful treatment** that you give data.

> Aren't you supposed to be analyzing **data**, not people's minds? What about **data models**?

Always make your mental models as explicit as possible.

Your statistical model depends on your mental model

Mental models determine what you see. They're your lens for viewing reality.

Your mental model is like the lens you use to view the world.

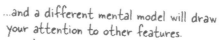

You look at the world.

You can't see *everything*, so your brain has to be selective in what it chooses to focus your attention on. So your mental model largely **determines what you see**.

One mental model will draw your attention to some features of the world...

...and a different mental model will draw your attention to other features.

The world looks one way.

The world looks slightly different!

If you're **aware** of your mental model, you're more likely to see what's important and develop the most relevant and useful statistical models.

Your statistical model **depends** on your mental model. If you use the wrong mental model, your analysis fails before it even begins.

You'd better get the mental model right!

Define ⟶ Disassemble ⟶ Evaluate ⟶ Decide

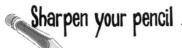

Sharpen your pencil

Let's take another look at the data and think about what other mental models would fit the data.

	September	October	November	December	January	February
Gross sales	$5,280,000	$5,501,000	$5,469,000	$5,480,000	$5,533,000	$5,554,000
Target sales	$5,280,000	$5,500,000	$5,729,000	$5,968,000	$6,217,000	$6,476,000
Ad costs	$1,056,000	$950,400	$739,200	$528,000	$316,800	$316,800
Social network costs	$0	$105,600	$316,800	$528,000	$739,200	$739,200
Unit prices (per oz.)	$2.00	$2.00	$2.00	$1.90	$1.90	$1.90

1 List some assumptions that would be true if MoisturePlus is actually the preferred lotion for tweens.

Use your creativity!

....

....

....

....

....

2 List some assumptions that would be true if MoisturePlus was in serious danger of losing customers to their competition.

....

....

....

....

....

Sharpen your pencil
Solution

You just looked at your summary data with a new perspective: how would *different* mental models fit?

	September	October	November	December	January	February
Gross sales	$5,280,000	$5,501,000	$5,469,000	$5,480,000	$5,533,000	$5,554,000
Target sales	$5,280,000	$5,500,000	$5,729,000	$5,968,000	$6,217,000	$6,476,000
Ad costs	$1,056,000	$950,400	$739,200	$528,000	$316,800	$316,800
Social network costs	$0	$105,600	$316,800	$528,000	$739,200	$739,200
Unit prices (per oz.)	$2.00	$2.00	$2.00	$1.90	$1.90	$1.90

1 List some assumptions that would be true if MoisturePlus is actually the preferred lotion for tweens.

Tween girls spend almost all their moisturizer dollars on MoisturePlus.

Here's a happy world.

Acme needs to find new markets for MoisturePlus to increase sales.

There are no meaningful competitors to MoisturePlus. It's by far the best product.

Social networks are the most cost-effective way to sell to people nowadays.

Price increases on MoisturePlus would reduce market share.

2 List some assumptions that would be true if MoisturePlus was in serious danger of losing customers to their competition.

Tween girls shifting to new moisturizer product, and Acme needs to fight back.

This is a challenge.

MoisturePlus is considered "uncool" and "just for dorks."

The "dry" skin look is becoming popular among young people.

Social network marketing is a black hole, and we need to go back to ads.

Tween girls are willing to spend much more money on moisturizer.

It's not unusual for your client to have the completely wrong mental model. In fact, it's really common for people to ignore what might be the most important part of the mental model...

Define → Disassemble → Evaluate → Decide

Mental models should always include what you don't know

Always specify **uncertainty**. If you're explicit about uncertainty, you'll be on the lookout for ways to use data to fill gaps in your knowledge, and you will make better recommendations.

Thinking about uncertainties and blind spots can be uncomfortable, but the payoff is huge. This "anti-resume" talks about what someone **doesn't** know rather than what they do know. If you want to hire a dancer, say, the dances they don't know might be more interesting to you than the dances they do know.

This would be a painful resume to write.

When you hire people, you often find out what they don't know only when it's too late.

It's the same deal with data analysis. Being clear about your knowledge gaps is essential.

Specify uncertainty up front, and you won't get nasty surprises later on.

Head First Anti-Resume

Experiences I haven't had:

Being arrested
Eating crawfish
Riding a unicycle
Shoveling snow

Things I don't know:

The first fifty digits of Pi
How many mobile minutes I used today
The meaning of life

Things I don't know how to do:

Make a toast in Urdu
Dance merengue
Shred on the guitar

Books I haven't read:

James Joyce's *Ulysses*
The Da Vinci Code

Sharpen your pencil

What questions would you ask the CEO to find out what he **doesn't know**?

....

....

....

....

....

....

The CEO tells you what he doesn't know

From: CEO, Acme Cosmetics
To: Head First
Subject: Re: Managing uncertainty

Where would you say are the biggest gaps in your knowledge about MoisturePlus sales?

> Well that's an interesting question. I'd always thought we really understood how customers felt about our product. But since we don't sell direct to consumers, we really don't know what happens after we send our product to our resellers. So, yeah, we don't really know what happens once MoisturePlus leaves the warehouse.

It's fine to get the client to speculate.

How confident are you that advertising has increased sales in the past?

> Well, like they always say, half of it works, half of it doesn't, and you never know which half is which. But it's pretty clear that the MoisturePlus brand is most of what our customers are buying, because MoisturePlus isn't terribly different from other moisturizers, so ads are key to establishing the brand.

Not a lot of certainty here on how well advertising works.

Who else might buy the product besides tween girls?

> I just have no idea. No clue. Because the product is so brand-driven we only think about tween girls. We've never reached out to any other consumer group.

This is a big blind spot!

Are there any other lingering uncertainties that I should know about?

> Sure, lots. You've scared the heck out of me. I don't feel like I know anything about my product any more. Your data analysis makes me think I know less than I ever knew.

Who else might be buying MoisturePlus?

Are there other buyers besides tween girls?

Define → **Disassemble** → Evaluate → Decide

there are no
Dumb Questions

Q: That's a funny thing the CEO said at the end: data analysis makes you feel like you know *less*. He's wrong about that, right?

A: It depends on how you look at it. Nowadays, more and more problems can be solved by using the techniques of data analysis. These are problems that, in the past, people would solve using gut instincts, flying by the seat of their pants.

Q: So mental models feel more and more flimsy compared to how they felt in the past?

A: A lot of what mental models do is help you fill in the gaps of what you don't know. The good news is that the tools of data analysis empower you to fill those gaps in a systematic and confidence-inspiring way. So the point of the exercise of specifying your uncertainty in great detail is to help you see the blind spots that require hard-nosed empirical data work.

Q: But won't I always need to use mental models to fill in the gaps of knowledge in how I understand the world?

A: Absolutely...

Q: Because even if I get a good understanding of how things work right now, ten minutes from now the world will be different.

A: That's exactly right. You can't know everything, and the world's constantly changing. That's why specifying your problem rigorously and managing the uncertainties in your mental model is so important. You have only so much time and resources to devote to solving your analytical problems, so answering these questions will help you do it efficiently and effectively.

Q: Does stuff you learn from your statistical models make it into your mental models?

A: Definitely. The facts and phenomena you discover in today's research often become the assumptions that take you into tomorrow's research. Think of it this way: you'll inevitably draw wrong conclusions from your statistical models. Nobody's perfect. And when those conclusions become part of your mental model, you want to keep them **explicit,** so you can recognize a situation where you need to double back and change them.

Q: So mental models are things that you can test empirically?

A: Yes, and you should test them. You can't test everything, but everything in your model should be testable.

Q: How do you change your mental model?

A: You're about to find out...

The CEO ordered more data to help you look for market segments besides tween girls. Let's take a look.

Acme just sent you a huge list of <u>raw data</u>

When you get new data, and you haven't done anything to change it yet, it's considered **raw data**. You willl **almost always need to manipulate data** you get from someone else in order to get it into a useful form for the number crunching you want to do.

Just be sure to **save your originals**. And keep them separate from any data manipulation you do. Even the best analysts make mistakes, and you always need to be able to compare your work to the raw data.

This is a lot of stuff... maybe more than you need.

Date	Vendor	Lot size (units)	Shipping ZIP	Cost
9/1/08	Sassy Girl Cosmetics	5253	20817	$75,643
9/3/08	Sassy Girl Cosmetics	6148	20817	$88,531
9/4/08	Prissy Princess	8931	20012	$128,606
9/14/08	Sassy Girl Cosmetics	2031	20817	$29,246
9/14/08	Prissy Princess	8029	20012	$115,618
9/15/08	General American Wholesalers	3754	20012	$54,058
9/20/08	Sassy Girl Cosmetics	7039	20817	$101,362
9/21/08	Prissy Princess	7478	20012	$107,683
9/25/08	General American Wholesalers	2646	20012	$38,102
9/26/08	Sassy Girl Cosmetics	6361	20817	$91,598
10/4/08	Prissy Princess	9481	20012	$136,526
10/7/08	General American Wholesalers	8598	20012	$123,811
10/9/08	Sassy Girl Cosmetics	6333	20817	$91,195
10/12/08	General American Wholesalers	4813	20012	$69,307
10/15/08	Prissy Princess	1550	20012	$22,320
10/20/08	Sassy Girl Cosmetics	3230	20817	$46,512
10/25/08	Sassy Girl Cosmetics	2064	20817	$29,722
10/27/08	General American Wholesalers	8298	20012	$119,491
10/28/08	Prissy Princess	8300	20012	$119,520
11/3/08	General American Wholesalers	6791	20012	$97,790
11/4/08	Prissy Princess	3775	20012	$54,360
11/10/08	Sassy Girl Cosmetics	8320	20817	$119,808
11/10/08	Sassy Girl Cosmetics	6160	20817	$88,704
11/10/08	General American Wholesalers	1894	20012	$27,274
11/15/08	Prissy Princess	1697	20012	$24,437
11/24/08	Prissy Princess	4825	20012	$69,480
11/28/08	Sassy Girl Cosmetics	6188	20817	$89,107
11/28/08	General American Wholesalers	4157	20012	$59,861
12/3/08	Sassy Girl Cosmetics	6841	20817	$98,510
12/4/08	Prissy Princess	7483	20012	$107,755
12/6/08	General American Wholesalers	1462	20012	$21,053
12/11/08	General American Wholesalers	8680	20012	$124,992
12/14/08	Sassy Girl Cosmetics	3221	20817	$46,382
12/14/08	Prissy Princess	6257	20012	$90,101
12/24/08	General American Wholesalers	4504	20012	$64,858
12/25/08	Prissy Princess	6157	20012	$88,661
12/28/08	Sassy Girl Cosmetics	5943	20817	$85,579
1/7/09	Sassy Girl Cosmetics	4415	20817	$63,576
1/10/09	Prissy Princess	2726	20012	$39,254
1/10/09	General American Wholesalers	4937	20012	$71,093
1/15/09	Sassy Girl Cosmetics	9602	20817	$138,269
1/18/09	General American Wholesalers	7025	20012	$101,160
1/20/09	Prissy Princess	4726	20012	$68,054

That's sooo much data! What do I do? Where do I begin?

A lot of data is usually a good thing.

Relax

Just stay focused on what you're trying to accomplish with the data. If you lose track of your goals and assumptions, it's easy to get "lost" messing around with a large data set. But good data analysis is all about keeping focused on what you want to learn about the data.

Define → **Disassemble** → Evaluate → Decide

Exercise

Take a close look at this data and think about the **CEO's mental model**.
Does this data fit with the idea that the customers are all tween girls, or
might it suggest other customers?

Date	Vendor	Lot size (units)	Shipping ZIP	Cost
9/1/08	Sassy Girl Cosmetics	5253	20817	$75,643
9/3/08	Sassy Girl Cosmetics	6148	20817	$88,531
9/4/08	Prissy Princess	8931	20012	$128,606
9/14/08	Sassy Girl Cosmetics	2031	20817	$29,246
9/14/08	Prissy Princess	8029	20012	$115,618
9/15/08	General American Wholesalers	3754	20012	$54,058
9/20/08	Sassy Girl Cosmetics	7039	20817	$101,362
9/21/08	Prissy Princess	7478	20012	$107,683
9/25/08	General American Wholesalers	2646	20012	$38,102
9/26/08	Sassy Girl Cosmetics	6361	20817	$91,598
10/4/08	Prissy Princess	9481	20012	$136,526
10/7/08	General American Wholesalers	8598	20012	$123,811
10/9/08	Sassy Girl Cosmetics	6333	20817	$91,195
10/12/08	General American Wholesalers	4813	20012	$69,307
10/15/08	Prissy Princess	1550	20012	$22,320
10/20/08	Sassy Girl Cosmetics	3230	20817	$46,512
10/25/08	Sassy Girl Cosmetics	2064	20817	$29,722
10/27/08	General American Wholesalers	8298	20012	$119,491
10/28/08	Prissy Princess	8300	20012	$119,520
11/3/08	General American Wholesalers	6791	20012	$97,790
11/4/08	Prissy Princess	3775	20012	$54,360
11/10/08	Sassy Girl Cosmetics	8320	20817	$119,808
11/10/08	Sassy Girl Cosmetics	6160	20817	$88,704
11/10/08	General American Wholesalers	1894	20012	$27,274
11/15/08	Prissy Princess	1697	20012	$24,437
11/24/08	Prissy Princess	4825	20012	$69,480
11/28/08	Sassy Girl Cosmetics	6188	20817	$89,107
11/28/08	General American Wholesalers	4157	20012	$59,861
12/3/08	Sassy Girl Cosmetics	6841	20817	$98,510
12/4/08	Prissy Princess	7483	20012	$107,755
12/6/08	General American Wholesalers	1462	20012	$21,053
12/11/08	General American Wholesalers	8680	20012	$124,992
12/14/08	Sassy Girl Cosmetics	3221	20817	$46,382
12/14/08	Prissy Princess	6257	20012	$90,101
12/24/08	General American Wholesalers	4504	20012	$64,858
12/25/08	Prissy Princess	6157	20012	$88,661
12/28/08	Sassy Girl Cosmetics	5943	20817	$85,579
1/7/09	Sassy Girl Cosmetics	4415	20817	$63,576
1/10/09	Prissy Princess	2726	20012	$39,254
1/10/09	General American Wholesalers	4937	20012	$71,093
1/15/09	Sassy Girl Cosmetics	9602	20817	$138,269
1/18/09	General American Wholesalers	7025	20012	$101,160
1/20/09	Prissy Princess	4726	20012	$68,054

Write your answer here.

Exercise Solution

What did you see in the data? Is the CEO right that only tween girls purchase MoisturePlus, or might there be someone else?

These companies sound like they sell to tween girls.

We can certainly see that Acme is selling to companies that go on to sell to younger girls. Sassy Girl Cosmetics and Prissy Princess definitely seem to fit the bill. But there's another reseller on the list: "General American Wholesalers." The name alone doesn't say who its clients are, but it might be worth researching.

Who are these people?

Date	Vendor	Lot size (units)	Shipping ZIP	Cost
9/1/08	Sassy Girl Cosmetics	5253	20817	$75,643
9/3/08	Sassy Girl Cosmetics	6148	20817	$88,531
9/4/08	Prissy Princess	8931	20012	$128,606
9/14/08	Sassy Girl Cosmetics	2031	20817	$29,246
9/14/08	Prissy Princess	8029	20012	$115,618
9/15/08	General American Wholesalers	3754	20012	$54,058
9/20/08	Sassy Girl Cosmetics	7039	20817	$101,362
9/21/08	Prissy Princess	7478	20012	$107,683
9/25/08	General American Wholesalers	2646	20012	$38,102
9/26/08	Sassy Girl Cosmetics	6361	20817	$91,598
10/4/08	Prissy Princess	9481	20012	$136,526
10/7/08	General American Wholesalers	8598	20012	$123,811
10/9/08	Sassy Girl Cosmetics	6333	20817	$91,195
10/12/08	General American Wholesalers	4813	20012	$69,307
10/15/08	Prissy Princess	1550	20012	$22,320
10/20/08	Sassy Girl Cosmetics	3230	20817	$46,512
10/25/08	Sassy Girl Cosmetics	2064	20817	$29,722
10/27/08	General American Wholesalers	8298	20012	$119,491
10/28/08	Prissy Princess	8300	20012	$119,520
11/3/08	General American Wholesalers	6791	20012	$97,790
11/4/08	Prissy Princess	3775	20012	$54,360
11/10/08	Sassy Girl Cosmetics	8320	20817	$119,808
11/10/08	Sassy Girl Cosmetics	6160	20817	$88,704
11/10/08	General American Wholesalers	1894	20012	$27,274
11/15/08	Prissy Princess	1697	20012	$24,437
11/24/08	Prissy Princess	4825	20012	$69,480
11/28/08	Sassy Girl Cosmetics	6188	20817	$89,107
11/28/08	General American Wholesalers	4157	20012	$59,861
12/3/08	Sassy Girl Cosmetics	6841	20817	$98,510
12/4/08	Prissy Princess	7483	20012	$107,755
12/6/08	General American Wholesalers	1462	20012	$21,053
12/11/08	General American Wholesalers	8680	20012	$124,992
12/14/08	Sassy Girl Cosmetics	3221	20817	$46,382
12/14/08	Prissy Princess	6257	20012	$90,101
12/24/08	General American Wholesalers	4504	20012	$64,858
12/25/08	Prissy Princess	6157	20012	$88,661
12/28/08	Sassy Girl Cosmetics	5943	20817	$85,579
1/7/09	Sassy Girl Cosmetics	4415	20817	$63,576
1/10/09	Prissy Princess	2726	20012	$39,254
1/10/09	General American Wholesalers	4937	20012	$71,093
1/15/09	Sassy Girl Cosmetics	9602	20817	$138,269
1/18/09	General American Wholesalers	7025	20012	$101,160
1/20/09	Prissy Princess	4726	20012	$68,054

Define → Disassemble → **Evaluate** → Decide

Time to drill further into the data

You looked at the mass of data with a very clear task: find out who's buying besides tween girls.

You found a company called General American Wholesalers. Who are they? And who's buying from them?

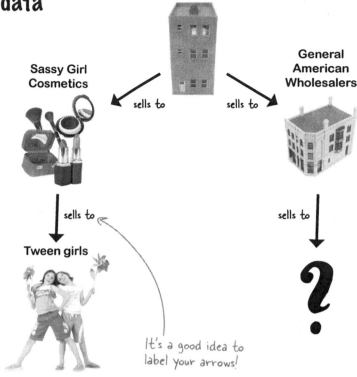

Acme

Sassy Girl Cosmetics

sells to

sells to

General American Wholesalers

sells to

Tween girls

sells to

?

It's a good idea to label your arrows!

Exercise

At Acme's request, General American Wholesalers sent over this breakdown of their customers for MoisturePlus. Does this information help you figure out who's buying?

Write down what this data tells you about who's buying MoisturePlus.

GAW vendor breakdown for six months ending 2/2009
MoisturePlus sales only

Vendor	Units	%
Manly Beard Maintenance, Inc.	9785	23%
GruffCustomer.com	20100	46%
Stu's Shaving Supply LLC	8093	19%
Cosmetics for Men, Inc.	5311	12%
Total	43289	100%

Exercise Solution

What did General American Wholesaler's vendor list tell you about who's buying MoisturePlus?

GAW vendor breakdown for six months ending 2/2009
MoisturePlus sales only

Vendor	Units	%
Manly Beard Maintenance, Inc.	9785	23%
GruffCustomer.com	20100	46%
Stu's Shaving Supply LLC	8093	19%
Cosmetics for Men, Inc.	5311	12%
Total	43289	100%

It looks like men are buying MoisturePlus! Looking at the original Acme vendor list, you couldn't tell that there were men buying. But General American Wholesalers is reselling MoisturePlus to shaving supply vendors!

General American Wholesalers confirms your impression

Yeah, the old guys like it, too, even though they're embarrassed that it's a tween product. It's great for post-shave skin conditioning.

This could be huge.

It looks like there's a whole group of people out there buying MoisturePlus that Acme hasn't recognized.

With any luck, this group of people could be where you have the potential to grow Acme's sales.

Define → Disassemble → **Evaluate** → Decide

I'm intrigued. This intelligence might bring about a huge shift in how we do business. Could you just walk me through how you came to this conclusion? And what should we do with this new information?

You've made it to the final stage of this analysis.

It's time to write your report. Remember, walk your client through your thought process in detail. How did you come to the insights you've achieved?

Finally, what do you suggest that he do to improve his business on the basis of your insights? How does this information help him **increase sales?**

Sharpen your pencil

How has the mental model changed?

What evidence led you to your conclusion?

Do you have any lingering uncertainties?

....

....

....

....

....

....

Sharpen your pencil Solution

How did you recap your work, and what do you recommend that the CEO do in order to increase sales?

I started off trying to figure out how to increase sales to tween girls, because we believed that those girls were MoisturePlus's sole client base. When we discovered that the tween girl market was saturated, I dug deeper into the data to look for sources of increased sales. In the process, I changed the mental model. Turns out there are more people than we realized who are enthusiastic about our product—especially older men. Since this group of customers is quiet about their enthusiasm for the product, I recommend that we increase our advertising to them dramatically, selling the same product with a more men-friendly label. This will increase sales.

there are no Dumb Questions

Q: If I have to get more detailed data to answer my questions, how will I know when to stop? Do I need to go as far as interviewing customers myself?

A: How far to go chasing new and deeper data sources is ultimately a question about your own best judgement. In this case, you searched until you found a new market segment, and that was enough to enable you to generate a compelling new sales strategy. We'll talk more about when to stop collecting data in future chapters.

Q: Is seems like getting that wrong mental model at the beginning was devastating to the first analysis I did.

A: Yeah, getting that assumption incorrect at the beginning doomed your analysis to the wrong answers. That's why it's so important to make sure that your models are based on the right assumptions from the very beginning and be ready to go back and refine them as soon as you get data that upsets your assumptions.

Q: Does analysis ever stop? I'm looking for some finality here.

A: You certainly can answer big questions in data analysis, but you can never know everything. And even if you knew everything today, tomorrow would be different. Your recommendation to sell to older men might work today, but Acme will always need analysts chasing sales.

Q: Sounds depressing.

A: On the contrary! Analysts are like detectives, and there are always mysteries to be solved. That's what makes data analysis so much fun! Just think of going back, refining your models, and looking at the world through your new models as being a fundamental part of your job as data analyst, not an exception the rule.

Define → Disassemble → Evaluate → **Decide**

Here's what you did

Here's one last look at the steps you've gone through to reach your conclusion about how to increase the sales of Acme's MoisturePlus.

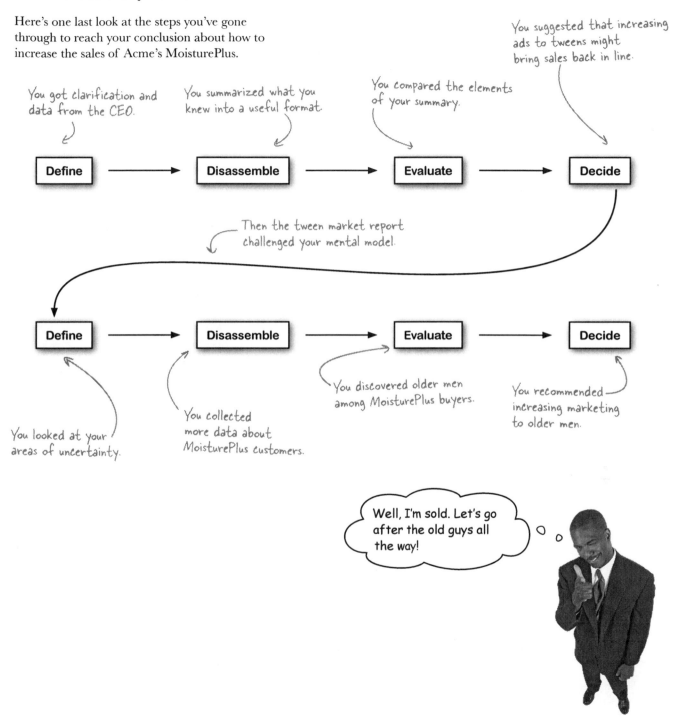

You got clarification and data from the CEO.

You summarized what you knew into a useful format.

You compared the elements of your summary.

You suggested that increasing ads to tweens might bring sales back in line.

Define → **Disassemble** → **Evaluate** → **Decide**

Then the tween market report challenged your mental model.

Define → **Disassemble** → **Evaluate** → **Decide**

You looked at your areas of uncertainty.

You collected more data about MoisturePlus customers.

You discovered older men among MoisturePlus buyers.

You recommended increasing marketing to older men.

Well, I'm sold. Let's go after the old guys all the way!

Your analysis led your client to a brilliant decision

After he received your report, the CEO quickly mobilized his marketing team and created a SmoothLeather brand moisturizer, which is just MoisturePlus under a new name.

Acme immediately and aggressively marketed SmoothLeather to older men. Here's what happened:

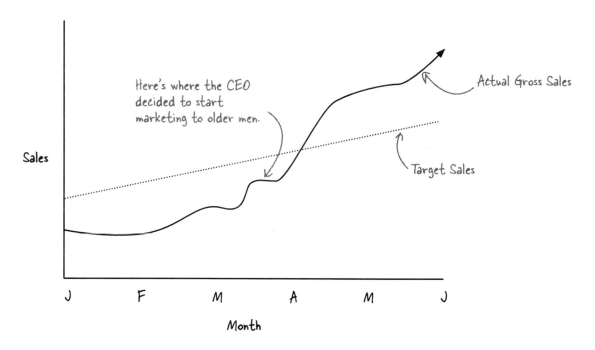

Sales took off! Within two months sales figures had exceeded the target levels you saw at the beginning of the chapter.

Looks like your analysis paid off!

2 experiments

Test your theories

They always say, "Ben, you'll never learn anything flying that kite all day," but I've got a hunch that I'll prove them all wrong...

Can you show what you believe?

In a real **empirical** test? There's nothing like a good experiment to solve your problems and show you the way the world really works. Instead of having to rely exclusively on your **observational data**, a well-executed experiment can often help you make **causal connections**. Strong empirical data will make your analytical judgments all the more powerful.

It's a coffee recession!

Times are tough, and even **Starbuzz Coffee** has felt the sting. Starbuzz has been the place to go for premium gourmet coffee, but in the past few months, sales have plummeted relative to their projections.

Sales are way down, and we need a plan to get back on track. It's up to you to make a recommendation to the board.

Today   Projected

Sales

Actual

Time

This isn't good at all!

The Starbuzz CEO

The Starbuzz CEO has called you in to help figure out how to get sales back up.

The Starbuzz board meeting is in three months

That's not a lot of time to pull a turnaround plan together, but it must be done.

We don't totally know why sales are down, but we're pretty sure the economy has something to do with it. Regardless, you need to figure out how to **get sales back up**.

What would you do for starters?

From: CEO, Starbuzz
To: Head First
Subject: Fwd: Upcoming board meeting

Did you see this?!?

> **From: Chairman of the Board, Starbuzz**
> **To: CEO**
> **Subject: Upcoming board meeting**
>
> **The board is expecting a complete turnaround plan at the next meeting. We're sorely disappointed by the sales decline.**
>
> **If your plan for getting numbers back up is insufficient, we'll be forced to enact *our* plan, which first involve the replacement of all high-level staff.**
>
> **Thanks.**

Yikes!

Sharpen your pencil

Take a look at the following options. Which do you think would be the best ways to **start**? Why?

Interview the CEO to figure out how Starbuzz works as a business.

....

....

Do a survey of customers to find out what they're thinking.

....

....

Find out how the projected sales figures were calculated.

....

....

Interview the Chairman of the Board

....

....

Pour yourself a tall, steamy mug of Starbuzz coffee.

....

....

Write in the blanks what you think about each of these options.

Sharpen your pencil
Solution

Where do you think is the best place to start figuring out how to increase Starbuzz sales?

Interview the CEO to figure out how Starbuzz works as a business.

Definitely a good place to start. He'll have all sorts of intelligence about the business.

Interview the Chairman of the Board

Going out on a limb here. Your client is really the CEO, and going over his head is dicey.

Do a survey of customers to find out what they're thinking.

This would also be good. You'll have to get inside their heads to get them to buy more coffee.

Pour yourself a tall, steamy mug of Starbuzz coffee.

Starbuzz is awfully tasty. Why not have a cup?

Find out how the projected sales figures were calculated.

This would be interesting to know, but it's probably not the first thing you'd look at.

> I like the idea of looking at our surveys. Give them a gander and tell me what you see.

Marketing runs surveys monthly.

They take a *random*, representative sample of their coffee consumers and ask them a bunch of pertinent questions about how they feel about the coffee and the coffee-buying experience.

"Random"... remember that word!

What people **say** in surveys does not always fit with how they **behave** in reality, but it never hurts to ask people how they feel.

The Starbuzz Survey

Here it is: the survey the marketing department administers monthly to a large sample of Starbuzz customers.

If you're a Starbuzz customer, there's a good chance someone will hand you one of these to fill out.

Starbuzz Survey

Thank you for filling out our Starbuzz survey! Once you're finished, our manager will be delighted to give you a $10 gift card for use at any Starbuzz location. Thank you for coming to Starbuzz!

Date _____January 2009_____

Starbuzz store # _____04524_____

Circle the number that corresponds to how you feel about each statement. 1 means strongly disagree, 5 means strongly agree.

"Starbuzz coffee stores are located conveniently for me."

1   2   3   4   (5)

"My coffee is always served at just the right temperature."

1   2   3   (4)   5

"Starbuzz employees are courteous and get me my drink quickly."

1   2   3   4   (5)

"I think Starbuzz coffee is a great value."

1   (2)   3   4   5

"Starbuzz is my preferred coffee destination."

1   2   3   4   (5)

A higher score means you agree strongly. This customer really prefers Starbuzz.

How would you summarize this survey data?

Always use the method of comparison

One of the most fundamental principles of analysis and statistics is the **method of comparison**, which states that data is interesting only in comparison to other data.

In this case, the marketing department takes the average answer for each question and compares those averages month by month.

Each monthly average is useful *only* when you compare it to numbers from other months.

Statistics are illuminating only in relation to other statistics.

Here's a summary of marketing surveys for the 6 months ending January 2009. The figures represent the average score given to each statement by survey respondents from participating stores.

	Aug-08	Sept-08	Oct-08	Nov-08	Dec-08	Jan-09
Location convenience	4.7	4.6	4.7	4.2	4.8	4.2
Coffee temperature	4.9	4.9	4.7	4.9	4.7	4.9
Courteous employees	3.6	4.1	4.2	3.9	3.5	4.6
Coffee value	4.3	3.9	3.7	3.5	3.0	2.1
Preferred destination	3.9	4.2	3.7	4.3	4.3	3.9

Participating stores	100	101	99	99	101	100

The answers to the questions are all averaged and grouped into this table.

This number is only useful when you <u>compare</u> it to these numbers.

Always make comparisons explicit.

Watch it!

*If a statistic seems interesting or useful, you need to explain **why** in terms of how that statistic compares to others. If you're not explicit about it, you're assuming that your client will make the comparison on their own, and that's **bad analysis**.*

Comparisons are key for observational data

The **more comparative the analysis is, the better**. And this is true especially in **observational studies** like the analysis of Starbuzz's marketing data.

In observational data, you just watch people and let them decide what groups they belong to, and taking an inventory of observational data is often the **first step** to getting better data through experiments.

Groups of people might be "big spenders," "tea drinkers," etc.

In experiments, on the other hand, you decide which groups people go into.

the Scholar's Corner

Observational study A study where the people being described decide on their own which groups they belong to.

Exercise

Look at the survey data on the facing page and compare the averages across the months.

Do you notice any patterns?

....

....

....

....

Is there anything that might explain to you why sales are down?

....

....

....

....

Exercise Solution

Now you've looked closely at the data to figure out what patterns the data contains.

Do you notice any patterns?

All the variables except for "Coffee value" bounce around within a narrow range. "Coffee temperature," for example, has a high score of 4.9 and a low score of 4.7, which isn't much variation. "Coffee value," on the other hand, shows a pretty significant decline. The December score is half of the August score, which could be a big deal.

Is there anything that might explain to you why sales are down?

It would make sense to say that, if people on average think that the coffee isn't a good value for the money, they'd tend to spend less money at Starbuzz. And because the economy's down, it makes sense that people have less money and that they'd find Starbuzz to be less of a value.

Could value perception be causing the revenue decline?

According to the data, everything's going along just fine with Starbuzz customers, except for one variable: perceived Starbuzz coffee value.

It looks like people might be buying less because they don't think Starbuzz is a good bang for the buck. Maybe the economy has made people a little more cash-strapped, so they're more sensitive to prices.

Let's call this theory the "value problem."

Starbuzz Coffee

Summary of marketing surveys for six months ending January 2009. The figures represents the average score given to each statement by survey respondents from participating stores.

	Aug-08	Sept-08	Oct-08	Nov-08	Dec-08	Jan-09
Location convenience	4.7	4.6	4.7	4.2	4.8	4.2
Coffee temperature	4.9	4.9	4.7	4.9	4.7	4.9
Courteous employees	3.6	4.1	4.2	3.9	3.5	4.6
Coffee value	**4.3**	**3.9**	**3.7**	**3.5**	**3.0**	**2.1**
Preferred destination	3.9	4.2	3.7	4.3	4.3	3.9
Participating stores	100	101	99	99	101	100

This variable shows a pretty steady decline over the past six months.

Do you think that the decline in perceived value is the reason for the sales decline?

there are no
Dumb Questions

Q: How do I know that a decline in value actually caused coffee sales to go down?

A: You don't. But right now the perceived value data is the only data you have that is congruent with the decline in sales. It looks like sales and perceived value are going down together, but you don't **know** that the decline in value has caused the decline in sales. Right now, it's just a theory.

Q: Could there be other factors at play? Maybe the value problem isn't as simple as it looks.

A: There almost certainly *are* other factors at play. With observational studies, you should assume that other factors are

confounding your result, because you can't **control for** them as you can with experiments. More on those buzzwords in a few pages.

Q: Could it be the other way around? Maybe declining sales caused people to think the coffee is less valuable.

A: That's a great question, and it could definitely be the other way around. A good rule of thumb for analysts is, when you're starting to suspect that causes are going in one direction (like value perception decline causing sales decline), flip the theory around and see how it looks (like sales decline causes value perception decline).

Q: So how do I figure out what causes what?

A: We're going to talk a lot throughout this book about how to draw conclusions about causes, but for now, you should know that observational studies aren't that powerful when it comes to drawing causal conclusions. Generally, you'll need other tools to get those sorts of conclusions.

Q: It sounds like observational studies kind of suck.

A: Not at all! There is a ton of observational data out there, and it'd be crazy to ignore it because of the shortcomings of observational studies. What's really important, however, is that you understand the limitations of observational studies, so that you don't draw the wrong conclusions about them.

The manager of Starbuzz's SoHo stores.

> Your so-called "value problem" is no problem at all at my stores! Our Starbuzz is hugely popular, and no one thinks that Starbuzz is a poor value. There must be some sort of mistake.

The manager of the SoHo stores does not agree

SoHo is a wealthy area and the home of a bunch of really lucrative Starbuzz stores, and the manager of those stores does not believe it's true that there's a value perception problem. Why do you think she'd disagree?

Are her customers lying? Did someone record the data incorrectly? Or is there something problematic about the observational study itself?

A typical customer's thinking

Jim: Forget about Starbuzz SoHo. Those guys just don't know how to read the numbers, and numbers don't lie.

Frank: I wouldn't be so quick to say that. Sometimes the instincts of the people on the ground tell you more than the statistics.

Joe: You're so right on. In fact, I'm tempted to just scrap this entire data set. Something seems fishy.

Jim: What specific reason do you have to believe that this data is flawed?

Joe: I dunno. The fishy smell?

Frank: Look, we need to go back to our interpretation of the typical or average customer.

Joe: Fine. Here it is. I drew a picture.

Frank: Is there any reason why this chain of events wouldn't apply to people in SoHo?

Jim: Maybe the SoHo folks are not hurting economically. The people who live there are sickly rich. And full of themselves, too.

Joe: Hey, my girlfriend lives in SoHo.

Frank: How you persuaded someone from the fashionable set to date you I have no idea. Jim, you may be on to something. If you're doing well money-wise, you'd be less likely to start believing that Starbuzz is a poor value.

Everyone's affected by this.

Economy down

I have less money

Starbuzz is less of a value

Starbuzz sales go down

It's always a good idea to draw pictures of how you think things relate.

People's actions are making this happen.

It looks like the SoHo Starbuzz customers may be **different** from all the other Starbuzz customers...

Observational studies are full of confounders

A **confounder** is a difference among the people in your study other than the factor you're trying to compare that ends up making your results less sensible.

In this case, you're comparing Starbuzz customers to each other at different points in **time**. Starbuzz customers are obviously different from each other—they're different people.

But if they're different from each other in respect to a variable you're trying to understand, the difference is a confounder, and in this case the confounder is **location**.

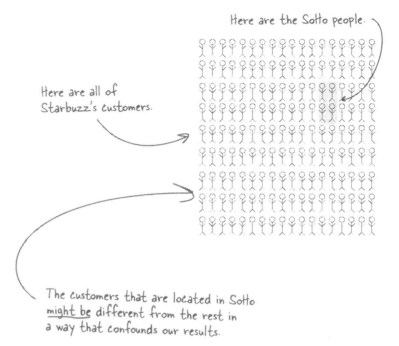

Here are the SoHo people.

Here are all of Starbuzz's customers.

The customers that are located in SoHo might be different from the rest in a way that confounds our results.

Sharpen your pencil

Redraw the causal diagram from the facing page to distinguish between SoHo stores and all the other stores., **correcting for the location confounder.**

Assume that the SoHo manager is correct and that SoHo customers don't perceive a value problem. How might that phenomenon affect sales?

How location might be confounding your results

Here's a refined diagram to show how things might be happening. It's a really good idea to **make your theories visual** using diagrams like this, which help both you and your clients keep track of your ideas.

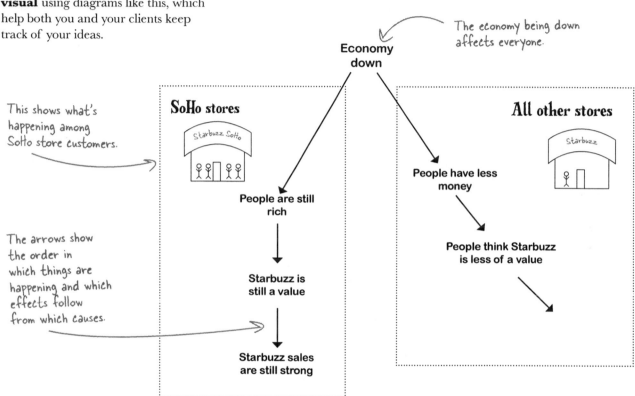

This shows what's happening among SoHo store customers.

The arrows show the order in which things are happening and which effects follow from which causes.

Economy down

The economy being down affects everyone.

SoHo stores

Starbuzz SoHo

People are still rich

Starbuzz is still a value

Starbuzz sales are still strong

All other stores

Starbuzz

People have less money

People think Starbuzz is less of a value

BRAIN BARBELL

What would you do to the data to show whether Starbuzz value perception in SoHo is still going strong? More generally, what would you do to observational study data to keep your confounders under control?

there are no
Dumb Questions

Q: In this case, isn't it really the *wealth* of the customers rather than the *location* that confounds the results?

A: Sure, and they're probably related. If you had the data on how much money each customers has, or how much money each customer feels comfortable spending, you could run the analysis again to see what sort of results wealth-based grouping gets you. But since we don't have that information, we're using location. Besides, location makes sense, because our theory says that wealthier people tend to shop in SoHo.

Q: Could there be other variables that are confounding this data besides location?

A: Definitely. Confounding is always a problem with observational studies. Your job as the analyst is always to think about how confounding might be affecting your results. If you think that the effect of confounders is minimal, that's great, but if there's reason to believe that they're causing problems, you need to adjust your conclusion accordingly.

Q: What if the confounders are hidden?

A: That's precisely the problem. Your confounders are usually not going to scream out to you. You have to dig them up yourself as you try to make your analysis as strong as possible. In this case, we are fortunate, because the location confounder was actually represented *in the data*, so we can manipulate the data to manage it. Often, the confounder information won't be there, which seriously undermines the ability of the entire study to give you useful conclusions.

Q: How far should I go to figure out what the confounders are?

A: It's really more art than science. You should ask yourself commonsense questions about what it is you're studying to imagine what variables might be confounding your results. As with everything in data analysis and statistics, no matter how fancy your quantitative techniques are, it's always really important that your conclusions **make sense**. If your conclusions make sense, and you've thoroughly searched for confounders, you've done all you can do for **observational studies**. Other types of studies, as you'll see, enable you to draw some more ambitious conclusions.

Q: Is it possible that location wouldn't be a confounder in this same data if I were looking at something besides value perception?

A: Definitely. Remember, location being a confounder makes sense in this context, but it might not make sense in another context. We have no reason to believe, for example, that people's feelings about whether their coffee temperature is right vary from place to place.

Q: I'm still feeling like observational studies have big problems.

A: There are big limitations with observational studies. This particular study has been useful to you in terms of understanding Starbuzz customers better, and when you control for location in the data the study will be even more powerful.

Manage confounders by breaking the data into chunks

To get your observational study confounders **under control**, sometimes it's a good idea to divide your groups into smaller chunks.

These smaller chunks are more **homogenous**. In other words, they don't have the internal variation that might skew your results and give you the wrong ideas.

Here is the Starbuzz survey data once again, this time with tables to represent other regions.

Here's the original data summary.

Starbuzz Coffee: All stores
Summary of marketing surveys for six months ending January 2009. The figures represents the average score given to each statement by survey respondents from participating stores.

	Aug-08	Sept-08	Oct-08	Nov-08	Dec-08	Jan-09
Location convenience	4.7	4.6	4.7	4.2	4.8	4.2
Coffee temperature	4.9	4.9	4.7	4.9	4.7	4.9
Courteous employees	3.6	4.1	4.2	3.9	3.5	4.6
Coffee value	4.3	3.9	3.7	3.5	3.0	2.1
Preferred destination	3.9	4.2	3.7	4.3	4.3	3.9

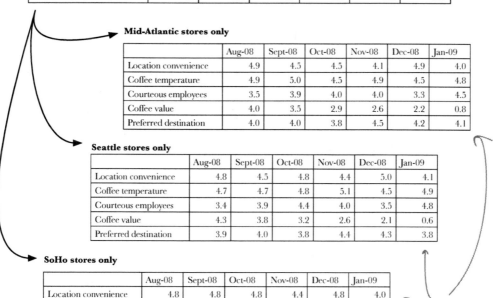

Mid-Atlantic stores only

	Aug-08	Sept-08	Oct-08	Nov-08	Dec-08	Jan-09
Location convenience	4.9	4.5	4.5	4.1	4.9	4.0
Coffee temperature	4.9	5.0	4.5	4.9	4.5	4.8
Courteous employees	3.5	3.9	4.0	4.0	3.3	4.5
Coffee value	4.0	3.5	2.9	2.6	2.2	0.8
Preferred destination	4.0	4.0	3.8	4.5	4.2	4.1

Seattle stores only

	Aug-08	Sept-08	Oct-08	Nov-08	Dec-08	Jan-09
Location convenience	4.8	4.5	4.8	4.4	5.0	4.1
Coffee temperature	4.7	4.7	4.8	5.1	4.5	4.9
Courteous employees	3.4	3.9	4.4	4.0	3.5	4.8
Coffee value	4.3	3.8	3.2	2.6	2.1	0.6
Preferred destination	3.9	4.0	3.8	4.4	4.3	3.8

SoHo stores only

	Aug-08	Sept-08	Oct-08	Nov-08	Dec-08	Jan-09
Location convenience	4.8	4.8	4.8	4.4	4.8	4.0
Coffee temperature	4.8	5.0	4.6	4.9	4.8	5.0
Courteous employees	3.7	4.1	4.4	3.7	3.3	4.8
Coffee value	4.9	4.8	4.8	4.9	4.9	4.8
Preferred destination	3.8	4.2	3.8	4.2	4.1	4.0

These groups internally homogenous.

Exercise

Take a look at the data on the facing page, which has been broken into groups.

How much of a difference is there between the Mid-Atlantic store subgroup average scores and the average scores for all the Starbuzz stores?

....

....

....

....

How does perceived coffee value compare among all the groups?

....

....

....

....

Was the SoHo manager right about her customers being happy with the value of Starbuzz coffee?

....

....

....

....

Exercise Solution

When you looked at the survey data that had been grouped by location, what did you see?

How much of a difference is there between the Mid-Atlantic store subgroup average scores and the average scores for all the Starbuzz stores?

All the scores wiggle around in the same narrow range, except for the value perception score. Value

perception just falls off a cliff in the Mid-Atlantic region compared to the all-region average!

How does perceived coffee value compare among all the groups?

Seattle has a precipitous drop, just like the Mid-Atlantic region. SoHo, on the other hand, appears

to be doing just fine. SoHo's value perception scores beat the all-region average handily. It looks like

the customers in this region are pretty pleased with Starbuzz's value.

Was the SoHo manager right about her customers being happy with the value of Starbuzz coffee?

The data definitely confirm the SoHo manager's beliefs about what her customers think about

Starbuzz's value. It was certainly a good idea to listen to her feedback and look at the data in a

different way because of that feedback.

It's worse than we thought!

The big guns have all come out to deal
with the problems you've identified.

Chief
Financial
Officer

CFO: This situation is worse than we had anticipated,
by a long shot. The value perception in our regions other
than SoHo has absolutely fallen through the floor.

Marketing: That's right. The first table, which
showed all the regions together, actually made the
value perception look *better* than it is. SoHo skewed the
averages upward.

CFO: When you break out SoHo, where everyone's
rich, you can see that SoHo customers are pleased with
the prices but that everyone else is about to jump ship, if
they haven't already.

Marketing: So we need to figure out what to do.

CFO: I'll tell you what to do. Slash prices.

Marketing: What?!?

CFO: You heard me. We slash prices. Then people will
see it as a better value.

Marketing: I don't know what planet you're from, but
we have a brand to worry about.

CFO: I come from Planet Business, and we call this
supply and demand. You might want to go back to
school to learn what those words mean. Cut prices and
demand goes up.

Marketing: We might get a jump in sales in the short
term, but we'll destroy our brand image if we cut costs.
We need to figure out a way to *persuade* people that
Starbuzz is a value and keep prices the same.

CFO: This is insane. I'm talking economics. Money.
People respond to incentives. Your fluffy little ideas won't
get us out of *this* jam.

VP Marketing

**Is there anything in the data
you have that tells you which
strategy will increase sales?**

You need an experiment to say which strategy will work best

Look again at that last question on the previous page:

Is there anything in the data you have that tells you which strategy will increase sales?

Observational data by itself can't tell you what will happen in the future.

You have no observational data that will tell you what **will** happen if you try out what either the VP of Marketing or the CFO suggests.

If you want to draw conclusions about things that overlap with your data but aren't completely described in the data, you need **theory** to make the connection.

These theories might be true or totally false, but your data doesn't say.

Marketing's Branding Theory

People respond to persuasion.

CFO's Economic Theory

People respond to price.

Marketing's strategy

Appeal to people's judgement. Starbuzz really is a good value, if you think about it in the right way. Persuading people to change their beliefs will get sales back up.

CFO's strategy

Slash the cost of coffee. This will cause people to perceive more value in Starbuzz coffee, which will drive sales back up.

You have no data to support either of these theories, no matter how passionately the others believe in them and in the strategies that follow from them.

In order to get more clarity about which strategy is better, you're going to need to run an **experiment**.

You need to experiment with these strategies in order to know which will increase sales.

I've run out of patience. I like CFO's argument. Cut prices and see what happens.

The Starbuzz CEO is in a big hurry

And he's going to pull the trigger whether you're ready or not!

Let's see how his gambit works out...

Starbuzz drops its prices

Taking a cue from the CFO, the CEO ordered
a price drop across the board for the month of
February. All prices in all Starbuzz stores are
reduced by $0.25.

$4.00 $3.75

**Will this change create
a spike in sales?**

How will you know?

One month later...

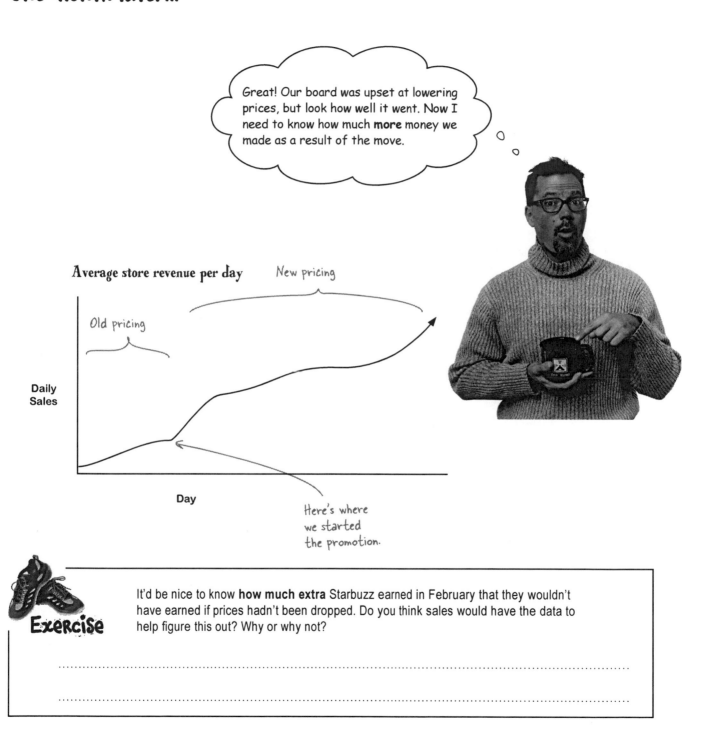

Great! Our board was upset at lowering prices, but look how well it went. Now I need to know how much **more** money we made as a result of the move.

Average store revenue per day

Old pricing

New pricing

Daily Sales

Day

Here's where we started the promotion.

Exercise

It'd be nice to know **how much extra** Starbuzz earned in February that they wouldn't have earned if prices hadn't been dropped. Do you think sales would have the data to help figure this out? Why or why not?

....

....

Exercise

Does sales have the data that would help you figure out how much more money you made off the cheaper $3.75 coffee?

Sales couldn't have the data. They only have data for $3.75 coffee and they can't compare that

data to hypothetical data about what kind of revenue $4.00 coffee would have brought them.

Control groups give you a baseline

You have **no idea** how much extra you made. Sales could have skyrocketed relative to what they would have been had the CEO not cut prices. Or they could have plummeted. You just don't know.

You don't know because by slashing prices across the board the CEO failed to follow the **method of comparison**. Good experiments always have a **control group** that enables the analyst to compare what you want to test with the status quo.

the Scholar's Corner

Control group A group of treatment subjects that represent the status quo, not receiving any new treatment.

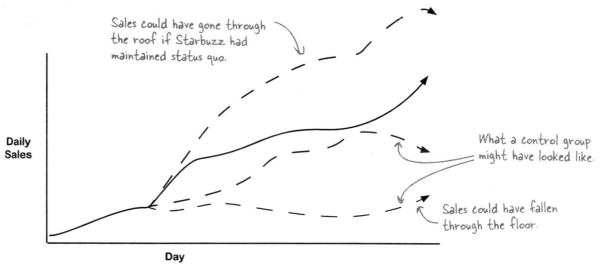

Sales could have gone through the roof if Starbuzz had maintained status quo.

Daily Sales

Day

What a control group might have looked like.

Sales could have fallen through the floor.

No control group means no comparison.
No comparison means no idea what happened.

there are no Dumb Questions

Q: Can't we compare February's sales with January's sales?

A: Sure, and if all you're interested in is whether sales in February are higher than January, you'll have your answer. But without a control, the data doesn't say whether your price-cutting had anything to do with it.

Q: What about comparing this February's sales with last year's February's sales?

A: In this question and the last one you're talking about using **historical controls**, where you take past data and treat it as the control, as opposed to **contemporaneous controls**, where your control group has its experience at the same time as your experimental group. Historical controls usually tend to favor the success of whatever it is you're trying to test because it's so hard to select a control that is really like the group you're testing. In general, you should be suspicious of historical controls.

Q: Do you always need a control? Is there ever a case where you can get by without one?

A: A lot of events in the world can't be controlled. Say you're voting in an election: you can't elect two candidates simultaneously, see which one fares better relative to the other, and then go back and elect the one that is more successful. That's just not how elections work, and it doesn't mean that you can't analyze the implications of one choice over the other. But if you *could* run an experiment like that you'd be able to get a lot more confidence in your choice!

Q: What about medical tests? Say you want to try out a new drug and are pretty sure it works. Wouldn't you just be letting people be sick or die if you stuck them in a control group that didn't receive treatment?

A: That's a good question with a legitimate ethical concern. Medical studies that lack controls (or use historical controls) have very often favored treatments that are later shown by contemporaneous controlled experiment to have no effect or even be harmful. No matter what your feelings are about a medical treatment, you don't really know that it's better than nothing until you do the controlled experiment. In the worst case, you could end up promoting a treatment that actually hurts people.

Q: Like the practice of bleeding people when they were sick?

A: Exactly. In fact, some of the first controlled experiments in history compared medical bleeding against just letting people be. Bleeding was a frankly disgusting practice that persisted for hundreds of years. We know now that it was the wrong thing to do because of controlled experiments.

Q: Do observational studies have controls?

A: They sure do. Remember the definition of observational studies: they're studies where the subjects themselves decide what group they're in, rather than having you decide it. If you wanted to do a study on smoking, for example, you couldn't tell some people to be smokers and some people not to be smokers. People decide issues like smoking on their own, and in this case, people who chose to be nonsmokers would be the control group of your observational study.

Q: I've been in all sorts of situations where sales have trended upwards in one month because we supposedly did something in the previous month. And everyone feels good because we supposedly did well. But you're saying that we have no idea whether we did well?

A: Maybe you did. There's definitely a place for gut instincts in business, and sometimes you can't do controlled experiments and have to rely on observational data-based judgements. But if you can do an experiment, do it. There's nothing like hard data to supplement your judgement and instincts when you make decisions. In this case, you don't have the hard data yet, but you have a CEO that expects answers.

The CEO still wants to know how much extra money the new strategy made... How will you answer his request?

Jim: The CEO asked us to figure out how much money we made in February that we wouldn't have made if we hadn't cut costs. We need to give the guy an answer.

Frank: Well, the answer is a problem. We have no idea how much extra money we made. It could have been a lot, but we could have lost money. Basically, we've fallen flat on our faces. We're screwed.

Joe: No way. We can definitely compare the revenue to historical controls. It might not be statistically perfect, but he'll be happy. That's all that counts.

Frank: A happy client is all that counts? Sounds like you want us to sacrifice the war to win the day. If we give him the wrong answers, it'll eventually come back on us.

Joe: Whatever.

Frank: We're going to have to give it to him straight, and it won't be pretty.

Jim: Look, we're actually in good shape here. All we have to do is set up a control group for March and run the experiment again.

Frank: But the CEO is feeling good about what happened in February, and that's because he has the wrong idea about what happened. We need to disabuse him of that good feeling.

Jim: I think we can get him thinking clearly without being downers about it.

Not getting fired 101

Having to deliver bad news is part of being a data analyst. But there are a bunch of different ways of going about delivering the same information.

Let's get straight to the point. How do you present bad news without getting fired?

The best data analysts know the right way to deliver potentially upsetting messages.

This event doesn't give us the information we want, but the good news is that I know how we fix it.

We've blown our brains out. Catastrophic meltdown. Please don't fire me.

You're right! Sales are rocking and rolling. We're up 100%. You're a genius!

Option 3: There's bad news, but if we use it correctly it's good news.

Option 2: The news is bad, so let's panic!

Option 1: There is no bad news.

Which of these approaches won't get you fired...

Today?

Tomorrow?

For your next gig?

Let's experiment ~~again~~ for real!

We're running the experiment again for the month of March. This time, Marketing divided the universe of Starbuzz stores into control and experimental groups.

The experimental group consists of stores from the Pacific region, and the control group consists of stores from the SoHo and Mid-Atlantic regions.

That was a close one!

From: CEO, Starbuzz
To: Head First
Subject: Need to re-run experiment

I get the picture. We still have two months before the board meeting. Just do what you need to do and get it right this time.

Experimental Group
Pacific region

$4.00 → $3.75

Control Group
SoHo and Mid-Atlantic regions

$4.00   *Keep this price the same.* $4.00

One month later...

Things aren't looking half bad! Your experiment might have given you the answer you want about the effectiveness of price cutting.

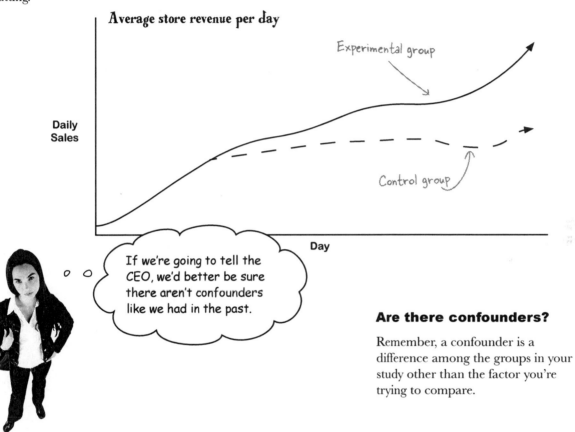

Average store revenue per day

Experimental group

Daily Sales

Control group

Day

If we're going to tell the CEO, we'd better be sure there aren't confounders like we had in the past.

Are there confounders?

Remember, a confounder is a difference among the groups in your study other than the factor you're trying to compare.

Sharpen your pencil

Look at the design on the facing page and the results above. Could any of these variables be confounding your results?

Culture

....

Coffee temperature

....

Location

....

Weather

....

Sharpen your pencil
Solution

Is it possible that these variables are confounding your results?

Culture

The culture ought to be the same all over.

Coffee temperature

This should be the same everywhere, too.

Location

Location could definitely confound.

Weather

Could be! Weather is part of location.

Confounders also plague experiments

Just because you've stepped out of the world of observational studies to do an experiment you're not off the hook with confounders.

In order for your comparison to be valid, your **groups need to be the same**. Otherwise, you're comparing apples to oranges!

You're comparing these two, but they're different in more ways than the treatment.

Control group
SoHo and Mid-Atlantic stores

Experimental group
Pacific stores

All Starbuzz Customers

Split stores into groups by <u>Region</u>

Confounding Up Close

Your results show your experimental group making more revenue. It could be because people spend more when the coffee cost less. But **since the groups aren't comparable**, it could be for any number of other reasons. The weather could be keeping people on the east coast indoors. The economy could have taken off in the Pacific region. What happened? You'll never know, because of **confounders**.

Avoid confounders by selecting groups carefully

Just as it was with observational studies, avoiding confounders is all about splitting the stores into groups correctly. But how do you do it?

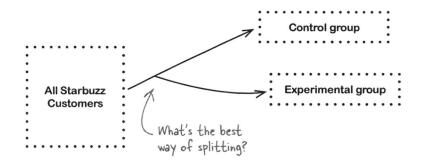

All Starbuzz Customers

Control group

Experimental group

What's the best way of splitting?

Sharpen your pencil

Here are four methods for selecting groups. How do you think each will fare as a method for avoiding confounders. Which one do you think will work best?

Charge every other customer differently as they check out. That way, half of your customers are experimental, half are control, and location isn't a confounder.

....

....

....

Use historical controls, making all the stores the control group this month and all the stores the experimental group next month.

....

....

....

Randomly assign different stores to control and experimental groups.

....

....

....

Divide big geographic regions into small ones and randomly assign the micro-regions to control and experimental groups.

....

....

....

Sharpen your pencil
Solution

Which method for selecting groups do you think is best?

Charge every other customer differently as they check out. That way, half of your customers are experimental, half are control, and location isn't a confounder.

The customers would freak out. Who wants to have to pay more than the person standing next to them? Customer anger would confound your results.

Use historical controls, making all the stores the control group this month and all the stores the experimental group next month.

We've already seen why historical controls are a problem. Who knows what could happen on the different months to throw off results?

Randomly assign different stores to control and experimental groups.

This looks kind of promising, but it doesn't quite fit the bill. People would just go to the cheaper Starbuzz outlets rather than the control group. Location would still confound.

Divide big geographic regions into small ones and randomly assign the micro-regions to control and experimental groups.

If your regions were big enough that people wouldn't travel to get cheaper coffee, but small enough to be similar to each other, you could avoid location confounding. This is the best bet.

Looks like there is something to this randomization method. Let's take a closer look...

Randomization selects similar groups

Randomly selecting members from your pool of subjects is a great way to avoid confounders.

What ends up happening when you randomly assign subjects to groups is this: the factors that might otherwise become confounders end up getting **equal representation** among your control and experimental groups.

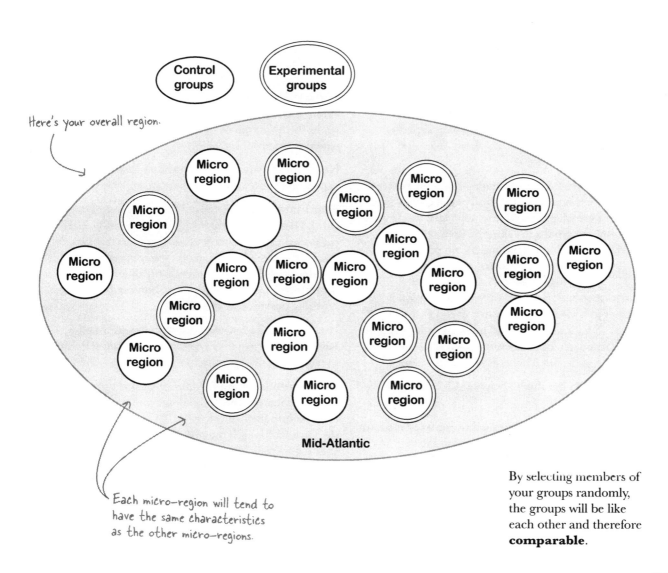

Control groups

Experimental groups

Here's your overall region.

Micro region

Mid-Atlantic

Each micro-region will tend to have the same characteristics as the other micro-regions.

By selecting members of your groups randomly, the groups will be like each other and therefore **comparable**.

Randomness Exposed

**This week's interview:
OMG that was so random!**

Head First: Randomness, thank you for joining us. You're evidently a big deal in data analysis and it's great to have you.

Randomness: Well, my schedule from one second to the next is kind of open. I have no real plan per se. My being here is, well, like the roll of the dice.

Head First: Interesting. So you have no real plan or vision for how you do things?

Randomness: That's right. Willy-nilly is how I roll.

Head First: So why are you useful in experimental design? Isn't data analysis all about order and method?

Randomness: When an analyst uses my power to select which experimental and control groups people or stores (or whatever) go into, my black magic makes the resulting groups the same as each other. I can even handle hidden confounders, no problem.

Head First: How's that?

Randomness: Say half of your population is subject to a hidden confounder, called Factor X. Scary, right? Factor X could mess up your results big time. You don't know what it is, and you don't have any data on it. But it's there, waiting to pounce.

Head First: But that's always a risk in observational studies.

Randomness: Sure, but say in your **experiment** you use me to divide your population into experimental and control groups. What'll happen is that your two groups will end up both containing Factor X to the same degree. If half of your overall population has it, then half of each of your groups will have it. That's the power of randomization.

Head First: So Factor X may still affect your results, but it'll affect both groups in the exact same way, which means you can have a valid comparison in terms of whatever it is you're testing for?

Randomness: Exactly. **Randomized controlled** is the gold standard for experiments. You can do analysis without it, but if you have it at your disposal you're going to do the best work. Randomized controlled experiments get you as close as you can get to the holy grail of data analysis: demonstrating causal relationships.

Head First: You mean that randomized controlled experiments can *prove* causal relationships?

Randomness: Well, "proof" is a very, very strong word. I'd avoid it. But think about what randomized controlled experiments get you. You're testing two groups that are identical in every way except in the variable you're testing. If there's any difference in the outcome between the groups, how could it be anything besides that variable?

Head First: So how do I do randomness? Say I have a spreadsheet list I want to split in half, selecting the members of the list randomly. How do I do it?

Randomness: Easy. In your spreadsheet program, create a column called "Random" and type this formula into the first cell: =RAND(). Copy and paste the formula for each member of your list. Then sort your list by your "Random" column. That's it! You can then divide your list into your control group and as many experimental groups as you need, and you're good to go!

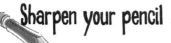

Sharpen your pencil

It's time to design your experiment. Now that you understand observational and experimental studies, control and experimental groups, confounding, and randomization, you should be able to design just the experiment to tell you what you want to know.

What are you trying to demonstrate? Why?

....
....
....
....

What are your control and experimental groups going to be?

....
....
....
....

How will you avoid confounders?

....
....
....
....

> Hey! You should add an experimental group for persuading people that Starbuzz is a good value. That way we'll know who's right—me or the CFO!

What will your results look like?

....
....
....
....

Sharpen your pencil
Solution

You've just designed your first randomized controlled experiment.
Will it work as you had hoped?

What are you trying to demonstrate? Why?

The purpose of the experiment is to figure out which will do a better job of increasing sales:
maintaining the status quo, cutting prices, or trying to persuade customers that Starbuzz coffee is a
good value. We're going to run the experiment over the course of one month: March.

What are your control and experimental groups going to be?

The control group will be stores that are functioning as they always function—no specials or
anything. One experimental group will consist of stores that have a price drop for March. The other
experimental group will consist of stores where employees try to persuade customers that Starbuzz is
a good value.

How will you avoid confounders?

By selecting groups carefully. We're going to divide each major Starbuzz region into micro-regions,
and we'll randomly assign members of that pool of micro-regions to the control and experimental
groups. That way, our three groups will be about the same.

What will your results look like?

It's impossible to know until we run the experiment, but what might happen is that one or both of the
experimental groups shows higher sales than the control group.

Your experiment is ready to go

Before we run it, let's take one last look at the process we're going through to show once and for all which strategy is best.

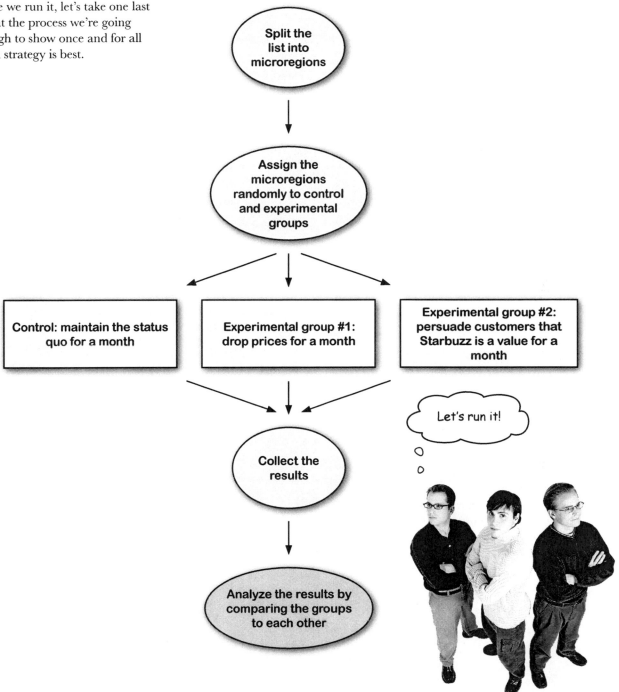

Split the list into microregions

Assign the microregions randomly to control and experimental groups

Control: maintain the status quo for a month

Experimental group #1: drop prices for a month

Experimental group #2: persuade customers that Starbuzz is a value for a month

Collect the results

Let's run it!

Analyze the results by comparing the groups to each other

The results are in

Starbuzz set up your experiment and let it run over the course of several weeks. The daily revenue levels for the value persuasion group immediately went up compared to the other two groups, and the revenue for the lower prices group actually matched the control.

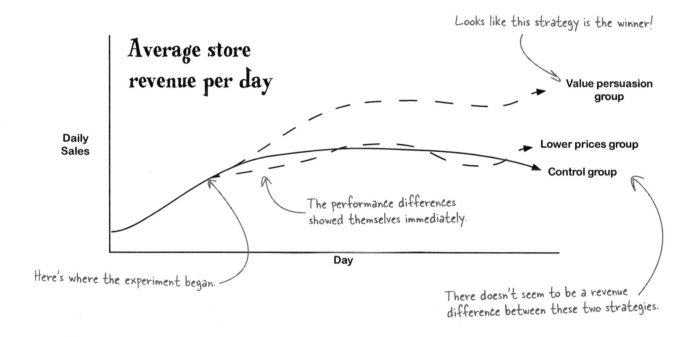

Average store revenue per day

Daily Sales

Day

Looks like this strategy is the winner!

Value persuasion group

Lower prices group

Control group

The performance differences showed themselves immediately.

Here's where the experiment began.

There doesn't seem to be a revenue difference between these two strategies.

This chart is so useful because it makes an excellent **comparison**. You selected identical groups and gave them separate treatments, so now you can really attribute the differences in revenue from these stores to the factors you're testing.

These are great results!

Value persuasion appears to result in significantly higher sales than either lowering prices or doing nothing. It looks like you have your answer.

Starbuzz has an empirically tested sales strategy

When you started this adventure in experiments, Starbuzz was in disarray. You carefully evaluated observational survey data and learned more about the business from several bright people at Starbuzz, which led you to create a **randomized controlled experiment**.

That experiment made a powerful **comparison**, which showed that persuading people that Starbuzz coffee is a more effective way to increase sales than lowering prices and doing nothing.

I'm really happy about this finding! I'm giving the order to implement this strategy in all our stores. Except for the SoHo stores. If the SoHo customers are happy to spend more, let them!

3 optimization

 # *Take it to the max* *

> Oh man, this is a blast! If only I had a rubber ducky, it'd be even better!

We all want more of something.

And we're always trying to figure out how to get it. *If* the things we want more of—profit, money, efficiency, speed—can be represented numerically, then chances are, there's a tool of data analysis to help us tweak our *decision variables,* which will help us find the **solution** or *optimal point* where we get the most of what we want. In this chapter, you'll be using one of those tools and the powerful spreadsheet **Solver** package that implements it.

You're now in the bath toy game

You've been hired by Bathing Friends Unlimited, one of the country's premier manufactures of rubber duckies and fish for bath-time entertainment purposes. Believe it or not, bath toys are a serious and profitable business.

They want to make more money, and they hear that managing their business through data analysis is all the rage, so they called you!

The rubber fish is an unconventional choice, but it's been a big seller.

Some call it the classic, some say it's too obvious, but one thing is clear: the rubber ducky is here to stay.

I'll give your firm top consideration as I make my toy purchases this year.

Duckies make me giggle.

You have demanding, discerning customers.

 Sharpen your pencil

Here's an email from your client at Bathing Friends Unlimited, describing why they hired you.

From: Bathing Friends Unlimited
To: Head First
Subject: Requested analysis of product mix

Dear Analyst,

We're excited to have you!

We want to be as profitable as possible, and in order to get our profits up, we need to make sure we're making the right amount of ducks and the right amount of fish. What we need you to help us figure out is our ideal *product mix*: how much of each should we manufacture?

Looking forward to your work. We've heard great things.

Regards,

BFU

Here's what your client says about what she needs.

What **data** do you need to solve this problem?

....

....

....

....

....

....

Sharpen your pencil
Solution

From: Bathing Friends Unlimited
To: Head First
Subject: Requested analysis of product mix

Dear Analyst,

We're excited to have you!

We want to be as profitable as possible, and in order to get our profits up we need to make sure we're making the right amount of ducks and the right amount of fish. What we need you to help us figure out is our ideal product mix: how much of each should we manufacture?

Looking forward to your work. We've heard great things.

Regards,

BFU

What *data* do you need to solve this problem?

First of all, it'd be nice to have data on just how profitable ducks

and fish are. Is one more profitable than the other? But more than

that, it'd be nice to know what other factors constrain the problem.

How much rubber does it take make these products? And how much

time does it take to manufacture these products?

Your Data Needs Up Close

Take a closer look at what you need to know. You can divide those data needs into two categories: **things you can't control**, and things you can.

These are things you can't control.

- How profitable fish are
- How much rubber they have to make fish
- How much rubber they have to make ducks

- How profitable ducks are
- How much time it takes to make fish
- How much time it takes to make ducks

And the basic thing the client wants you to find out in order to get the profit as high as possible. Ultimately, the answers to these two questions you **can control**.

These are things you can control.

- How many fish to make
- How many ducks to make

You need the hard numbers on what you can and can't control.

Constraints limit the variables you control

These considerations are called **constraints**, because they will define the parameters for your problem. What you're ultimately after is *profit*, and finding the right product mix is how you'll determine the right level of profitability for next month.

But your options for product mix will be *limited* by your constraints.

These are your actual constraints for this problem.

Decision variables are things you can control

Constraints don't tell you how to maximize profit; they only tell you what you *can't* do to maximize profit.

Decision variables, on the other hand, are the things you *can* control. You get to choose how many ducks and fish will be manufactured, and as long as your constraints are met, your job is to choose the combination that creates the most profit.

From: Bathing Friends Unlimited
To: Head First
Subject: Potentially useful info

Dear Analyst,

Great questions. Re rubber supply: we have enough rubber to manufacture 500 ducks or 400 fish. If we did make 400 fish, we wouldn't have any rubber to make ducks, and vice versa.

We have time to make 400 ducks or 300 fish. That has to do with the time it takes to set the rubber. No matter what the product mix is, we can't make more than 400 ducks and 300 fish if we want the product on shelves next month.

Finally, each duck makes us $5 in profit, and each fish makes us $4 in profit. Does that help?

Regards,

BFU

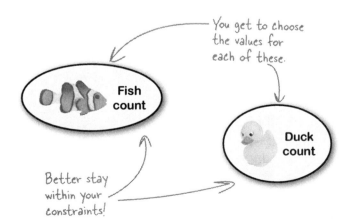

You get to choose the values for each of these.

Fish count

Duck count

Better stay within your constraints!

BRAIN POWER

So, what do you think you *do* with constraints and decision variables to figure out how to maximize profit?

You have an optimization problem

When you want to get as much (or as little) of something as possible, and the way you'll get it is by changing the values of other quantities, you have an **optimization problem**.

Here you want to maximize *profit* by changing your decision variables: the number of ducks and fish you manufacture.

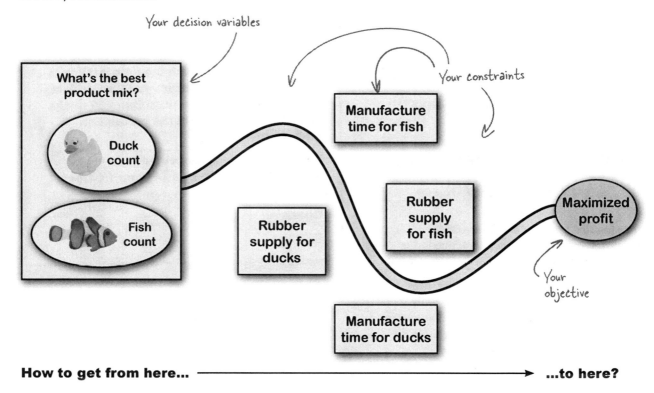

How to get from here... ⟶ **...to here?**

But to maximize profit, you have to stay within your constraints: the manufacture time and rubber supply for both toys.

To solve an optimization problem, you need to combine your decision variables, constraints, and the thing you want to maximize together into an **objective function**.

Find your objective with the objective function

The **objective** is the thing you want to maximize or minimize, and you use the **objective function** to find the optimum result.

Here's what your objective function looks like, if you state it algebraically:

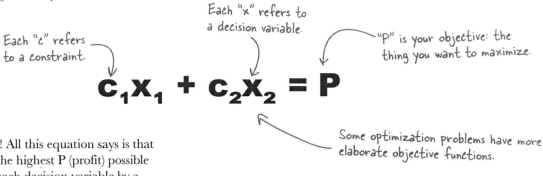

Each "c" refers to a constraint.

Each "x" refers to a decision variable.

"P" is your objective: the thing you want to maximize.

$$c_1 x_1 + c_2 x_2 = P$$

Some optimization problems have more elaborate objective functions.

Don't be scared! All this equation says is that you should get the highest P (profit) possible by multiplying each decision variable by a constraint.

Your constraints and decision variables in this equation combine to become the profit of ducks and fish, and those together form your objective: the total profit.

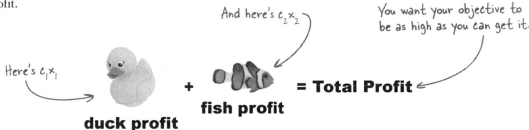

Here's $c_1 x_1$

And here's $c_2 x_2$

You want your objective to be as high as you can get it.

duck profit + **fish profit** = **Total Profit**

All optimization problems have constraints and an objective function.

BRAIN BARBELL

What specific values do you think you should use for the constraints, c_1 and c_2?

Your objective function

The constraints that you need to put into your objective function are the **profit for each toy**. Here's another way to look at that algebraic function:

(💵 * 🦆) + (💵 * 🐠) = 👩

Here's your client from Bathing Friends Unlimited.

The profit you get from selling fish and ducks is equal to the profit per duck multiplied by the number of ducks plus the profit per fish multiplied by the number of fish.

(**profit per duck** * **count of ducks**) + (**profit per fish** * **count of fish**) = **Profit**

Total duck profit.

Total fish profit.

Now you can start trying out some product mixes. You can fill in this equation with the values you know represent the profit per item along with some hypothetical count amounts.

This is what your profit would be if you decide to make 100 ducks and 50 fish.

(**$5 profit** * **100 ducks**) + (**$4 profit** * **50 fish**) = **$700**

This objective function projects a $700 profit for *next month*. We'll use the objective function to try out a number of other product mixes, too.

Hey! What about all those other constraints? Like rubber and time?

Show product mixes with your other constraints

Rubber and time place limits on the count of fish you can manufacture, and the best way to start thinking about these constraints is to envision different hypothetical **product mixes**. Let's start with the constraint of *time*.

Here's what they say about their time constraint.

ducks, and vice versa.

We have time to make 400 ducks or 300 fish. That has to do with the time it takes to set the rubber. No matter what the product mix is, we can't make more than 400 ducks and 300 fish if we want the product on shelves next month.

Finally, each duck makes us $5 in profit.

A hypothetical "Product mix 1" might be where you manufacture 100 ducks and 200 fish. You can plot the time constraints for that product mix (and two others) on these bar graphs.

This line shows the maximum number of ducks you can produce.

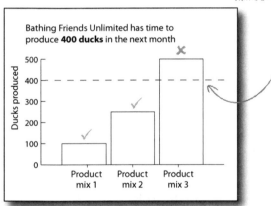

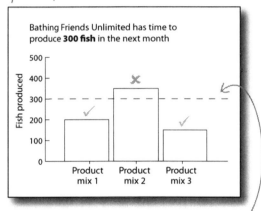

This line shows how many fish you have time to produce.

Product mix 1 doesn't violate any constraints, but the other two do: product mix 2 has too many fish, and product mix 3 has too many ducks.

Seeing the constraints in this way is progress, but we need a better visualization. We have yet more constraints to manage, and it'd be clearer if we could view them **both** on a single chart.

BRAIN BARBELL

How would you visualize the constraints on hypothetical product mixes of ducks *and* fish with one chart?

Plot multiple constraints on the same chart

We can plot both time constraints on a single chart, representing each product mix with a dot rather than a bar. The resulting chart makes it easy to **visualize both time constraints together**.

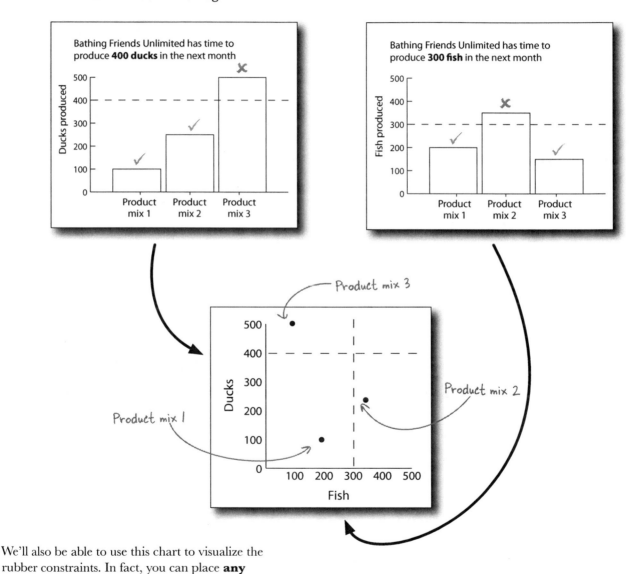

We'll also be able to use this chart to visualize the rubber constraints. In fact, you can place **any number of constraints** on this chart and get an idea of what product mixes are possible.

Your good options are all in the feasible region

Plotting ducks on a y-axis and fish on an x-axis makes it easy to see what product mixes are *feasible*. In fact, the space where product mixes are within the constraint lines is called the **feasible region**.

When you add constraints to your chart, the feasible region will change, and you'll use the feasible region to figure out which point is *optimal*.

This is the feasible region.

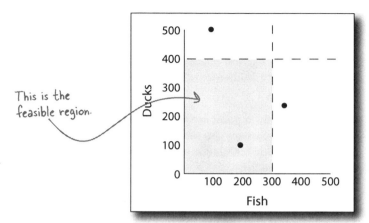

Sharpen your pencil

Let's add our other constraint, which states how many fish and ducks can be produced given the quantity of rubber they have. Bathing Friends Unlimited said:

Each fish takes a little more rubber to make than each duck.

Great questions. Re rubber supply: we have enough rubber to manufacture 500 ducks or 400 fish. If we did make 400 fish, we wouldn't have any rubber to make ducks, and vice versa.

You have a fixed supply of rubber, so the number of ducks you make will limit the number of fish you can make.

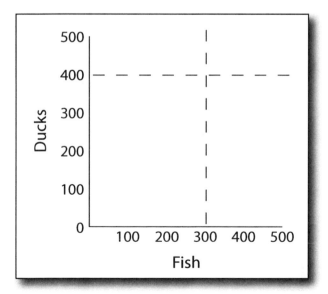

1 Draw a point representing a product mix where you make 400 fish. As she says, if you make 400 fish, you won't have rubber to make any ducks.

2 Draw a point representing a product mix where you make 500 ducks. If you made 500 ducks, you'd be able to make zero fish.

3 Draw a line through the two points.

Sharpen your pencil
Solution

How does the new constraint look on your chart?

1 Draw a point representing a product mix where you make 400 fish. As she says, if you make 400 fish, you won't have rubber to make any ducks.

2 Draw a point representing a product mix where you make 500 ducks. If you made 500 ducks, you'd be able to make zero fish.

3 Draw a line through the two points.

Great questions. Re rubber supply: we have enough rubber to manufacture 500 ducks or 400 fish. If we did make 400 fish, we wouldn't have any rubber to make ducks, and vice versa.

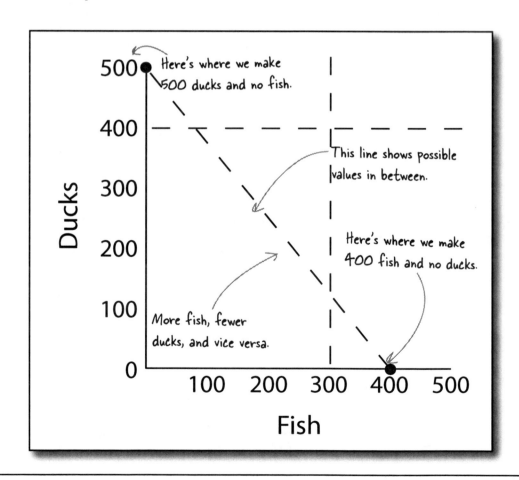

Here's where we make 500 ducks and no fish.

This line shows possible values in between.

Here's where we make 400 fish and no ducks.

More fish, fewer ducks, and vice versa.

Your new constraint changed the feasible region

When you added the rubber constraint, you **changed the shape** of the feasible region.

Before you added the constraint, you might have been able to make, say, 400 ducks and 300 fish. But now your rubber scarcity has ruled out that product mix as a possibility.

You can't use duck/fish combinations that exist in any of these spaces.

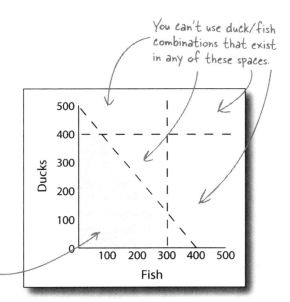

Your potential product mixes all need to be inside here.

Sharpen your pencil

Draw where each product mix goes on the chart.

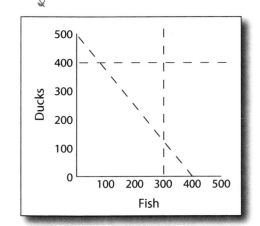

Here are some possible product mixes.

Are they inside the feasible region?
Draw a dot for each product mix on the chart.

How much profit will the different product mixes create?
Use the equation below to determine the profit for each.

300 ducks and 250 fish

Profit: ....

100 ducks and 200 fish

Profit: ....

50 ducks and 300 fish

Profit: ....

Use your objective function to determine profit.

$$\left(\begin{array}{c} \textbf{\$5} \\ \textbf{profit} \end{array} * \begin{array}{c} \textbf{count of} \\ \textbf{ducks} \end{array} \right) + \left(\begin{array}{c} \textbf{\$4} \\ \textbf{profit} \end{array} * \begin{array}{c} \textbf{count} \\ \textbf{of fish} \end{array} \right) = \textbf{Profit}$$

Sharpen your pencil
Solution

You just graphed and calculated the profit for three different product mixes of ducks and fish. What did you find?

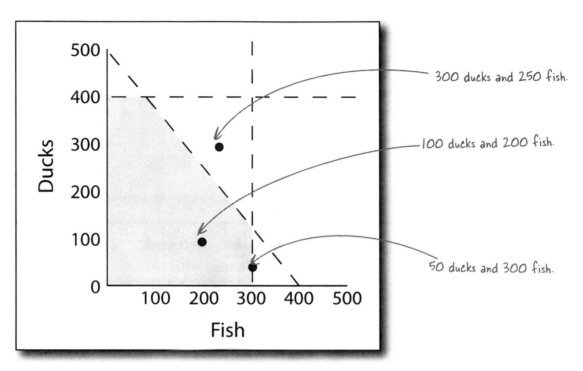

300 ducks and 250 fish.

100 ducks and 200 fish.

50 ducks and 300 fish.

300 ducks and 250 fish.

Profit: (¦5 profit*300 ducks)+(¦4 profit*250 fish) = ¦2500

Too bad this product mix isn't in the feasible region.

100 ducks and 200 fish.

Profit: (¦5 profit*100 ducks)+(¦4 profit*200 fish) = ¦1300

This product mix definitely works.

50 ducks and 300 fish.

Profit: (¦5 profit*50 ducks)+(¦4 profit*300 fish) = ¦1450

This product mix works and makes even more money.

Now all you have to do is try every possible product mix and see which one has the most profit, right?

Even in the small space of the feasible region there are tons and tons of possible product mixes. There's no way you're going to get me to try them all.

You don't have to try them all.

Because both Microsoft Excel and OpenOffice have a handy little function that makes short order of optimization problems. Just turn the page to find out how…

Your spreadsheet does optimization

Microsoft Excel and OpenOffice both have a handy little utility called **Solver** that can make short order of your optimization problems.

If you plug in the constraints and write the objective function, Solver does the algebra for you. Take a look at this spreadsheet, which describes all the information you received from Bathing Friends Unlimited.

Load this!

www.headfirstlabs.com/books/hfda/ bathing_friends_unlimited.xls

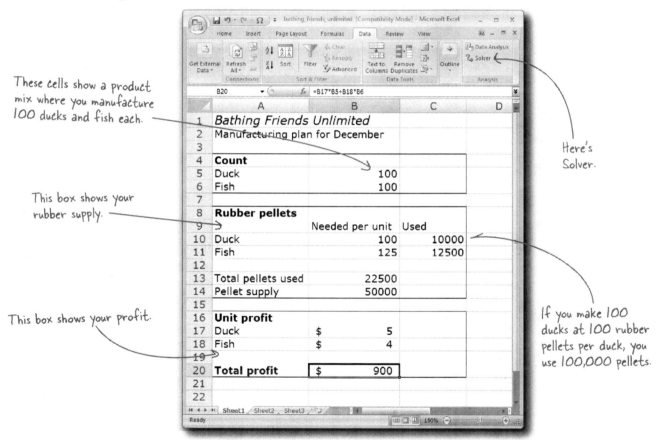

These cells show a product mix where you manufacture 100 ducks and fish each.

This box shows your rubber supply.

This box shows your profit.

Here's Solver.

If you make 100 ducks at 100 rubber pellets per duck, you use 100,000 pellets.

There are a few simple formulas on this spreadsheet. First, here are some numbers to quantify your rubber needs. The bath toys are made out of rubber pellets, and cells B10:B11 have formulas that calculate how many pellets you need.

Second, cell B20 has a formula that multiplies the count of fish and ducks by the profit for each to get the total profit.

Take a look at Appendix iii if you use OpenOffice or if Solver isn't on your Excel menu.

> **Try clicking the Solver button under the Data tab. What happens?**

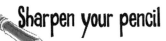

Sharpen your pencil

Let's take a look at the Solver dialog box and figure out how it works with the concepts you've learned.

Draw an arrow from each element to where it goes in the Solver dialogue box.

Rubber and time

Decision variables   Constraints ⟵   Objective

The number of ducks to make

Profit

Solver Parameters

Set Target Cell: [   ]

Equal To: ⦿ Max   ○ Min   ○ Value of: [0   ]

By Changing Cells:

[   ]   Guess

Subject to the Constraints:

[   ]   Add
                                    Change
                                    Delete

Solve
Close
Options
Reset All
Help

Draw an arrow from each element to where it should go on the Solver.

Where do you think the **objective function** goes?

....

....

Sharpen your pencil
Solution

How do the spaces in the Solver dialog box match up with the optimization concepts you've learned?

Draw an arrow from each element to where it goes in the Solver dialogue box.

Decision variables   Constraints   Objective

Excel calls your objective
the Target Cell.

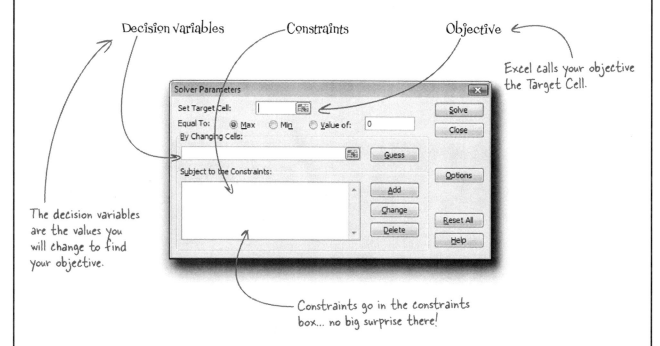

The decision variables
are the values you
will change to find
your objective.

Constraints go in the constraints
box... no big surprise there!

Where do you think the **objective function** goes?

The objective function goes in a cell on the spreadsheet and returns the objective as the result.

The objective that this objective function calculates is the total profit.

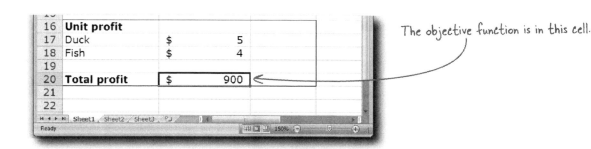

The objective function is in this cell.

16	**Unit profit**		
17	Duck	$	5
18	Fish	$	4
19			
20	**Total profit**	$	900
21			
22			

TEST DRIVE

Now that you've defined your optimization model, it's time to plug the elements of it into Excel and let the Solver do your number crunching for you.

1 Set your target cell to point to your objective function.

2 Find your decision variables and add them to the Changing Cells blank.

3 Add your constraints.

4 Click Solve!

Here's your rubber constraint.

Don't forget your time constraints!

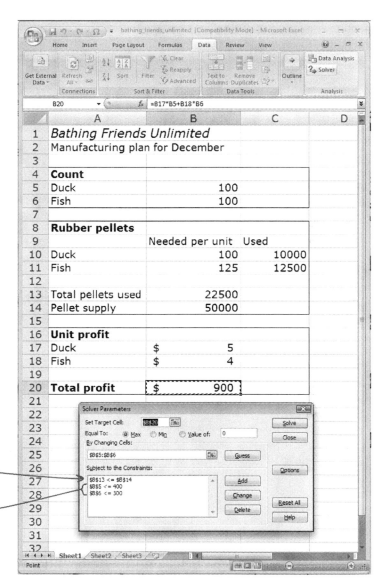

What happens when you click Solve?

Solver crunched your optimization problem in a snap

Nice work. Solver took all of about a millisecond to find the solution to your optimization problem. If Bathing Friends Unlimited wants to maximize its profit, it need only manufacture 400 ducks and 80 fish.

Solver tried out a bunch of Count values and found the ones that maximize profit.

Looks like you're using all your rubber, too.

What's more, if you compare Solver's result to the graph you created, you can see that the precise point that Solver considers the best is on the outer limit of your feasible region.

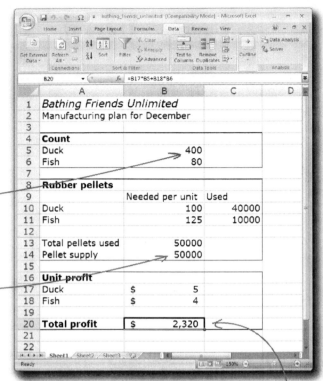

	A	B	C	D
1	*Bathing Friends Unlimited*			
2	Manufacturing plan for December			
3				
4	**Count**			
5	Duck	400		
6	Fish	80		
7				
8	**Rubber pellets**			
9		Needed per unit	Used	
10	Duck	100	40000	
11	Fish	125	10000	
12				
13	Total pellets used	50000		
14	Pellet supply	50000		
15				
16	**Unit profit**			
17	Duck	$ 5		
18	Fish	$ 4		
19				
20	**Total profit**	$ 2,320		
21				
22				

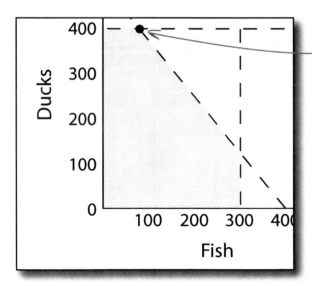

Here's your solution.

Here's the profit you can expect.

Looks like great work. Now how did you get to that solution again?

Better explain to the client what you've been up to...

Sharpen your pencil

How would you explain to the client what you're up to? Describe each of these visualizations. What do they mean, and what do they accomplish?

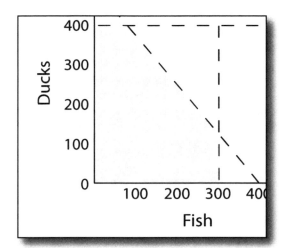

....

....

....

....

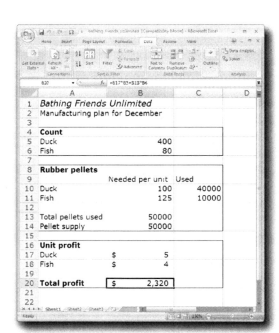

....

....

....

....

Sharpen your pencil
Solution

How did you interpret your findings to your client?

The shaded part of this graph shows all the possible

duck/fish product mixes given our constraints, which

are represented by the dashed lines. But this chart

does not point out the solution itself.

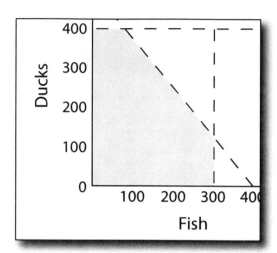

This spreadsheet shows the product mix computed by

Excel to be the optimum. Of all possible product mixes,

manufacturing 400 ducks and 80 fish produces the

most profit while staying inside our constraints.

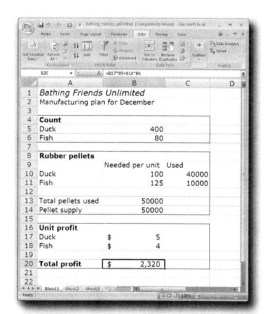

Profits fell through the floor

You just got this note from Bathing
Friends Unlimited about the
results of your analysis…

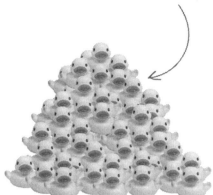

There are lots of ducks left over!

> **From: Bathing Friends Unlimited**
> **To: Head First**
> **Subject: Results of your "analysis"**
>
> **Dear Analyst,**
>
> **Frankly, we're shocked. We sold all 80 of
> the fish we produced, but we only sold 20
> ducks. That means our gross profit is only
> $420, which you might realize is way below
> the estimate you gave us of $2,320. Clearly,
> we wanted something better than this.**
>
> **We haven't ever had this sort of experience
> before with our duck sales, so for the
> moment we're not blaming you for this until
> we can do our own internal evaluation of
> what happened. You might want to do your
> own analysis, too.**
>
> **Regards,**
>
> **BFU**

This is pretty **bad news**. The fish sold out,
but no one's buying the ducks. Looks like you
may have made a mistake.

I want to see
your explanation.

**How does *your
model* explain
this situation?**

Your model only describes what you put into it

Your model tells you how to maximize profits only **under the constraints you specified.**

Your models approximate reality and are never perfect, and sometimes their imperfections can cause you problems.

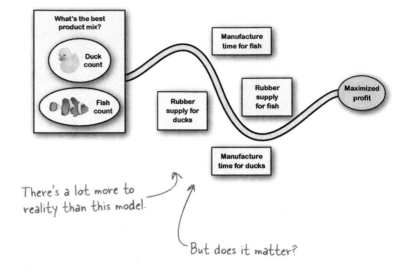

There's a lot more to reality than this model.

But does it matter?

It's a good idea to keep in mind this cheeky quote from a famous statistician:

"All models are wrong, but some are useful."

– George Box

Your analytical tools inevitably simplify reality, but if your **assumptions** are accurate and your data's good the tools can be pretty reliable.

Your goal should be to create the ***most useful models*** you can, making the imperfections of the models unimportant relative to your analytical objectives.

So how will I know if my model has the right assumptions?

Calibrate your assumptions to your analytical objectives

You can't specify all your assumptions, but if you miss an important one it could ruin your analysis.

You will always be asking yourself how far you need to go specifying assumptions. It depends on how important your analysis is.

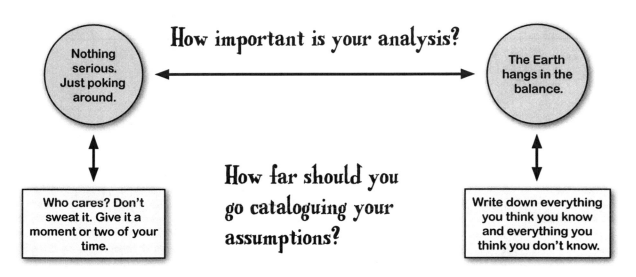

How important is your analysis?

Nothing serious. Just poking around.

The Earth hangs in the balance.

How far should you go cataloguing your assumptions?

Who cares? Don't sweat it. Give it a moment or two of your time.

Write down everything you think you know and everything you think you don't know.

Sharpen your pencil

What assumption do you need to include in order to get your optimization model working again?

....

....

....

....

Sharpen your pencil
Solution

Is there an assumption that would help you refine your model?

There's nothing in the current model that says <u>what people will actually buy</u>. The model describes time, rubber, and profit, but in order for the model to work, people would have to buy everything we make. But, as we saw, this isn't happening, so we need an assumption about what people will buy.

there are no
Dumb Questions

Q: **What if the bad assumption were true, and people *would* buy everything we manufactured? Would the optimization method have worked?**

A: Probably. If you can **assume** that everything you make will sell out, then maximizing your profitability is going to be largely about fine-tuning your product mix.

Q: **But what if I set up the objective function to figure out how to maximize the amount of ducks and fish we made overall? It would seem that, if everything was selling out, we'd want to figure out how to make more.**

A: That's a good idea, but remember your constraints. Your contact at Bathing Friends Unlimited said that you were limited in the amount of fish and ducks you could produce by both time and rubber supply. Those are your constraints.

Q: **Optimization sounds kind of narrow. It's a tool that you only use when you have a single number that you want to maximize and some handy equations that you can use to find the right value.**

A: But you can think of optimization more broadly than that. The optimizing mentality is all about figuring out what you want and carefully identifying the constraints that will affect how you are able to get it. Often, those constraints will be things you can represent quantitatively, and in that case, an algebraic software tool like Solver will work well.

Q: **So Solver will do my optimizations if my problems can be represented quantitatively.**

A: A lot of quantitative problems can be handled by Solver, but Solver is a tool that specializes in problems involving *linear programming*. There are other types of optimization problems and a variety of algorithms to solve them. If you'd like to learn more, run a search on the Internet for **operations research**.

Q: **Should I use optimization to deal with this new model, will we sell people what they want?**

A: Yes, if we can figure out how to incorporate people's preferences into our optimization model.

Exercise

Here's some historical sales data for rubber fish and ducks. With this information, you might be able to figure out why no one seemed interested in buying all your ducks.

Load this!

www.headfirstlabs.com/books/hfda/
historical_sales_data.xls

Is there a pattern in the sales over time that hints at why ducks didn't sell well last month?

....

....

....

....

This sales data is for the whole rubber toy industry, not just BFU, so it's a good indicator of what people prefer to buy and when they prefer to buy it.

Do you see any month-to-month patterns?

	A	B	C	D	E
1	Month	Year	Fish	Ducks	Total
2	J	2006	71	25	96
3	F	2006	76	29	105
4	M	2006	73	29	102
5	A	2006	81	29	110
6	M	2006	83	32	115
7	J	2006	25	81	106
8	J	2006	35	89	124
9	A	2006	32	91	123
10	S	2006	25	87	112
11	O	2006	21	96	117
12	N	2006	113	51	164
13	D	2006	125	49	174
14	J	2007	90	34	124
15	F	2007	91	30	121
16	M	2007	90	30	120
17	A	2007	35	97	132
18	M	2007	34	96	130
19	J	2007	34	97	131
20	J	2007	43	105	148
21	A	2007	38	105	143
22	S	2007	119	43	162
23	O	2007	134	45	179
24	N	2007	139	58	197
25	D	2007	148	60	208
26	J	2008	103	37	140
27	F	2008	37	106	143
28	M	2008	34	103	137
29	A	2008	45	114	159
30	M	2008	40	117	157
31	J	2008	37	113	150
32	J	2008	129	48	177
33	A	2008	127	45	172
34	S	2008	137	45	182
35	O	2008	160	56	216
36	N	2008	125	175	300
37	D	2008	137	201	338

Exercise
Solution

What do you see when you look at this new data?

Is there a pattern in the sales over time that hints at why Ducks didn't sell well last month?

Duck sales and fish sales seem to go in opposite

directions. When one's up, the other's down. Last

month, everyone wanted fish.

There are big drops in sales every January.

Here's a switch, where ducks sell well and then fish jump ahead..

Here's another switch!

	A	B	C	D	E
1	Month	Year	Fish	Ducks	Total
2	J	2006	71	25	96
3	F	2006	76	29	105
4	M	2006	73	29	102
5	A	2006	81	29	110
6	M	2006	83	32	115
7	J	2006	25	81	106
8	J	2006	35	89	124
9	A	2006	32	91	123
10	S	2006	25	87	112
11	O	2006	21	96	117
12	N	2006	113	51	164
13	D	2006	125	49	174
14	J	2007	90	34	124
15	F	2007	91	30	121
16	M	2007	90	30	120
17	A	2007	35	97	132
18	M	2007	34	96	130
19	J	2007	34	97	131
20	J	2007	43	105	148
21	A	2007	38	105	143
22	S	2007	119	43	162
23	O	2007	134	45	179
24	N	2007	139	58	197
25	D	2007	148	60	208
26	J	2008	103	37	140
27	F	2008	37	106	143
28	M	2008	34	103	137
29	A	2008	45	114	159
30	M	2008	40	117	157
31	J	2008	37	113	150
32	J	2008	129	48	177
33	A	2008	127	45	172
34	S	2008	137	45	182
35	O	2008	160	56	216
36	N	2008	125	175	300
37	D	2008	137	201	338

Watch out for negatively linked variables

We don't know *why* rubber duck and fish sales seem to go in opposite directions from each other, but it sure looks like they are **negatively linked**. More of one means less of the other.

Together, they have an increasing trend, with holiday season sales spikes, but always one is ahead of the other.

Sometimes, fish are down and ducks are up.

Fish   Ducks

Sometimes, ducks are down and fish are up.

Fish   Ducks

But nowhere in the data are they both up.

Fish   Ducks

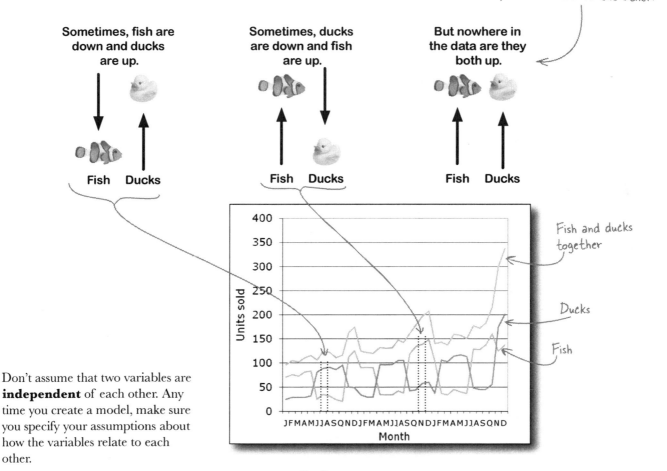

Fish and ducks together

Ducks

Fish

Don't assume that two variables are **independent** of each other. Any time you create a model, make sure you specify your assumptions about how the variables relate to each other.

**BRAIN POWER**

What sort of constraint would you add to your optimization model to account for the negatively linked fish and duck sales?

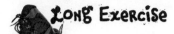

Long Exercise

You need a new constraint that **estimates demand** for ducks and fish for the month in which you hope to sell them.

1 Looking at the historical sales data, estimate what you think the highest amount of sales for ducks and fish will be next month. **Assume** also that the next month will follow the trend of the months that precede it.

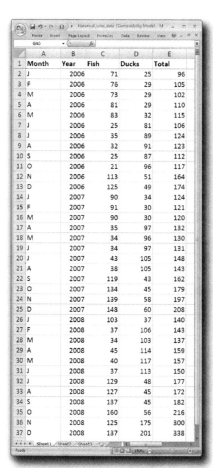

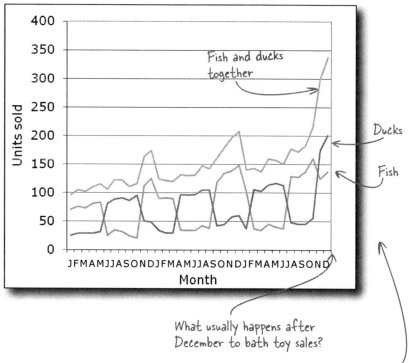

Fish and ducks together

Ducks

Fish

What usually happens after December to bath toy sales?

Which toy do you think will be on top next month?

2 Run the Solver again, adding your estimates as new constraints. For both ducks and fish, what do you think is the **maximum number** of units you could hope to sell?

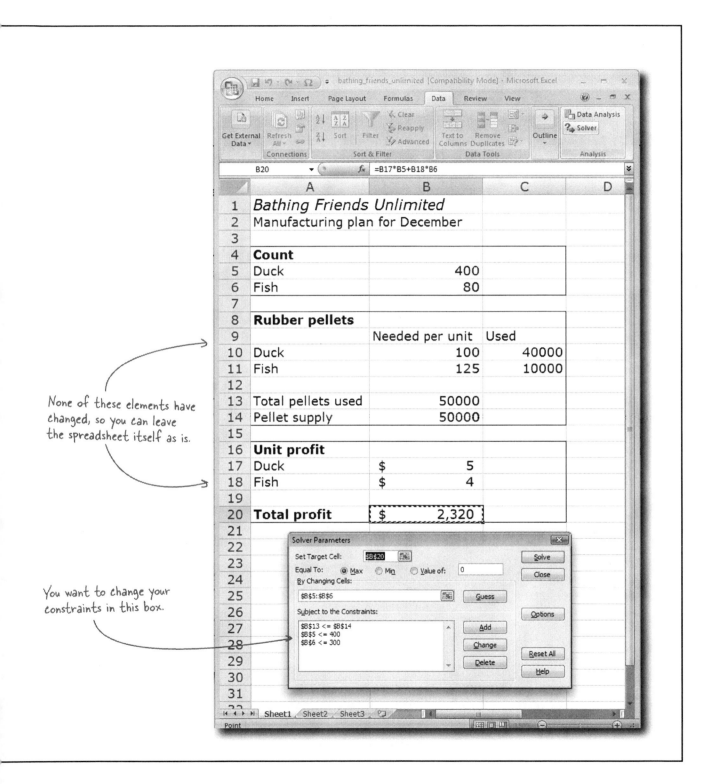

None of these elements have changed, so you can leave the spreadsheet itself as is.

You want to change your constraints in this box.

LONG EXERCISE SOLUTION

You ran your optimization model again to incorporate estimates about rubber duck and fish sales. What did you learn?

1 Looking at the historical sales data, estimate what you think the highest amount of sales for ducks and fish will be next month. **Assume** that the next month will be similar to the months that preceded it.

We should prepare for a big drop in January sales, and it looks like ducks will still be on top.

We probably won't be able to sell more than 150 ducks.

Fish and ducks together

Ducks

Fish

We probably won't be able to sell more than 50 fish.

2 Run the Solver again, adding your estimates as new constraints. For example, if you don't think that more than 50 fish will sell next month, make sure you add a constraint that tells Solver not to suggest manufacturing more than 50 fish.

Here are your new constraints.

Ducks

Fish

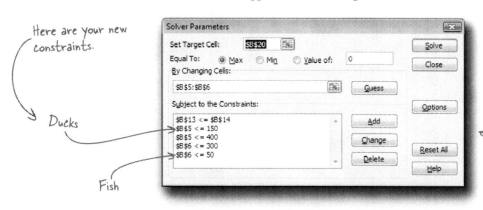

Your specific numbers may vary a little... these are estimates after all.

Here's what Solver returned:

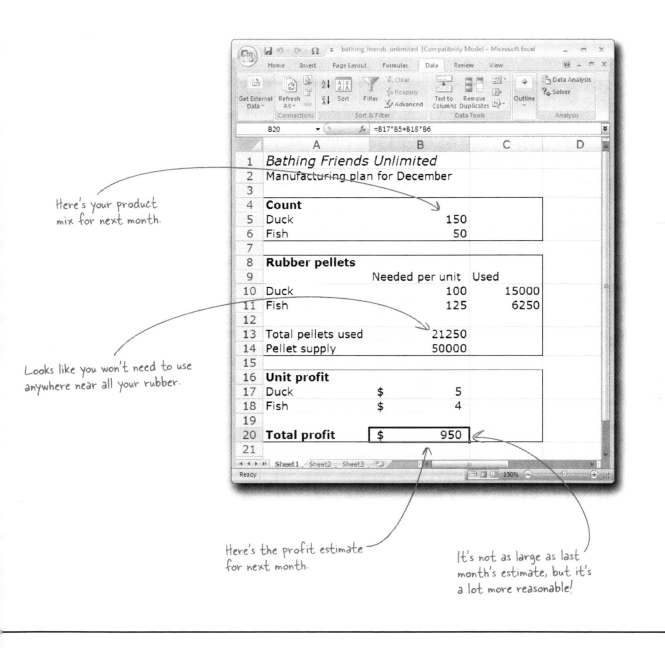

Here's your product mix for next month.

Looks like you won't need to use anywhere near all your rubber.

Here's the profit estimate for next month.

It's not as large as last month's estimate, but it's a lot more reasonable!

Your new plan is working like a charm

The new plan is working brilliantly. Nearly every duck and fish that comes out of their manufacturing operation is sold immediately, so they have no excess inventory and every reason to believe that the profit maximization model has them where they need to be.

Not too shabby

> **From: Bathing Friends Unlimited**
> **To: Head First**
> **Subject: Thank you!!!**
>
> **Dear Analyst,**
>
> **You gave us *exactly* what we wanted, and we really appreciate it. Not only have you optimized our profit, you've made our operations more intelligent and data-driven. We'll definitely use your model for a long time to come. Thank you!**
>
> **Regards,**
>
> **BFU**
>
> **P.S. Please accept this little token of our appreciation, a special Head First edition of our timeless rubber duck.**

Enjoy your duck!

Good job! One question: the model works because you got the relationship right between duck demand and fish demand. But what if that relationship changes? What if people start buying them together, or not at all?

Your assumptions are based on an ever-changing reality

All your data is observational, and you don't know what will happen in the future.

Your model is working now, but it might break suddenly. You need to be ready and able to reframe your analysis as necessary. This perpetual, iterative framework is what analysts do.

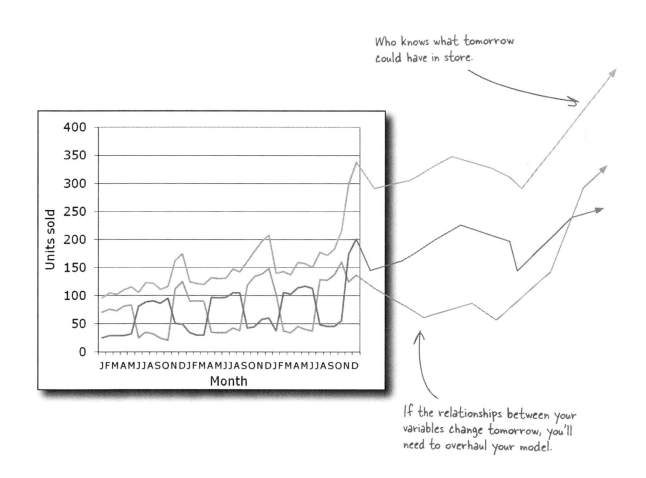

Who knows what tomorrow could have in store.

If the relationships between your variables change tomorrow, you'll need to overhaul your model.

Be ready to change your model!

4 data visualization

Pictures make you smarter

Now hold still... we want to get all the variables together in one shot.

You need more than a table of numbers.

Your data is brilliantly complex, with more variables than you can shake a stick at. Mulling over mounds and mounds of spreadsheets isn't just boring; it can actually be a waste of your time. A clear, highly multivariate visualization can in a small space show you the forest that you'd miss for the trees if you were just looking at spreadsheets all the time.

New Army needs to optimize their website

New Army is an online clothing retailer that just ran an experiment to test web layouts. For one month, everyone who came to the website was randomly served one of these three **home page designs**.

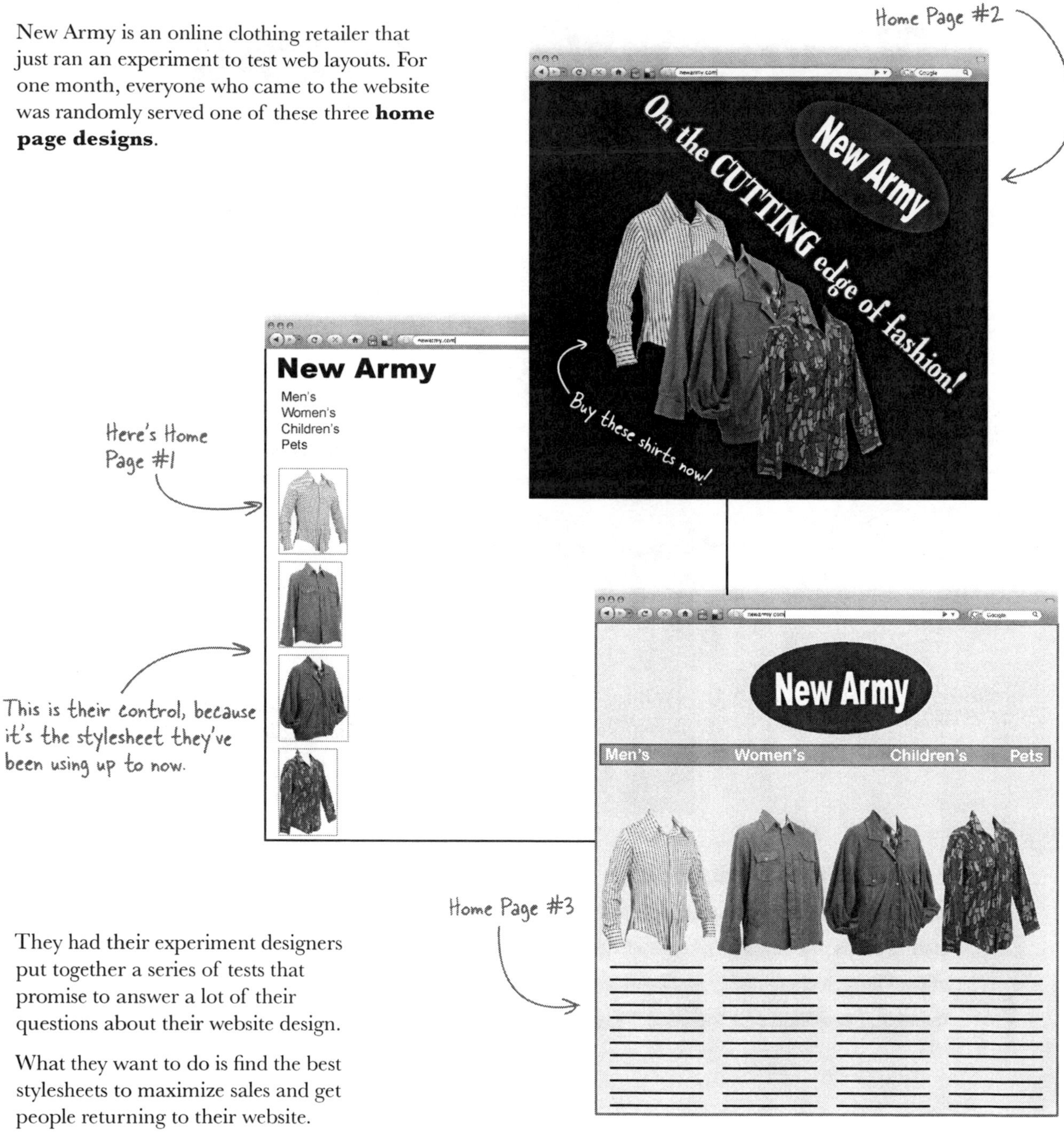

Home Page #2

Here's Home Page #1

This is their control, because it's the stylesheet they've been using up to now.

Home Page #3

They had their experiment designers put together a series of tests that promise to answer a lot of their questions about their website design.

What they want to do is find the best stylesheets to maximize sales and get people returning to their website.

The results are in, but the information designer is out

Now that they have a store of fantastic data from a controlled, randomized experiment, they need a way to visualize it all together.

So they hired a fancy **information designer** and asked him to pull together something that helped them understand the implications of their research. Unfortunately, all did not work out as planned.

We got a lot of crap back from the information designer we hired. It didn't help us understand our data at all, so he got the ax. Can you create data visualizations for us that help us build a better website?

What we want to see is which stylesheet or stylesheets maximize revenue, the time our visitors spend on the site, and return visits to the site.

Web guru from New Army

You'll need to redesign the visualizations for the analysis. It could be hard work, because the experiment designers at New Army are an exacting bunch and generated **a lot of solid data**.

But before we start, let's take a look at the rejected designs. We'll likely learn something by knowing what sort of visualizations *won't* work.

Let's take a look at the rejected designs...

The last information designer submitted these three infographics

The information designer submitted these three designs to New Army. Take a look at these designs. What are your impressions? Can you see why the client might not have been pleased?

Keyword clicks... what does that mean?

The size of the text must have something to do with the number of clicks.

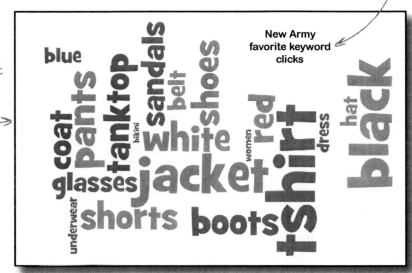

New Army favorite keyword clicks

You can make tag clouds like this for free at http://www.wordle.net.

Looks like this chart measures how many visits each home page got.

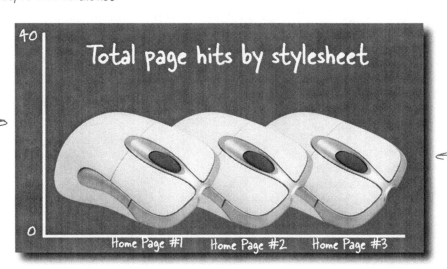

It seems that they're all about the same.

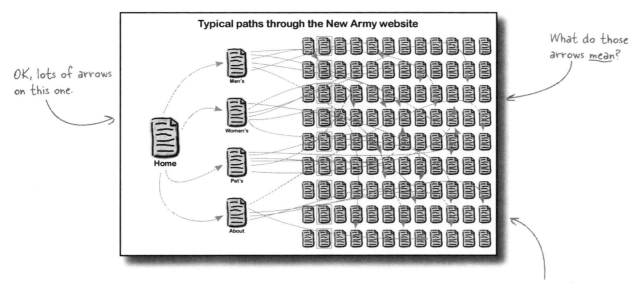

OK, lots of arrows on this one.

What do those arrows <u>mean</u>?

These visualizations are definitely flashy, but what's behind them?

What data is behind the visualizations?

"What is the data behind the visualizations?" is the very **first question** you should ask when looking at a new visualization. You care about the quality of the data and its interpretation, and you'd hate for a flashy design to get in the way of your own judgments about the analysis.

What d'ya got back there?

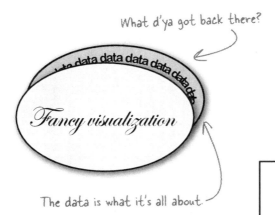

The data is what it's all about.

BRAIN POWER

What sort of data do you think is behind these visualizations?

Show the data!

You can't tell from these visualizations what data is behind them. If you're the client, how could you ever expect to be able to make useful judgments with the visualizations if they don't even say clearly what data they describe?

Show the data. Your first job in creating good data visualizations is to facilitate rigorous thinking and good decision making on the part of your clients, and good data analysis begins and ends with ***thinking with data***.

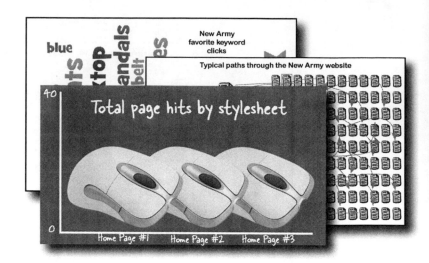

These graphics can fit a lot of different data.

You just don't know what's behind them until the designer tells you.

And these graphs are not solutions to the problems of New Army.

Here are some of New Army's data sheets.

New Army's actual data, however, is really rich and has all sorts of great material for your visualizations.

This is what it's all about.

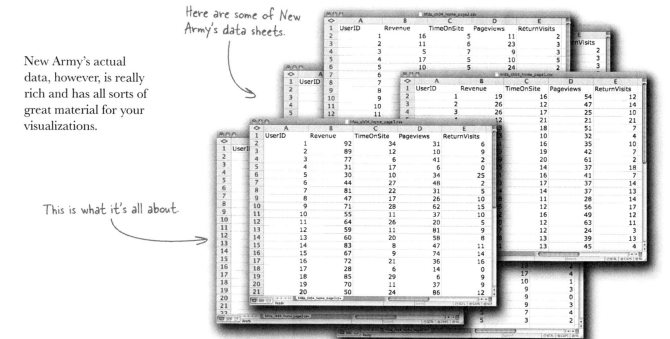

Here's some unsolicited advice from the last designer

You didn't ask for it, but it appears that you're getting it anyway: the outgoing information designer wants to put in his two cents about the project. Maybe his perspective help…

Well that's "nice" of him to say.

From the looks of the table on the facing page, it appears that Dan is correct.

Too much data to visualize it all, huh?

> To: **Head First**
> From: **Dan's Dizzying Data Designs**
> Re: **Website design optimization project**
>
> **Dear Head First,**
>
> **I want to wish you the best of luck on the New Army project. I didn't really want to do it anyway, so it's good for someone else to get a chance to give it a shot.**
>
> **One word of warning: they have a lot of data. Too much, in fact. Once you really dig into it, you'll know what I mean. I say, give me a nice little tabular layout, and I'll make you a pretty chart with it. But these guys? They have more data than they know what to do with.**
>
> **And they will expect you to make visuals of all of it for them. I just made a few nice charts, which I understand not everyone liked, but I'll tell you they've set forward an insurmountable task. They want to see it all, but there is just too much.**
>
> **Dan**

Sharpen your pencil

Dan seems to think that an excess of data is a real problem for someone trying to design good data visualizations. Do you think that what he is saying is plausible? Why or why not?

....

....

....

....

Sharpen your pencil
Solution

Is Dan being reasonable when he says it's too hard to do good visualizations when there is too much data?

This isn't very plausible. The whole point of data analysis is to summarize data, and summarizing

tools, like taking the average of a number, will work regardless of whether you have just a few

data points or millions. And if you have a bunch of different data sets to compare to each other,

really great visualizations facilitate this sort of data analysis just like all the other tools.

Too much data is never your problem

It's easy to get scared by looking at a lot of data.

So... much... data!!!

But knowing how to deal with what seems like a lot of data is easy, too.

If you've got a lot of data and aren't sure what to do with it, just remember your analytical objectives. With these in mind, stay focused on the data that speaks to your objectives and ignore the rest.

Some of this stuff is going to be useful to you.

And some of it won't be useful to you.

Duh. The problem is not too much data; the problem is figuring out how to make the data visually appealing.

Oh, really? Do you think it's your job as a **data analyst** to create an aesthetic experience for your clients?

Making the data pretty isn't your problem either

If the data visualization solves a client's problem, it's always attractive, whether it's something really elaborate and visually stimulating or whether it's just a plain ol' table of numbers.

Making good data visualizations is just like making any sort of good data analysis. You just need to know where to start.

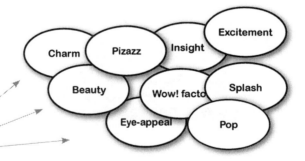

Charm Pizazz Insight Excitement

Beauty Wow! factor Splash

Eye-appeal Pop

What do you think the client's looking for?

⚛ BRAIN POWER

So *how* do you use a big pile of data with a bunch of different variables to evaluate your objectives? Where exactly do you begin?

Data visualization is all about making the right comparisons

To build good visualizations, first identify what are the fundamental comparisons that will address your client's objectives. Take a look at their most important spreadsheets:

What we want to see is which stylesheet or stylesheets maximize revenue, the time our visitors spend on the site, and return visits to the site.

Here's Home Page #3

Think about the comparisons that fulfill your client's objectives.

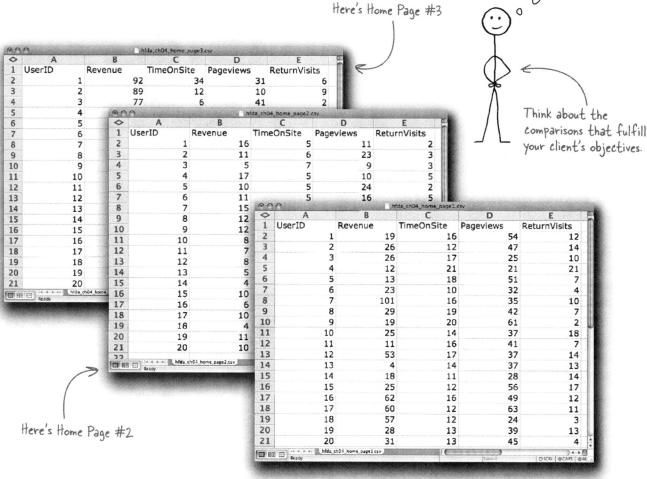

Here's Home Page #2

Here's Home Page #1

While New Army has more data than these three sheets, these sheets have the comparisons that will speak directly to what they want to know. Let's try out a comparison now...

Sharpen your pencil

Take look at the statistics that describe the results for Home Page #1.
Plot dots to represent each of the users on the axes below.

Use your spreadsheet's average formula (AVG) to calculate the average
Revenue and TimeOnSite figures for Home Page #1, and draw those
numbers as horizontal and vertical lines on the chart.

Load this!

www.headfirstlabs.com/books/hfda/
hfda_ch04_home_page1.csv

This value represents the New Army's goals for the average
number of minutes each user spends on the website.

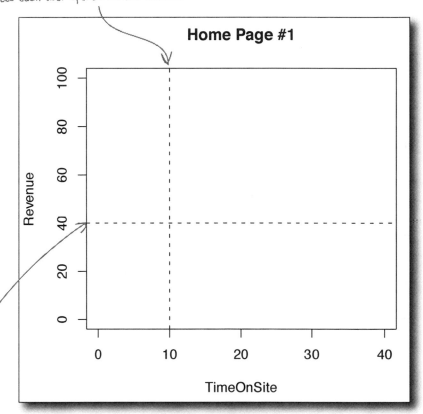

This value represents the
goal New Army has for
the average amount of
money each user spends.

How do the results you see compare to their
goals for revenue and time on site?

....

....

....

 Sharpen your pencil
Solution

How did you visualize the Revenue and
TimeOnSite variables for Home Page #1?

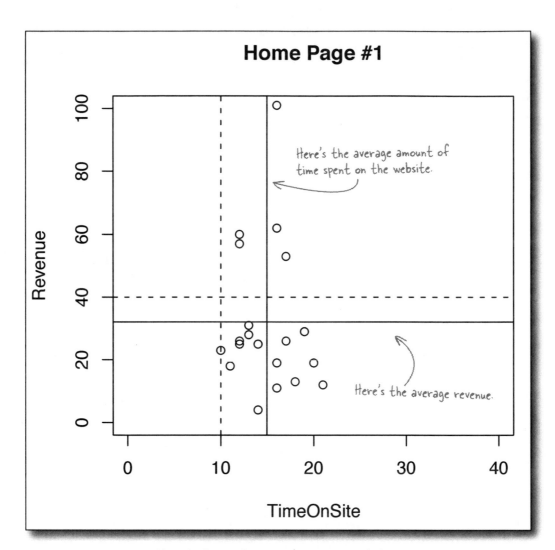

How do the results you see compare to their
goals for revenue and time on site?

On average, the time people spend looking at the website under Home Page #1

is greater than New Army's goal for that statistic. On the other hand, the

average amount of revenue for each user is less than their goal.

Your visualization is already more useful than the rejected ones

Now that's a nice chart, and it'll definitely be useful to your client. It's an example of a good data visualization because it…

Here's another feature of great visualizations.

- Shows the data
- Makes a smart comparison
- Shows multiple variables

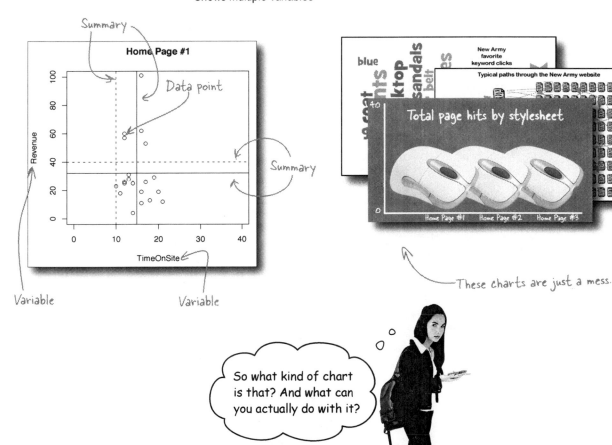

Summary

Data point

Summary

Variable

Variable

These charts are just a mess.

So what kind of chart is that? And what can you actually do with it?

Use scatterplots to explore causes

Scatterplots are great tools for **exploratory data analysis**, which is the term statisticians use to describe looking around in a set of data for hypotheses to test.

Analysts like to use scatterplots when searching for **causal relationships**, where one variable is affecting the other. As a general rule, the horizontal x-axis of the scatterplot represents the **independent variable** (the variable we imagine to be a cause), and the vertical y-axis of a scatterplot represents the **dependent variable** (which we imagine to be the effect).

Here's a scatterplot.

Here's the effect.

Dependent Variable

Each of these dots represents an observation, in this case a user on the website.

Independent Variable

It's a good idea to use little circles for your scatterplots, because they're easier to see when they overlap than dots.

Here's the cause.

You don't have to *prove* that the value of the independent variable causes the value of the dependent variable, because after all we're exploring the data. But causes are what you're looking for.

That's cool, but there is a lot more data than two variables, and a lot more comparisons to be made. Can we plot more variables than just two?

The best visualizations are highly multivariate

A visualization is **multivariate** if it compares three or more variables. And because making good comparisons is fundamental to data analysis, making your visualizations **as multivariate as possible** makes it most likely that you'll make the best comparisons.

And in this case you've got a bunch of variables.

You have multiple variables.

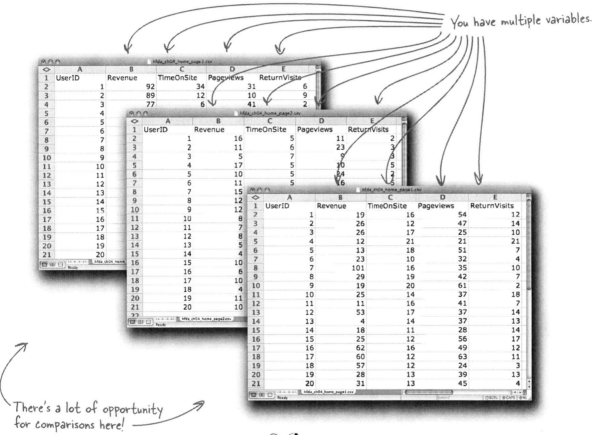

There's a lot of opportunity for comparisons here!

BRAIN POWER

How would you make the scatterplot visualization you've created *more multivariate*?

Show more variables by looking at charts together

One way of making your visualization more multivariate is just to show a bunch of similar scatterplots right next to each other, and here's an example of such a visualization.

All of your variables are plotted together in this format, which enables you to compare a huge array of information right in one place. Because New Army is really interested in revenue comparisons, we can just stick with the charts that compare TimeOnSite, Pageviews, and ReturnVisits to revenue.

The dotted lines represent New Army's goals.

The solid lines are the averages for that home page.

Here's the chart that you created.

This graphic was created with a open source software program called R, which you'll learn more about later.

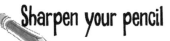

Sharpen your pencil

You've just created a pretty complex visualization. Look at it and think about what it tells you about the stylesheets that New Army decided to test.

Do you think that this visualization does a good job of showing the data? Why or why not?

....

....

....

....

Just looking at the dots, you can see that Home Page #2 has a very different sort of spread from the other two stylesheets. What do you think is happening with Home Page #2?

....

....

....

....

Which of the three stylesheets do you think does the best job of maximizing the variables that New Army cares about? Why?

....

....

....

....

Sharpen your pencil
Solution

Does the new visualization help you understand the comparative performance of the stylesheets?

Do you think that this visualization does a good job of showing the data? Why or why not?

Definitely. Each dot on each of the nine panels represents the experience of a single user, so even though the data points are summarized into averages, you can still see absolutely all of them. Seeing all the points makes it easy to evaluate the spread, and the average lines make it easy to see how each stylesheet performs relative to each other and relative to New Army's goals.

Just looking at the dots, you can see that Home Page #2 has a very different sort of spread from the other two stylesheets. What do you think is happening with Home Page #2?

It looks like Home Page #2 is performing terribly. Compared to the other two stylesheets, Home Page #2 isn't bringing in much revenue and also performs poorly on the Time on Site, Pageviews, and Return Visits figures. Every single user statistic is below New Army's goals. Home Page #2 is terrible and should be taken offline immediately!

Which of the three stylesheets do you think does the best job of maximizing the variables that New Army cares about? Why?

Home Page #3 is the best. While #1 performs above average when it comes to the metrics besides Revenue, #3 is way ahead in terms of revenue. When it comes to Return Visits, #1 is ahead, and they're neck-and-neck on Pageviews, but people spend more time on the site with #3. It's great that #1 gets a lot of return visits, but you can't argue with #3's superior revenue.

Q: What software tool should I use to create this sort of graphic?

A: Those specific graphs are created in a statistical data analysis program called R, which you're going to learn all about later in the book. But there are a number of charting tools you can use in statistical programs, and you don't even have to stop there. You can use illustration programs like Adobe Illustrator and just draw visualizations, if you have visual ideas that other software tools don't implement.

Q: What about Excel and OpenOffice? They have charting tools, too.

A: Yes, well, that's true. They have a limited range of charting tools you can use, and you can probably figure out a way to create a chart like this one in your spreadsheet program, but it's going to be an uphill battle.

Q: You don't sound too hot on spreadsheet data visualizations.

A: Many serious data analysts who use spreadsheets all the time for basic calculations and lists nevertheless wouldn't dream of using spreadsheet charting tools. They can be a real pain: not only is there a small range of charts you can create in spreadsheet programs, but often, the programs force you into formatting decisions that you might not otherwise make. It's not that you *can't* make good data graphics in spreadsheet programs; it's just that there's more trouble in it than you'd have if you learned how to use a program like R.

Q: So if I'm looking for inspiration on chart types, the spreadsheet menus aren't the place to look?

A: No, no, no! If you want inspiration on designs, you should probably pick up some books by Edward Tufte, who's the authority on data visualization by a long shot. His body of work is like a museum of excellent data visualizations, which he sometimes calls "cognitive art."

Q: What about magazine, newspapers, and journal articles?

A: It's a good idea to become sensitive to data visualization quality in publications. Some are better than others when it comes to designing illuminating visualizations, and when you pay attention to the publications, over time, you'll get a sense of which ones do a better job. A good way to start would be to count the variables in a graphic. If there are three or more variables in a chart, the publication is more likely to be making intelligent comparisons than if there's one variable to a chart.

Q: What should I make of data visualizations that are complex and artistic but not analytically useful?

A: There's a lot of enthusiasm and creativity nowadays for creating new computer-generated visualizations. Some of them facilitate good analytical thinking about the data, and some of them are just interesting to look at. There's absolutely nothing wrong with what some call **data art**. Just don't call it data *analysis* unless you can directly use it to achieve a greater understanding of the underlying data.

Q: So something can be visually interesting without being analytically illuminating. What about vice versa?

A: That's your judgement call. But if you have something at stake in an analysis, and your visualization is illuminating, then it's hard to imagine that the graphic **wouldn't** be visually interesting!

Let's see what the client thinks...

The visualization is great, but the web guru's not satisfied yet

You just got an email from your client, the web guru at New Army, assessing what you created for him. Let's see what he has to say…

Nice!

Here's a reasonable question.

To: **Head First**
From: **New Army Web Guru**
Re: **My explanation of the data**

Your designs are excellent and we're pleased we switched to you from the other guy. But tell me something: why does Home Page #3 perform so much better than the others?

All this looks really reasonable, but I still want to know *why* we have these results. I've got two pet theories. First, I think that Home Page #3 loads faster, which makes the experience of the website more snappy. Second, I think that its cooler color palette is really relaxing and makes for a good shopping experience. What do you think?

Looks like your client has some ideas of his own about why the data looks the way it looks.

He's short and sweet. What can you do with his request?

He wants to know about causality.

Knowing what designs work only takes him so far. In order to make his website as powerful as possible, he needs some idea of why people interact with the different home pages the way they do.

And, since he's the client, we definitely need to address the theories he put forward.

Good visual designs help you think about causes

Your and your client's preferred model will usually fit the data.

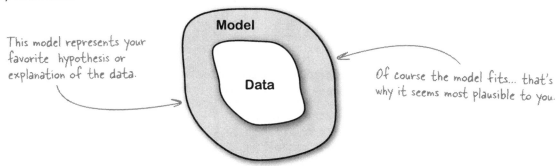

This model represents your favorite hypothesis or explanation of the data.

Model

Data

Of course the model fits... that's why it seems most plausible to you.

But there are always other possibilities, especially when you are willing to get imaginative about the explanations. What about other models?

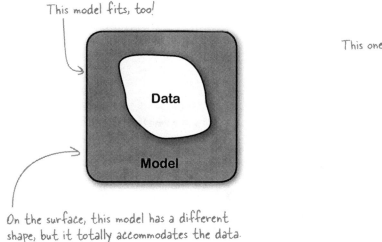

This model fits, too!

Data

Model

On the surface, this model has a different shape, but it totally accommodates the data.

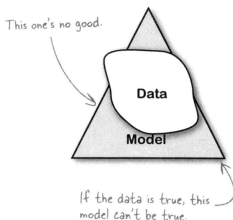

This one's no good.

Data

Model

If the data is true, this model can't be true.

You need to address alternative causal models or explanations as you describe your data visualization. Doing so is a real mark of integrity: it shows your client that you're not just showing the version of the story that you like best: you're thinking through possible failure points in your theories.

The experiment designers weigh in

The experiment designers saw the web guru's theories and sent you some of their thoughts. Perhaps their input will enable you to evaluate the web guru's hypotheses about why some home pages performed better than others.

To: **Head First**
From: **New Army experiment designers**
Re: **The boss's ideas**

He thinks that page loads count? That could be. We haven't taken a look at the data yet to see for sure. But in our testing, #2 was the fastest, followed by #3, and then #1. So, sure, he could be right.

As for the cooler color palette, we kind of doubt it. The color palette of Home Page #3 is coolest, followed by #2, then #1, by the way. There's research to show that people react differently, but none of it has really persuaded us.

Here's what the experiment designers think about the first hypothesis.

Here's their response to the second hypothesis.

We better take a look at the data to see whether it confirms or disconfirms these hypotheses.

Sharpen your pencil

Let's take a look at the data to see whether the bosses hypotheses fit. Does the data fit either of the hypotheses?

Hypothesis 1: The snappy performance of snappy web pages accounts for why Home Page #3 performed best.

....

....

....

....

....

Do the web guru's hypotheses fit this data?

Hypothesis 2: The relaxing, cool color palette of Home Page #3 accounts for why it performed best.

....

....

....

....

....

....

Home Page #1 — Revenue vs TimeOnSite

Home Page #1 — Revenue vs Pageviews

Home Page #1 — Revenue vs ReturnVisits

Home Page #2 — Revenue vs TimeOnSite

Home Page #2 — Revenue vs Pageviews

Home Page #2 — Revenue vs ReturnVisits

Home Page #3 — Revenue vs TimeOnSite

Home Page #3 — Revenue vs Pageviews

Home Page #3 — Revenue vs ReturnVisits

Sharpen your pencil
Solution

How well did you find the web guru's hypotheses to fit the data?

Hypothesis 1: The snappy performance of snappy web pages accounts for why Home Page #3 performed best.

This can't be true, since #3 isn't the fastest, according to the experiment designers. It might be that as general rule people prefer faster pages, but page load speed can't explain #3's success in the context of this experiment.

Do the web guru's hypotheses fit this data?

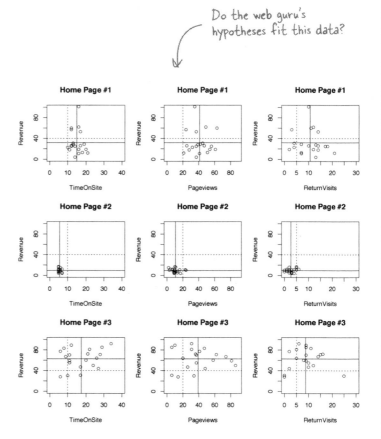

Hypothesis 2: The relaxing, cool color palette of Home Page #3 accounts for why it performed best.

This hypothesis fits the data. Home Page #3 is the highest-performing page, and it has the coolest color palette. The data don't prove that the color palette is the reason that #3 performed so well, but it fits the hypothesis.

The experiment designers have some hypotheses of their own

They've had an opportunity to take a look at your scatterplots and sent you some of their own thinking about what's going on. These people are data junkies, and their hypotheses definitely fit.

> **To:** **Head First**
> **From:** **New Army experiment designers**
> **Re:** **We don't know why Home Page #3 is stronger**
>
> We're delighted to hear that #3 is the best, but we really don't know why. Who knows what people are thinking? But that is actually OK: as long as we're showing improvement on the business fundamentals, we don't need to understand people in a deep way. Still, it's interesting to learn as much as we can.
>
> The stylesheets are really different from each other in many ways. So when it comes to isolating individual features that might account for the performance differential, it's hard. In the future, we'd like to take Home Page #3 and test a bunch of subtle permutations. That way, we might learn things like how button shape or font choice affect user behavior.
>
> But we conjecture that there are two factors. First, Home Page #3 is really readable. We use fonts and a layout that are easy on the eyes. Second, the page hierarchy is flatter. You can find pretty much everything in three clicks, when for Home Page #1 it takes you more like seven clicks to find what you want. Both could be affecting our revenue, but we need more testing to say for sure.

Here's what the experiment designers want to do next.

Maybe it's fonts and layout.

Maybe it's hierarchy of the pages.

Sharpen your pencil

On the basis of what you've learned, what would you recommend to your client that he do regarding his web strategy?

....

....

....

Sharpen your pencil
Solution

What would you tell your client to do with his website on the bases of the data you visualized and the explanatory theories you evaluated?

Stick with Home Page #3 and test for finer-grained elements of the user's experience, like variable

navigation, style, and content. There are a bunch of different possible explanations for #3's

performance that should be investigated and visualized, but it's clear that #3 is the victor here.

The client is pleased with your work

You created an excellent visualization that enabled New Army to quickly and simultaneously assess all the variables they tested in their experiment.

And you evaluated that visualization in light of a bunch of different hypotheses, giving them some excellent ideas about what to test for in the future.

> Very cool. I agree with your assessments of the hypotheses and your recommendation. I'm implementing Home Page #3 for our website. Job well done.

Orders are coming in from everywhere!

Because of the new website, traffic is greater than ever. Your visualization of the experimental results showed what they needed to know to spruce up their website.

New Army sent you these shirts as a thank-you.

Hope they fit!

Even better, New Army has embarked on a continuous program of experimentation to fine-tune their new design, using your visualization to see what works. Nice job!

New Army's optimized website is really paying off.

5 hypothesis testing

That marlin I caught was 10,000 pounds, and we had to let it go before it sank the boat... what? Well I'd like to see you prove me wrong!

The world can be tricky to explain.

And it can be fiendishly difficult when you have to deal with complex, heterogeneous data to anticipate future events. This is why analysts don't just take the obvious explanations and assume them to be true: the careful reasoning of data analysis enables you to meticulously evaluate a bunch of options so that you can incorporate all the information you have into your models. You're about to learn about **falsification**, an unintuitive but powerful way to do just that.

Gimme some skin...

You're with ElectroSkinny, a maker of phone skins. Your assignment is to figure out whether PodPhone is going to release a new phone next month. PodPhone is a huge product, and there's a lot at stake.

With my active lifestyle, I need a great skin for my PodPhone, that's why I'm all about ElectroSkinny!

ElectroSkinny hipster

PodPhone will release a phone at some point in the future, and ElectroSkinny needs to start manufacturing skins a month **before** the phone is released in order to get in on the first wave of phone sales.

If they don't have skins ready for a release, their competitors will **beat them to the punch** and sell a lot of skins before ElectroSkinny can put their own on the market. But if they manufacture skins and PodPhone *isn't* released, they'll have **wasted money** on skins that no one knows when they'll be able to sell.

When do we start making new phone skins?

The decision of when to start manufacturing a new line of skins is a big deal.

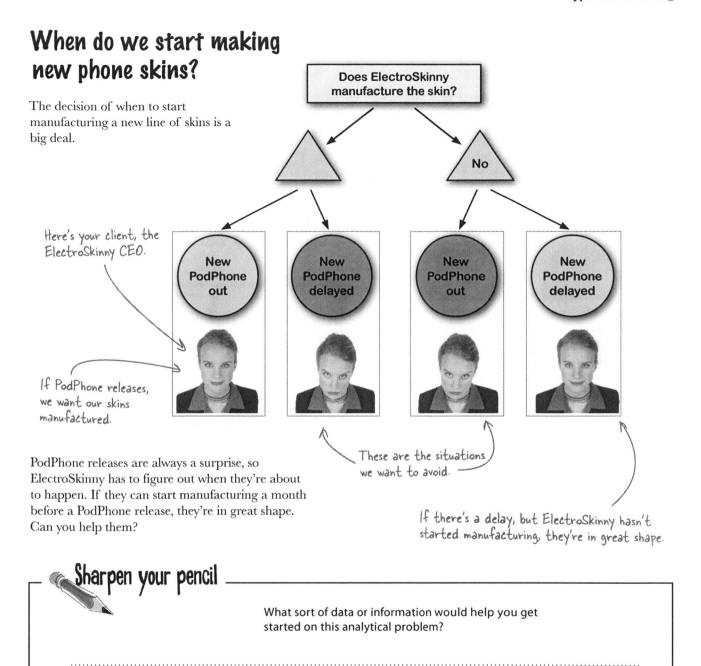

Does ElectroSkinny manufacture the skin?

No

Here's your client, the ElectroSkinny CEO.

New PodPhone out

New PodPhone delayed

New PodPhone out

New PodPhone delayed

If PodPhone releases, we want our skins manufactured.

These are the situations we want to avoid.

If there's a delay, but ElectroSkinny hasn't started manufacturing, they're in great shape.

PodPhone releases are always a surprise, so ElectroSkinny has to figure out when they're about to happen. If they can start manufacturing a month before a PodPhone release, they're in great shape. Can you help them?

Sharpen your pencil

What sort of data or information would help you get started on this analytical problem?

....

....

....

Sharpen your pencil Solution

What do you need to know in order to get started?

PodPhone wants their releases to be a surprise, so they'll probably take measures to avoid letting

people figure out when those releases happen. We'll need some sort of insight into how they think

about their releases, and we'll need to know what kind of information they use in their decision.

PodPhone doesn't want you to predict their next move

PodPhone knows you'll see all this information, so they won't want any of it to let on their release date.

PodPhone takes surprise seriously: they really
really don't want you to know what they're up to. So you
can't just look at publicly available data and expect
an answer of when they're releasing the PodPhone
to pop out at you.

These data points really aren't going to be of much help...

...unless you've got a really smart way to think about them.

You need to figure out how to ***compare*** the data
you do have with your **hypotheses** about when
PodPhone will release their new phone. But first,
let's take a look at the key pieces of information
we do have about PodPhone...

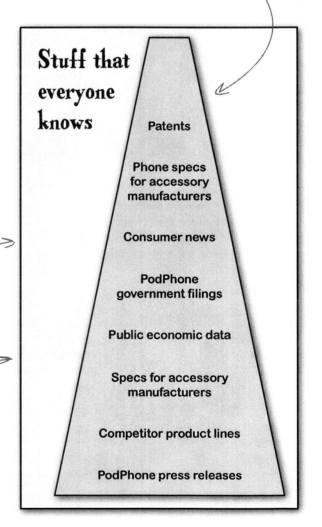

Stuff that everyone knows

Patents

Phone specs for accessory manufacturers

Consumer news

PodPhone government filings

Public economic data

Specs for accessory manufacturers

Competitor product lines

PodPhone press releases

Here's everything we know

Here's what little information ElectroSkinny has been able to piece together about the release. Some of it is publicly available, some of it is secret, and some of it is rumor.

PodPhone has invested more in the new phone than any other company ever has.

There is going to be a huge increase in features compared to competitor phones.

CEO of PodPhone said "No way we're launching the new phone tomorrow."

There was just a big new phone released from a competitor.

The economy and consumer spending are both up, so it's a good time to sell phones.

There is a rumor that the PodPhone CEO said there'd be no release for a year.

Internally, we don't expect a release, because their product line is really strong. They'll want to ride out their success with this line as long as possible. I'm thinking we should start several months from now...

CEO of ElectroSkinny

BRAIN POWER

Do you think her hypothesis makes sense in light of the above evidence we have to consider?

ElectroSkinny's analysis does fit the data

The CEO has a pretty straightforward account of step-by-step thinking on the part of PodPhone. Here's what she said in a schematic form:

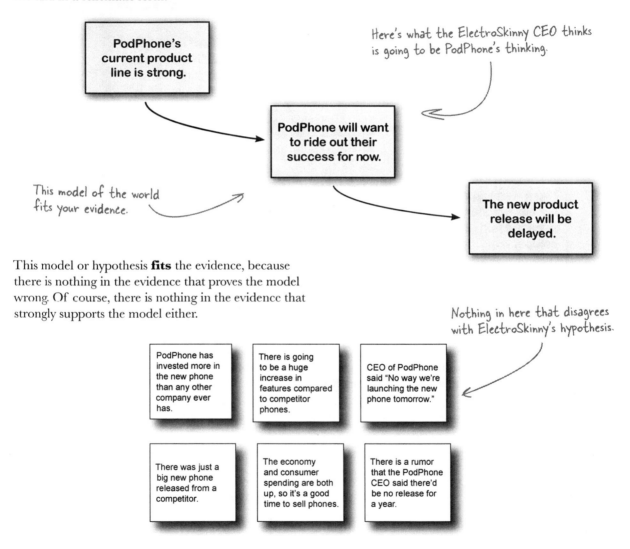

Here's what the ElectroSkinny CEO thinks is going to be PodPhone's thinking.

PodPhone's current product line is strong.

PodPhone will want to ride out their success for now.

This model of the world fits your evidence.

The new product release will be delayed.

This model or hypothesis **fits** the evidence, because there is nothing in the evidence that proves the model wrong. Of course, there is nothing in the evidence that strongly supports the model either.

Nothing in here that disagrees with ElectroSkinny's hypothesis.

PodPhone has invested more in the new phone than any other company ever has.

There is going to be a huge increase in features compared to competitor phones.

CEO of PodPhone said "No way we're launching the new phone tomorrow."

There was just a big new phone released from a competitor.

The economy and consumer spending are both up, so it's a good time to sell phones.

There is a rumor that the PodPhone CEO said there'd be no release for a year.

Seems like pretty solid reasoning...

ElectroSkinny obtained this confidential strategy memo

ElectroSkinny watches PodPhone *really* closely, and sometimes stuff like this just falls in your lap.

This strategy memo outlines a number of the factors that PodPhone considers when it's calculating its release dates. It's quite a bit more subtle than the reasoning the ElectroSkinny CEO imagined they are using.

> ### PodPhone phone release strategy memo
>
> We want to time our releases to maximize sales and to beat out our competitors. We have to take into account a variety of factors to do it.
>
> First, we watch the economy, because an increase in overall economic performance drives up consumer spending, while economic decline depresses consumer spending. And consumer spending is where all phone sales comes from. But we and our competitors are after the same pot of consumer spending. Every phone we sell is one they don't sell, and vice versa.
>
> We don't usually want to release a phone when they have a new phone on the market. We take a bigger bite out of competitor sales if we release when they have a stale product portfolio.
>
> Our suppliers and internal development team place limits on our ability to drop new phones, too.

Can this memo help you figure out when a new PodPhone will be released?

Sharpen your pencil

Think carefully about how PodPhone thinks the variables mentioned in the memo relate. Do the pairs below rise and fall together, or do they go in opposite directions? Write a "+" or "−" in each circle depending on your answer.

Put a "+" in each circle if the two variables rise and fall together.

Write a "−" sign if the variables move in opposite directions.

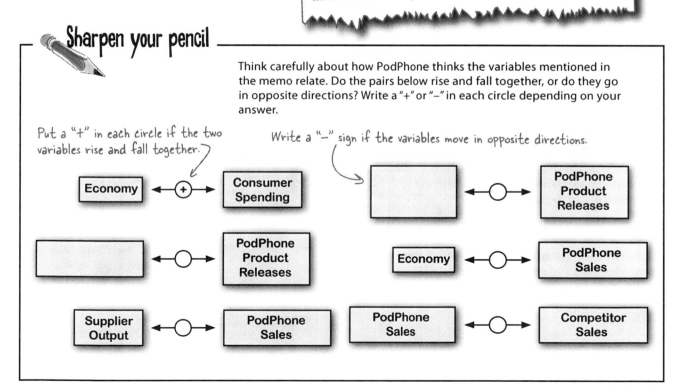

Sharpen your pencil
Solution

In the mind of PodPhone, how are the pairs of variables below linked to each other quantitatively?

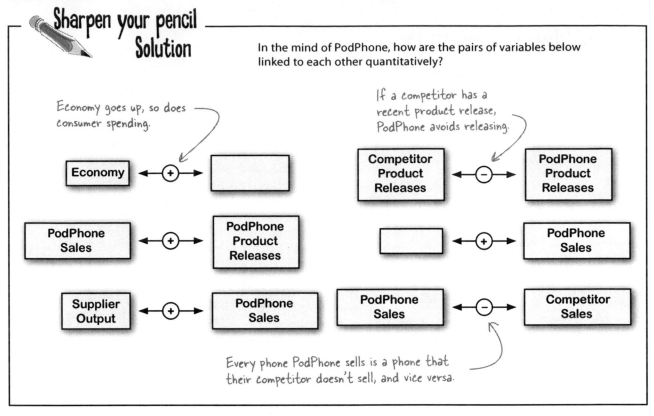

Economy goes up, so does consumer spending.

Economy ◀━(+)━▶ [   ]

If a competitor has a recent product release, PodPhone avoids releasing.

Competitor Product Releases ◀━(−)━▶ PodPhone Product Releases

PodPhone Sales ◀━(+)━▶ PodPhone Product Releases

[   ] ◀━(+)━▶ PodPhone Sales

Supplier Output ◀━(+)━▶ PodPhone Sales

PodPhone Sales ◀━(−)━▶ Competitor Sales

Every phone PodPhone sells is a phone that their competitor doesn't sell, and vice versa.

Variables can be negatively or positively linked

When you are looking at data variables, it's a good idea to ask whether they are **positively linked**, where more of one means more of the other (and vice versa), or **negatively linked**, where more of one means less of the other.

On the right are some more of the relationships PodPhone sees. How can you use these relationships to develop a **bigger model** of their beliefs, one that might predict when they're going to release their new phone?

Here are a few of the other relationships that can be read from PodPhone's strategy memo.

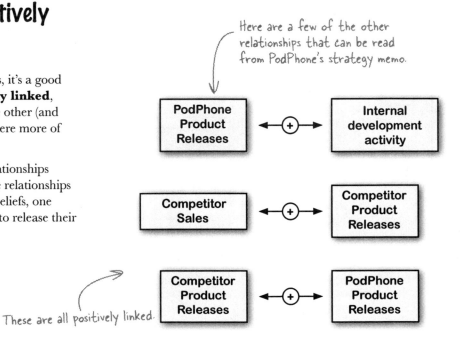

PodPhone Product Releases ◀━(+)━▶ Internal development activity

Competitor Sales ◀━(+)━▶ Competitor Product Releases

Competitor Product Releases ◀━(+)━▶ PodPhone Product Releases

These are all positively linked.

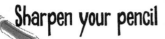

Sharpen your pencil

Let's tie those positive and negative links between variables into an integrated model.

Using the relationships specified on the facing page, draw a network that incorporates all of them.

These two relationships are already done.

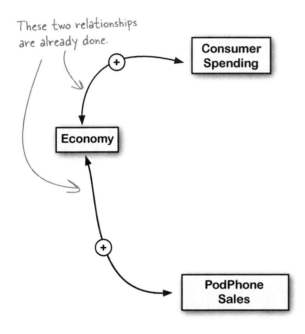

Sharpen your pencil
Solution

How does your model of PodPhone's worldview look once you've put it in the form of a network?

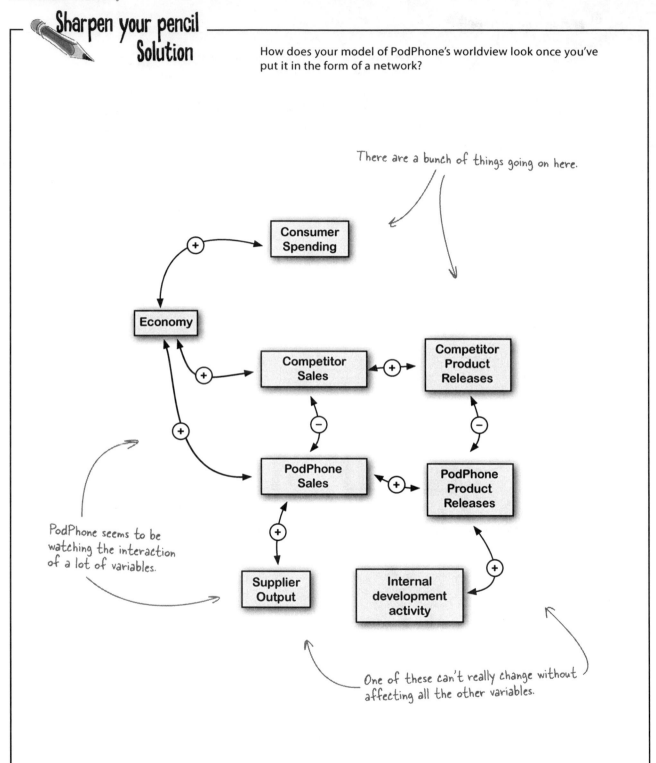

There are a bunch of things going on here.

PodPhone seems to be watching the interaction of a lot of variables.

One of these can't really change without affecting all the other variables.

Causes in the real world are networked, not linear

Linearity is intuitive. A linear explanation of the causes for why PodPhone might decide to delay their release is simple and straightforward.

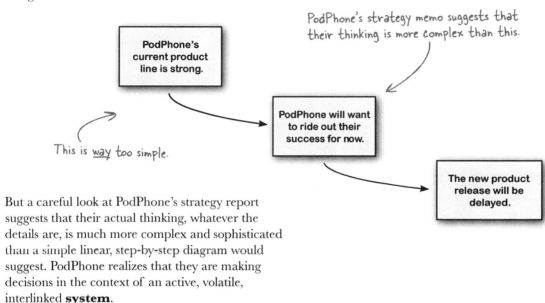

PodPhone's strategy memo suggests that their thinking is more complex than this.

PodPhone's current product line is strong.

This is <u>way</u> too simple.

PodPhone will want to ride out their success for now.

The new product release will be delayed.

But a careful look at PodPhone's strategy report suggests that their actual thinking, whatever the details are, is much more complex and sophisticated than a simple linear, step-by-step diagram would suggest. PodPhone realizes that they are making decisions in the context of an active, volatile, interlinked **system**.

As an analyst, you need to see beyond simple models like this and expect to see causal **networks**. In the *real world* causes propagate across a network of related variables… why should your models be any different?

So how do we use that to figure out when PodPhone is going to release their new phone? What about the data?

Hypothesize PodPhone's options

Sooner or later, PodPhone is going to release a new phone. The question is **when**.

And different answers to that question are your **hypotheses** for this analysis. Below are a few options that specify when a release might occur, and picking the right hypothesis is what ElectroSkinny needs you to do.

You'll somehow combine your hypotheses with this evidence and PodPhone's mental model to get your answer.

PodPhone has invested more in the new phone than any other company ever has.	There is going to be a huge increase in features compared to competitor phones.	CEO of PodPhone said "No way we're launching the new phone tomorrow."
There was just a big new phone released from a competitor.	The economy and consumer spending are both up, so it's a good time to sell phones.	There is a rumor that the PodPhone CEO said there'd be no release for a year.

Your evidence

Here are a few estimates of when the new PodPhone might be released.

H1: Release will be tomorrow

H2: Release will be next month

H3: Release will be in six months

H4: Release will be in a year

H5: No release, product canceled

Your hypotheses

The hypothesis that we consider strongest will determine ElectroSkinny's manufacturing schedule.

You have what you need to run a hypothesis test

Between your understanding of PodPhone's mental model and the evidence, you have amassed quite a bit of knowledge about the issue that ElectroSkinny cares about most: when PodPhone is going to release their product.

You just need a **method** to put all this intelligence together and form a solid prediction.

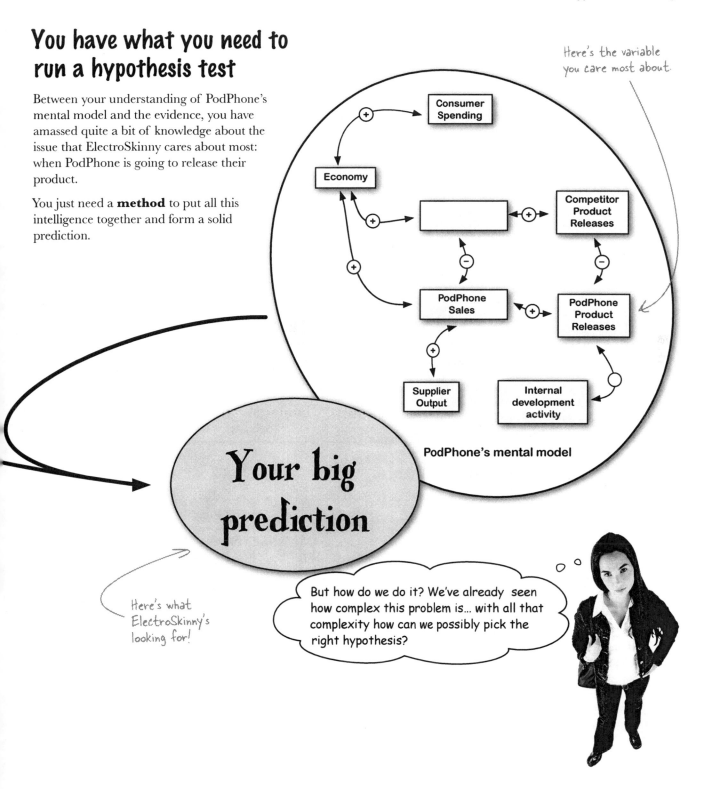

Here's the variable you care most about.

PodPhone's mental model

Your big prediction

Here's what ElectroSkinny's looking for!

But how do we do it? We've already seen how complex this problem is... with all that complexity how can we possibly pick the right hypothesis?

Falsification is the heart of hypothesis testing

Don't try to pick the right hypothesis; just **eliminate the disconfirmed hypotheses**. This is the method of **falsification**, which is fundamental to hypothesis testing.

Picking the first hypothesis that seems best is called **satisficing** and looks like this:

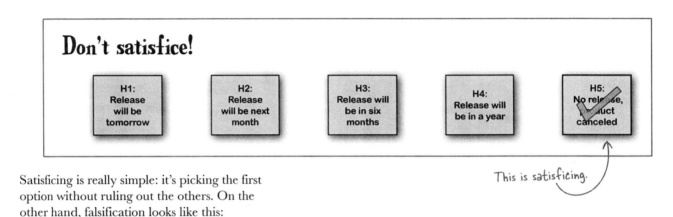

Satisficing is really simple: it's picking the first option without ruling out the others. On the other hand, falsification looks like this:

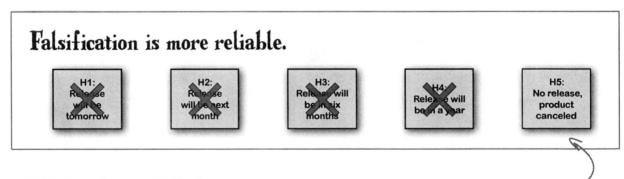

It looks like both satisficing and falsification get you the same answer, right? They don't always. The **big problem** with satisficing is that when people pick a hypothesis without thoroughly analyzing the alternatives, they often stick with it even as evidence piles up against it. Falsification enables you to have a **more nimble perspective** on your hypotheses and avoid a huge cognitive trap.

Use falsification in hypothesis testing and avoid the danger of satisficing.

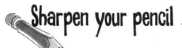

Sharpen your pencil

Give falsification a try and cross out any hypotheses that are falsified by the evidence below.

H1: Release will be tomorrow	H2: Release will be next month	H3: Release will be in six months	H4: Release will be in a year	H5: No release, product canceled

Here are your hypotheses.

Which ones do your evidence suggest are wrong?

Here's your evidence.

PodPhone has invested more in the new phone than any other company ever has.

There is going to be a huge increase in features compared to competitor phones.

CEO of PodPhone said "No way we're launching the new phone tomorrow."

There was just a big new phone released from a competitor.

The economy and consumer spending are both up, so it's a good time to sell phones.

There is a rumor that the PodPhone CEO said there'd be no release for a year.

Why do you believe that the hypotheses you picked are falsified by the evidence?

....

....

....

....

Sharpen your pencil Solution

Which hypotheses did you find to be falsified?

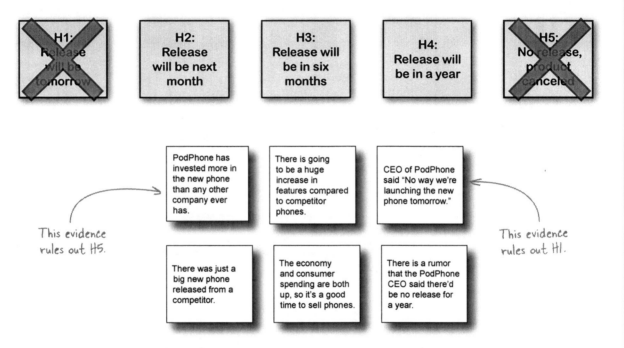

H1: Release will be tomorrow ~~(crossed out)~~

H2: Release will be next month

H3: Release will be in six months

H4: Release will be in a year

H5: No release, product canceled ~~(crossed out)~~

PodPhone has invested more in the new phone than any other company ever has.

There is going to be a huge increase in features compared to competitor phones.

CEO of PodPhone said "No way we're launching the new phone tomorrow."

This evidence rules out H5.

There was just a big new phone released from a competitor.

The economy and consumer spending are both up, so it's a good time to sell phones.

There is a rumor that the PodPhone CEO said there'd be no release for a year.

This evidence rules out H1.

Why do you believe that the hypotheses you picked are falsified by the evidence?

H1 is definitely falsified by the evidence, because the CEO has gone on record saying that there was no way it'll happen tomorrow. The CEO might be lying, but that would be so weird that we can still rule out H1. H5 is falsified because PodPhone has put so much money into the phone. The phone might be delayed or changed, but unless the company ceases to exist, it's hard to imagine that they'd cancel the new phone.

there are no
Dumb Questions

Q: Falsification seems like a really elaborate way to think about analyzing situations. Is it really necessary?

A: It's a great way to overcome the natural tendency to focus on the wrong answer and ignore alternative explanations. By forcing you to think in a really formal way, you'll be less likely to make mistakes that stem from your ignorance of important features of a situation.

Q: How does this sort of falsification relate to statistical hypothesis testing?

A: What you might have learned in statistics class (or better yet, in *Head First Statistics*) is a method of comparing a candidate hypothesis (the "alternate" hypothesis) to a baseline hypothesis (the "null" hypothesis). The idea is to identify a situation that, if true, would make the null hypothesis darn near impossible.

Q: So why aren't we using that method?

A: One of the virtues of this approach is that it enables you to aggregate

heterogenous data of widely varying quality. This method is falsification in a very general form, which makes it useful for very complex problems. But it's *definitely* a good idea to bone up on "frequentist" hypothesis testing described above, because for tests where the data fit its parameters, you would not want to use anything else.

Q: I think that if my coworkers saw me reasoning like this they'd think I was crazy.

A: They certainly won't think you're crazy if you catch something really important. The aspiration of good data analysts is to uncover unintuitive answers to complex problems. Would you hire a conventionally minded data analyst? If you are really interested in learning something new about your data, you'll go for the person who thinks outside the box!

Q: It seems like not all hypotheses could be falsified definitively. Like certain evidence might count against a hypothesis without *disproving* it.

A: That's totally correct.

Q: Where's the data in all this? I'd expect to see a lot more numbers.

A: Data is not just a grid of numbers. Falsification in hypothesis testing lets you take a more expansive view of "data" and aggregate a lot of heterogeneous data. You can put virtually any sort of data into the falsification framework.

Q: What's the difference between using falsification to solve a problem and using optimization to solve it?

A: They're different tools for different contexts. In certain situations, you'll want to break out Solver to tweak your variables until you have the optimal values, and in other situations, you'll want to use falsification to eliminate possible explanations of your data.

Q: OK. What if I can't use falsification to eliminate *all* the hypotheses?

A: That's the $64,000 question! Let's see what we can do...

Nice work! I definitely know more now than I did when I brought you on board. But can you do even better than this? What about eliminating two more?

We still have 3 hypotheses left. Looks like falsification didn't solve the whole problem. So what's the plan now?

How do you choose among the last three hypotheses?

You know that it's a bad idea to pick the one that looks like it has the most support, and falsification has helped you eliminate only two of the hypotheses, so what should you do now?

| H2:
Release will be next month | H3:
Release will be in six months | H4:
Release will be in a year |

Which one of these will you ultimately consider to be the strongest?

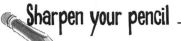
Sharpen your pencil

What are the benefits and drawbacks of each hypothesis-elimination technique?

Compare each hypothesis to the evidence and pick the one that has the most confirmation.

....

....

....

....

Just present all of the hypotheses and let the client decide whether to start manufacturing skins.

....

....

....

....

Use the evidence to rank hypotheses in the order of which has the fewest evidence-based knocks against it.

....

....

....

....

Sharpen your pencil
Solution

Did you pick a hypothesis elimination technique that you like best?

Compare each hypothesis to the evidence and pick the one that has the most confirmation.

This is dangerous. The problem is that the information I have is incomplete. It could be that there is something really important that I don't know. And if that's true, then picking the hypothesis based on what I do know will probably give me the wrong answer.

Just present all of the hypotheses and let the client decide whether to start manufacturing skins.

This is certainly an option, but the problem with it is that I'm not really taking any responsibility for the conclusions. In other words, I'm not really acting as a data analyst as much as someone who just delivers data. This is the wimpy approach.

Use the evidence to rank hypotheses in the order of which has the fewest evidence-based knocks against it.

This one is the best. I've already used falsification to rule out things that I'm sure can't be true. Now, even though I can't rule out my remaining hypotheses, I can still use the evidence to see which ones are the strongest.

Wait a second. By putting the hypothesis that seems strongest at the top of the list, don't we run the risk of satisficing and picking the one we like rather than the one that's best supported by the evidence?

Not if you compare your evidence to your hypotheses by looking at its diagnosticity.

Evidence is **diagnostic** if it helps you rank one hypothesis as stronger than another, and so our method will be to look at each hypothesis in comparison to each piece of evidence and each other and see which has the strongest support.

Let's give it a shot…

the Scholar's Corner

Diagnosticity is the ability of evidence to help you assess the relative likelihood of the hypotheses you're considering. If evidence is diagnostic, it helps you rank your hypotheses.

Diagnosticity helps you find the hypothesis with the least disconfirmation

Evidence and data are **diagnostic** if they help you assess the relative strengths of hypotheses. The tables below compare different pieces of evidence with several hypotheses. The "+" symbol indicates that the evidence **supports** that hypothesis, while the "–" symbol indicates that the evidence **counts against** the hypothesis.

In the first table, the evidence is diagnostic.

The weights you assign to these values are analytically rigorous but subjective, so use your best judgment.

This evidence is diagnostic.

This evidence counts in favor of H1...

...but it really counts in favor of H2.

	H1	H2	H3
Evidence #1	+	++	–

This evidence doesn't disconfirm H3 outright, but it leads us to doubt H3.

In the second table, on the other hand, the evidence is **not** diagnostic.

This evidence is not diagnostic.

It equally supports each of these hypotheses.

	H1	H2	H3
Evidence #2	+	+	+

It might seem like an otherwise interesting piece of evidence, but unless it helps us rank our hypotheses, it's not of much use.

When you are hypothesis testing, it's important to identify and seek out diagnostic evidence. Nondiagnostic evidence doesn't get you anywhere.

Let's try looking at the diagnosticity of our evidence...

Exercise

Take a close look at your evidence in comparison to each of your hypotheses. Use the plus and minus notation to rank hypotheses with diagnosticity.

1 Say whether each piece of evidence supports or hurts each hypothesis.

2 **Cross out** pieces of evidence that *aren't diagnostic*.

	H2: Release will be next month	H3: Release will be in six months	H4: Release will be in a year
The investment from PodPhone is the biggest investment in new phone tech ever.			
There is going to be a huge increase in features compared to competitor phones.			
CEO of PodPhone said "No way we're launching the new phone tomorrow."			
There was just a big new phone released from a competitor.			
The economy and consumer spending are both up.			
Rumor: PodPhone CEO said there'd be no release this year.			

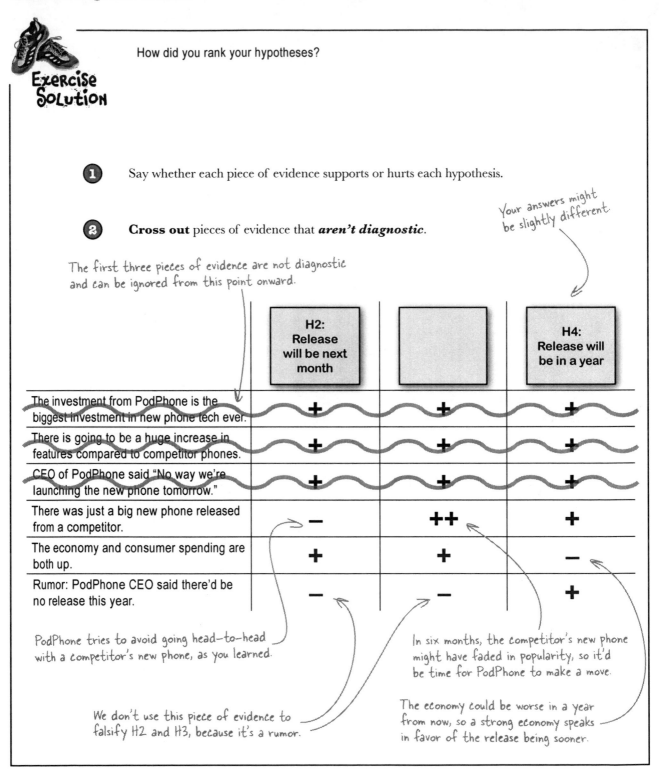

Exercise Solution

How did you rank your hypotheses?

1 Say whether each piece of evidence supports or hurts each hypothesis.

2 **Cross out** pieces of evidence that *aren't diagnostic*.

Your answers might be slightly different.

The first three pieces of evidence are not diagnostic and can be ignored from this point onward.

	H2: Release will be next month		H4: Release will be in a year
~~The investment from PodPhone is the biggest investment in new phone tech ever.~~	+	+	+
~~There is going to be a huge increase in features compared to competitor phones.~~	+	+	+
~~CEO of PodPhone said "No way we're launching the new phone tomorrow."~~	+	+	+
There was just a big new phone released from a competitor.	−	++	+
The economy and consumer spending are both up.	+	+	−
Rumor: PodPhone CEO said there'd be no release this year.	−	−	+

PodPhone tries to avoid going head-to-head with a competitor's new phone, as you learned.

In six months, the competitor's new phone might have faded in popularity, so it'd be time for PodPhone to make a move.

We don't use this piece of evidence to falsify H2 and H3, because it's a rumor.

The economy could be worse in a year from now, so a strong economy speaks in favor of the release being sooner.

You can't rule out all the hypotheses, but you can say which is strongest

While the evidence you have at your disposal doesn't enable you to rule out all hypotheses but one, you can take the three remaining and figure out which one has the least disconfirmation from the evidence.

That hypothesis is going to be your best bet until you know more.

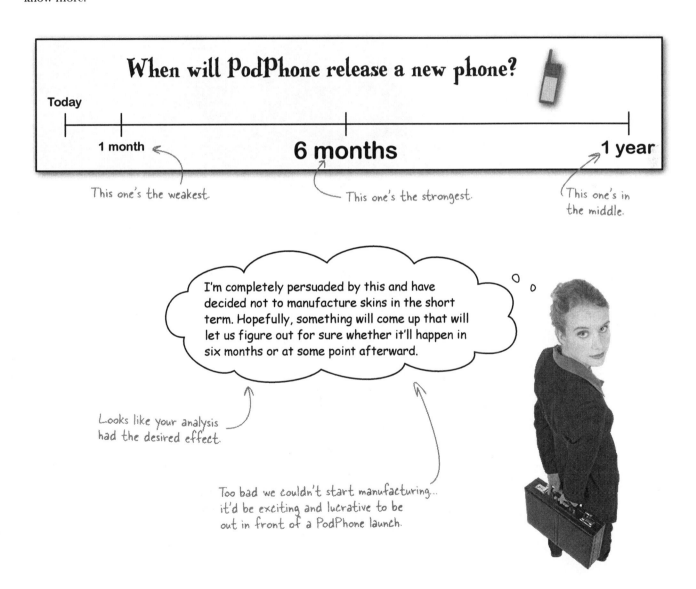

When will PodPhone release a new phone?

Today

1 month

6 months

1 year

This one's the weakest.

This one's the strongest.

This one's in the middle.

I'm completely persuaded by this and have decided not to manufacture skins in the short term. Hopefully, something will come up that will let us figure out for sure whether it'll happen in six months or at some point afterward.

Looks like your analysis had the desired effect.

Too bad we couldn't start manufacturing... it'd be exciting and lucrative to be out in front of a PodPhone launch.

You just got a picture message...

Your coworker saw this crew of PodPhone employees at a restaurant just now.

Everyone's **passing around new phones**, and although your contact can't get close enough to see one, he thinks it might be the one.

Why would all these PodPhone employees be out having a bash at a restaurant?

Passing around phones? Everyone's seen mock-ups, but why throw a party for mock-ups?

This is new evidence.

Better look at your hypothesis grid again. You can add this new information to your hypothesis test and then run it again. Maybe this information will help you distinguish among your hypotheses even further.

Sharpen your pencil

Do your hypothesis test again, this time with the new evidence.

	H2: Release will be next month	H3: Release will be in six months	H4: Release will be in a year
There was just a big new phone released from a competitor.	−	++	+
The economy and consumer spending are both up.	+	+	−
Rumor: PodPhone CEO said there'd be no release this year.	−	−	+

Write down the new piece of evidence here.

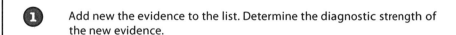

1 Add new the evidence to the list. Determine the diagnostic strength of the new evidence.

2 Does this new evidence change your assessment of whether PodPhone is about to announce its new phone (and whether ElectroSkinny should start manufacturing)?

....

....

....

Sharpen your pencil
Solution

Did your new evidence change your ideas about the relative strengths of your hypotheses? How?

	H2: Release will be next month		H4: Release will be in a year
There was just a big new phone released from a competitor.	–	++	+
The economy and consumer spending are both up.	+	+	–
There is a rumor that CEO isn't going to release this year at all.	–	–	+
The development team is seen having a huge celebration, holding new phones.	+++	–	–

This is a big one!

① Add new the evidence to the list. Determine the diagnostic strength of the new evidence.

② Does this new evidence change your assessment of whether PodPhone is about to announce its new phone (and whether ElectroSkinny should start manufacturing)?

Definitely. It's kind of hard to imagine that the team would be celebrating and passing around

copies of the phone if they weren't going to release a new phone soon. We've already ruled out

a launch tomorrow, and so it's really looking like H2 is our best hypothesis.

It's a launch!

Your analysis was spot on, and ElectroSkinny had a line of cool new skins for the new model of the PodPhone.

Thanks to you, we totally saw that launch coming and were ready for it with a bunch of awesome new skins. What's more, our competitors all thought PodPhone wasn't going to release a new phone, so we were the only ones ready and now we're cleaning up!

Nice work!

6 bayesian statistics

Get past first base

He says he's not like the other guys, but how different is he *exactly*?

You'll always be collecting new data.

And you need to make sure that every analysis you do incorporates the data you have that's relevant to your problem. You've learned how *falsification* can be used to deal with heterogeneous data sources, but what about **straight up probabilities**? The answer involves an extremely handy analytic tool called **Bayes' rule**, which will help you incorporate your **base rates** to uncover not-so-obvious insights with ever-changing data.

The doctor has disturbing news

Your eyes are not deceiving you. Your doctor has given you a diagnosis of **lizard flu**.

The **good news** is that lizard flu is not fatal and, if you have it, you're in for a full recovery after a few weeks of treatment. The **bad news** is that lizard flu is a big pain in the butt. You'll have to miss work, and you will have to stay away from your loved ones for a few weeks.

LIZARD FLU TEST RESULTS

Date: **Today**

Name: **Head First Data Analyst**

Diagnosis: **Positive**

Here's some information on lizard flu:

Lizard flu is a tropical disease first observed among lizard researchers in South America.

The disease is highly contagious, and affected patients need to be quarantined in their homes for no fewer than six weeks.

Patients diagnosed with lizard flu have been known to "taste the air" and in extreme cases have developed temporary chromatophores and zygodactylous feet.

Cough

You!

Your doctor is convinced that you have it, but because you've become so handy with data, you might want to take a look at the **test** and see just **how accurate** it is.

Sharpen your pencil

A quick web search on the lizard flu diagnostic test has yielded this result: an analysis of the test's accuracy.

MED-O-PEDIA

> *90%... that looks pretty solid.*

Lizard flu diagnostic test
Accuracy analysis

If someone has lizard flu, the probability that the test returns *positive* for it is 90 percent.

If someone doesn't have lizard flu, the probability that the test returns *positive* for it is 9 percent.

> *This is an interesting statistic.*

In light of this information, what do you think is the probability that you have lizard flu? How did you come to your decision?

....

....

....

....

Sharpen your pencil
Solution

You just looked at some data on the efficacy of the lizard flu diagnostic test. What did you decide were the chances that you have the disease?

Lizard flu diagnostic test
Accuracy analysis

If someone has lizard flu, the probability that the test returns **positive** for it is 90 percent.

If someone doesn't have lizard flu, the probability that the test returns **positive** for it is 9 percent.

In light of this information, what do you think is the probability that you have lizard flu? How did you come to your decision?

It looks like the chances would be 90% if I had the disease. But not everyone has the disease, as

the second statistic shows. So I should revise my estimate down a little bit. But it doesn't seem like

the answer is going to be exactly 90%-9%=81%, because that would be too easy, so, I dunno, maybe

75%?

The answer is way
lower than 75%!

Watch it!

75% is the answer that most people give to this sort of question. And they're *way* off.

Not only is 75% the wrong answer, but it's not anywhere near the right answer. And if you started making decisions with the idea that there's a 75% chance you have lizard flu, you'd be making an even bigger mistake!

There is so much at stake in getting the answer to this question correct.

We are *totally* going to get to the bottom of this…

Let's take the accuracy analysis one claim at a time

There are two different and obviously important claims being made about the test: the rate at which the test returns "positive" varies depending on whether the person has lizard flu or not.

So let's **imagine two different worlds**, one where a lot of people have lizard flu and one where few people have it, and then look at the claim about "positive" scores for people who **don't** have lizard flu.

Start here.

Lizard flu diagnostic test
Accuracy analysis

If someone has lizard flu, the probability that the test returns *positive* for it is 90 percent.

If someone doesn't have lizard flu, the probability that the test returns *positive* for it is 9 percent.

Let's really get the meaning of this statement...

Sharpen your pencil

Take a closer look at the second statement and answer the questions below.

Lizard flu diagnostic test
Accuracy analysis

If someone doesn't have lizard flu, the probability that the test returns *positive* for it is 9 percent.

Think really hard about this.

Scenario 1	
If **90 out of 100 people have it**, how many people who *don't* have it test positive?	If **10 out of 100 people** have it, how many people who *don't* have it test positive?
....	....
....	....
....	....

Sharpen your pencil
Solution

Does the number of people who have the disease affect how many people are wrongly told that they test positive?

Lizard flu diagnostic test
Accuracy analysis

If someone doesn't have lizard flu, the probability that the test returns ***positive*** for it is 9 percent.

Scenario 1

If **90 out of 100 people have it**, how many people who *don't* have it test positive?

This means that 10 people don't have it, so we take 9% of 10 people, which is about 1 person who tests positive but doesn't have it.

Scenario 2

If **10 out of 100 people** have it, how many people who *don't* have it test positive?

This means that 90 people don't have it, so we take 9% of 90 people, which is 10 people who test positive but don't have it.

How common is lizard flu really?

At least when it comes to situations where people who *don't* have lizard flu test positively, it seems that the prevalence of lizard flu in the general population makes a big difference.

In fact, unless we know **how many people *already* have lizard flu**, in addition to the accuracy analysis of the test, we simply cannot figure out how likely it is that you have lizard flu.

We need more data to make sense of that diagnostic test...

You've been counting false positives

In the previous exercise, you counted the number of people who *falsely* got a *positive* result. These cases are called **false positives**.

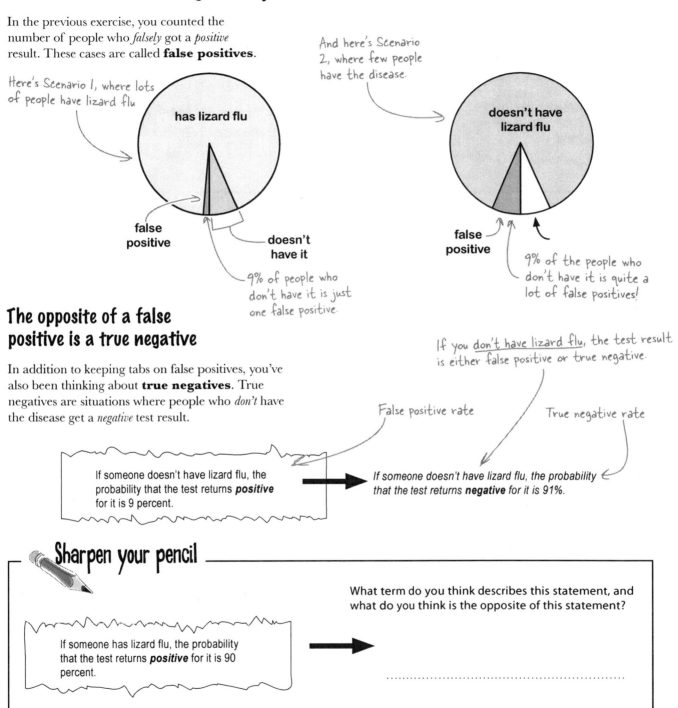

Here's Scenario 1, where lots of people have lizard flu

has lizard flu

And here's Scenario 2, where few people have the disease.

doesn't have lizard flu

false positive

doesn't have it

9% of people who don't have it is just one false positive.

false positive

9% of the people who don't have it is quite a lot of false positives!

The opposite of a false positive is a true negative

In addition to keeping tabs on false positives, you've also been thinking about **true negatives**. True negatives are situations where people who *don't* have the disease get a *negative* test result.

If you don't have lizard flu, the test result is either false positive or true negative.

False positive rate

True negative rate

> If someone doesn't have lizard flu, the probability that the test returns **positive** for it is 9 percent.

> *If someone doesn't have lizard flu, the probability that the test returns **negative** for it is 91%.*

Sharpen your pencil

What term do you think describes this statement, and what do you think is the opposite of this statement?

> If someone has lizard flu, the probability that the test returns **positive** for it is 90 percent.

....

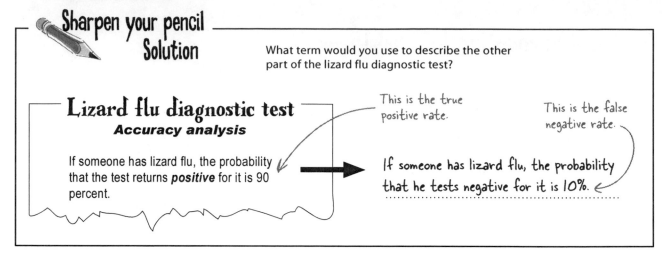

Sharpen your pencil Solution

What term would you use to describe the other part of the lizard flu diagnostic test?

Lizard flu diagnostic test
Accuracy analysis

If someone has lizard flu, the probability that the test returns *positive* for it is 90 percent.

This is the true positive rate.

This is the false negative rate.

If someone has lizard flu, the probability that he tests negative for it is 10%.

All these terms describe conditional probabilities

A **conditional probability** in the probability of some event, *given* that some other event has happened. *Assuming* that someone tests positive, what are the chances that he has lizard flu?

Here's how the statements you've been using look in conditional probability notation:

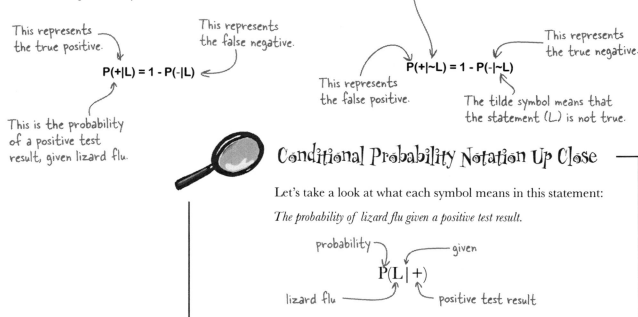

This represents the true positive.

This represents the false negative.

$$P(+|L) = 1 - P(-|L)$$

This is the probability of a positive test result, given lizard flu.

This is the probability of a positive test result, given that the person doesn't have lizard flu.

This represents the false positive.

This represents the true negative.

$$P(+|{\sim}L) = 1 - P(-|{\sim}L)$$

The tilde symbol means that the statement (L) is not true.

Conditional Probability Notation Up Close

Let's take a look at what each symbol means in this statement:

The probability of lizard flu given a positive test result.

probability — given

$$P(L \,|\, +)$$

lizard flu — positive test result

You need to count
→ false positives,
→ true positives,
→ false negatives, and
true negatives

Figuring out your probability of having lizard flu is all about knowing how many ***actual people*** are represented by these figures.

How many <u>actual people</u> fit into each of these probability groupings?

P(+|~L), the probability at someone tests **positive**, given that they **don't** have lizard flu

P(+|L), , the probability at someone tests **positive**, given that they **do** have lizard flu

P(-|L), the probability at someone tests **negative**, given that they **do** have lizard flu

P(-|~L), the probability at someone tests **negative** given that they **don't** have lizard flu.

But first you need to know how many people have lizard flu. Then you can use these percentages to calculate how many people actually fall into these categories.

Yeah, I get it. So how many people have lizard flu?

This is the figure you want!

P(L|+)

What is the probability of lizard flu, given a positive test result?

1 percent of people have lizard flu

Here's the number you need in order to interpret your test. Turns out that 1 percent of the population has lizard flu. In human terms, that's quite a lot of people. But as a percentage of the overall population, it's a pretty small number.

One percent is the **base rate**. Prior to learning anything new about individuals because of the test, you know that only 1 percent of the population has lizard flu. That's why base rates are also called **prior probabilities**.

Center for Disease Tracking is on top of lizard flu

Study finds that 1 percent of national population has lizard flu

The most recent data, which is current as of last week, indicates that 1 percent of the national population is infected with lizard flu. Although lizard flu is rarely fatal, these individuals need to be quarantined to prevent others from becoming infected.

Watch out for the base rate fallacy

I just thought that the 90% true positive rate meant it's really likely that you have it!

That's a fallacy!

Always be on the lookout for base rates. You might not have base rate data in every case, but if you do have a base rate and don't use it, you'll fall victim to the **base rate fallacy**, where you ignore your prior data and make the wrong decisions because of it.

In this case, your judgment about the probability that you have lizard flu depends ***entirely*** on the base rate, and because the base rate turns out to be 1 percent of people having lizard flu, **that 90 percent true positive rate on the test doesn't seem nearly so insightful**.

Sharpen your pencil

Calculate the probability that you have lizard flu. Assuming you start with 1,000 people, fill in the blanks, dividing them into groups according to your base rates and the specs of the test.

Lizard flu diagnostic test
Accuracy analysis

If someone has lizard flu, the probability that the test returns **positive** for it is 90 percent.

If someone doesn't have lizard flu, the probability that the test returns **positive** for it is 9 percent.

Remember, 1% of people have lizard flu.

1,000 people

....
The number of people who have it

....
The number of people who don't have it

....
The number who test positive

....
The number who test negative

....
The number who test positive

....
The number who test negative

The probability that you have it, given that you tested positive $=$ $\dfrac{\text{\# of people who have it and test positive}}{(\text{\# of people who have it and test positive}) + (\text{\# of people who don't have it and test positive})}$ $=$ ....

*things don't look **so bad***

Sharpen your pencil
Solution

What did you calculate your new probability
of having lizard flu to be?

Lizard flu diagnostic test
Accuracy analysis

If someone has lizard flu, the probability
that the test returns ***positive*** for it is 90
percent.

If someone doesn't have lizard flu, the
probability that the test returns ***positive***
for it is 9 percent.

1,000 people

*9% of people who've tested
positively have lizard flu.*

*91% of people who've tested
positively <u>don't</u> have lizard flu.*

10

The number of
people who have it

990

The number of people
who don't have it

9

The number who
test positive

1

The number who
test negative

89

The number who
test positive

901

The number who
test negative

The probability that
you have it, given that
you tested positive

=

$$\frac{\text{\# of people who have it and test positive}}{(\text{\# of people who have it and test positive}) + (\text{\# of people who don't have it and test positive})}$$

= $\frac{9}{9+89} = 0.09$

There's a 9% chance that I have lizard flu!

Your chances of having lizard flu are still pretty low

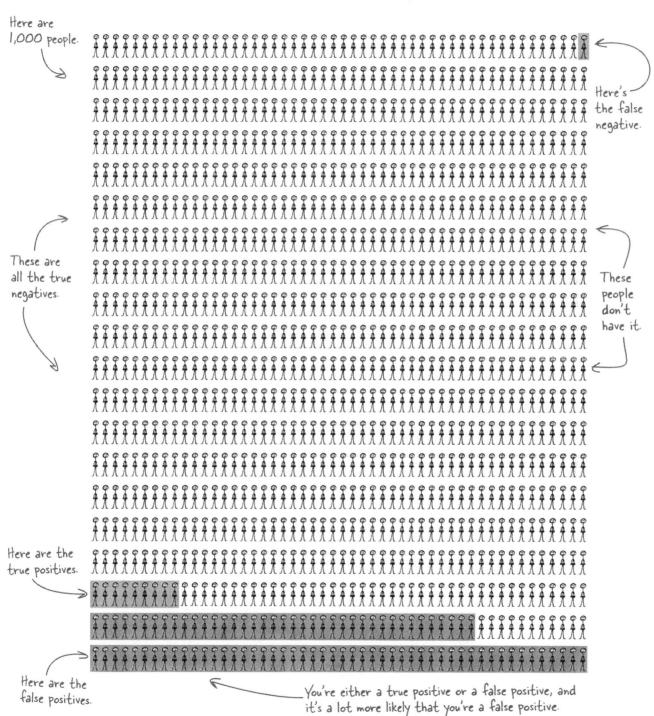

Here are 1,000 people.

Here's the false negative.

These are all the true negatives.

These people don't have it.

Here are the true positives.

Here are the false positives.

You're either a true positive or a false positive, and it's a lot more likely that you're a false positive.

Do complex probabilistic thinking with simple whole numbers

When you imagined that you were looking at 1,000 people, you switched from decimal probabilities to **whole numbers**. Because our brains aren't innately well-equipped to process numerical probabilities, converting probabilities to whole numbers and then thinking through them is a very effective way to avoid making mistakes.

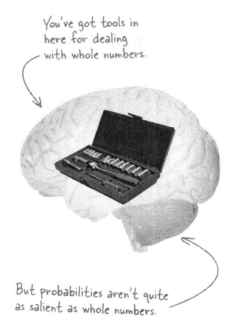

You've got tools in here for dealing with whole numbers.

But probabilities aren't quite as salient as whole numbers.

Bayes' rule manages your base rates when you get new data

Believe it or not, you just did a commonsense implementation of Bayes' rule, an incredibly powerful statistical formula that enables you to use base rates along with your conditional probabilities to estimate new conditional probabilities.

If you wanted to make the same calculation algebraically, you could use this monster of a formula:

This formula will give you the same result you just calculated.

The probability of lizard flu given a positive test result

The base rate (people who have the disease)

The true positive rate

$$P(L\,|\,+) = \frac{P(L)P(+\,|\,L)}{P(L)P(+\,|\,L) + P(\sim)P(+\,|\sim L)}$$

The base rate (people who don't have the disease)

The false positive rate

You can use Bayes' rule over and over

Bayes' rule is an important tool in data analysis, because it provides a precise way of incorporating new information into your analyses.

Bayes' rule lets you add more information over time.

My Analysis

Base rate

My Analysis

Base rate **+** **Test results**

My Analysis

Base rate **+** **Test results** **+** **More test results**

So the test isn't that accurate. You're still nine times more likely to have lizard flu than other people. Shouldn't you get another test?

Yep, you're 9x more likely to have lizard flu than the regular population.

The base rate: **1%**

Your chances of having lizard flu: **9%**

Your doctor took the suggestion and ordered another test. Let's see what it said...

Your second test result is negative

The doctor didn't order you the more powerful, *advanced* lizard flu test the first time because it's kind of expensive, but now that you tested positively on the first (cheaper, less accurate) test, it's time to bring out the big guns…

The doctor ordered a slightly different test: the "advanced" lizard flu diagnostic test.

ADVANCED LIZARD FLU TEST RESULTS

Date: **Today**

Name: **Head First Data Analyst**

Diagnosis: **Negative**

Here's some information on lizard flu:

Lizard flu is a tropical disease first observed among lizard researchers in South America.

The disease is highly contagious, and affected patients need to be quarantined in their homes for no fewer than six weeks.

Patients diagnosed with lizard flu have been known to "taste the air" and in extreme cases have developed temporary chromatophores and zygodactylous feet.

That's a relief!

You got these probabilities wrong before.

Better run the numbers again. By now, you know that responding to the test result (or even the test accuracy statistics) without looking at base rates is a recipe for confusion.

The new test has different accuracy statistics

Using your base rate, you can use the new test's statistics to calculate the new probability that you have lizard flu.

This is the first test you took.

This new test is more expensive but more powerful.

Lizard flu diagnostic test
Accuracy analysis

If someone has lizard flu, the probability that the test returns *positive* for it is 90 percent.

If someone doesn't have lizard flu, the probability that the test returns *positive* for it is 9 percent.

Advanced Lizard flu diagnostic test
Accuracy analysis

If someone has lizard flu, the probability that the test returns **positive** for it is 99 percent.

If someone doesn't have lizard flu, the probability that the test returns **positive** for it is 1 percent.

Should we use the same base rate as before? You tested positive. It seems like that should count for something.

These accuracy figures are a lot stronger.

✏ Sharpen your pencil

What do you think the base rate should be?

....

....

Sharpen your pencil
Solution

What do you think the base rate should be?

1% can't be the base rate. The new base rate is the 9% we just calculated,

because that figure is my own probability of having the disease.

New information can change your base rate

When you got your first test results back, you used as your base rate the incidence in the population of ***everybody*** for lizard flu.

1% of everybody has lizard flu

Old base rate

You used to be part of this group...

Everybody

Just a regular person... nothing remarkable

But you learned from the test that your probability of having lizard flu is higher than the base rate. That probability is your new base rate, because now you're part of the group of people who've tested positively.

...now you're part of this group.

9% of people who tested positively have lizard flu

Your new base rate

People who've tested positively once

Let's hurry up and run Bayes' rule again...

Sharpen your pencil

Using the new test and your revised base rate, let's calculate the probability that you have lizard flu given your results.

Advanced Lizard flu diagnostic test
Accuracy analysis

If someone has lizard flu, the probability that the test returns **positive** for it is 99 percent.

If someone doesn't have lizard flu, the probability that the test returns **positive** for it is 1 percent.

Remember, 9% of people like you will have lizard flu.

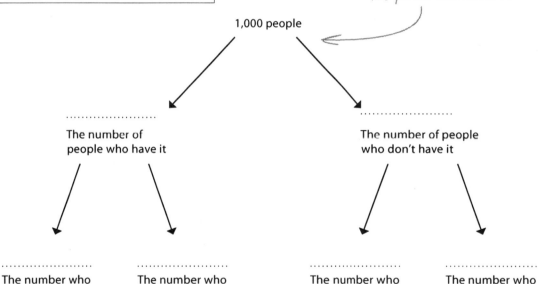

1,000 people

....
The number of people who have it

....
The number of people who don't have it

....
The number who test positive

....
The number who test negative

....
The number who test positive

....
The number who test negative

The probability that you have it, given that you tested negative $=$ $\dfrac{\text{\# of people who have it and test negative}}{\begin{array}{l}(\text{\# of people who have it and test negative}) + \\ \quad (\text{\# of people who don't have it and test negative})\end{array}}$ $=$ ....

Sharpen your pencil
Solution

What do you calculate your new probability of having lizard flu to be?

Advanced
Lizard flu diagnostic test
Accuracy analysis

If someone has lizard flu, the probability that the test returns **positive** for it is 99 percent.

If someone doesn't have lizard flu, the probability that the test returns **positive** for it is 1 percent.

1,000 people

9% of people who've tested positively have lizard flu.

91% of people who've tested positively <u>don't</u> have lizard flu.

90

910

The number of people who have it

The number of people who don't have it

89

1

9

901

The number who test positive

The number who test negative

The number who test positive

The number who test negative

The probability that you have it, given that you tested negative

=

$$\frac{\text{\# of people who have it and test negative}}{(\text{\# of people who have it and test negative}) + (\text{\# of people who don't have it and test negative})}$$

  = $\frac{1}{1+901} = 0.001$

There's a 0.1% chance that I have lizard flu!

What a relief!

You took control of the probabilities using Bayes' rule and now know how to manage base rates.

The only way to avoid the base rate fallacy is always to be on the lookout for base rates and to be sure to incorporate them into your analyses.

Your probability of having lizard flu is so low that you can pretty much rule it out.

Cough

No lizard flu for you!

Now you've just got to shake that cold...

7 subjective probabilities

Numerical belief

She's a perfect 10...

Before the ice cream, I gave him a 3, but now he's a 4.

Sometimes, it's a good idea to make up numbers.

Seriously. But only if those numbers describe your own mental states, expressing your beliefs. **Subjective probability** is a straightforward way of injecting some real *rigor* into your hunches, and you're about to see how. Along the way, you are going to learn how to evaluate the spread of data using **standard deviation** and enjoy a special guest appearance from one of the more powerful analytic tools you've learned.

Backwater Investments needs your help

Backwater Investments is a business that tries to make money by seeking out *obscure investments* in developing markets. They pick investments that other people have a hard time understanding or even finding.

Backwater owns companies here...

...and here...

...and even here!

Their strategy means that they rely heavily on the **expertise of their analysts,** who need to have impeccable judgment and good connections to be able to get BI the information they need for good investment decisions.

It's a cool business, except it's about to be **torn apart** by arguments among the analysts. The disagreements are so acrimonious that everyone's about to quit, which would be a disaster for the fund.

The internal crisis at Backwater Investments might force the company to shut down.

Their analysts are at each other's throats

The analysts at BI are having big disagreements over a number of geopolitical trends. And this is a big problem for the people trying to set investment strategy based on their analyses. There are a bunch of different issues that are causing splits.

> The analysts are in full revolt! If I don't get them agreeing on something, they'll all quit.

The boss

Where *precisely* are the disagreements? It would be really great if you could help figure out the scope of the dispute and help achieve a consensus among the analysts. Or, at the very least, it'd be nice if you could specify the disagreements in a way that will let the BI bosses figure out where they stand.

Let's take a look at the disputes...

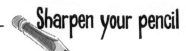

Sharpen your pencil

Take a look at these emails, which the analysts have sent you. Do they help you understand their arguments?

> **From: Senior Research Analyst, Backwater Investments**
> **To: Head First**
> **Subject: Rant on Vietnam**
>
> For the past six months, I've consistently argued to the staff that the Vietnamese government is probably going to reduce its taxes this year. And everything that we've seen from our people on the ground and in news reports confirms this.
>
> Yet others in the "analytical" community at BI seem to think this is crazy. I'm a considered dreamer by the higher-ups and told that such a gesture or the part of the government is "highly unlikely." Well, what do they base this assessment on? Clearly the government is encouraging foreign investment. I'll tell you this: if taxes go down, there will be a flood of private investment, and we need to increase our presence in Vietnam before the

These analysts are kind of bent out of shape.

> **From: Political Analyst, Backwater Investments**
> **To: Head First**
> **Subject: Investing in obscure places: A Manifesto**
>
> Russia, Indonesia, Vietnam. The community at BI has become obsessed with these three places. Yet aren't the answers to all our questions abundantly clear? Russia will continue to subsidize oil next quarter like it always has, and they're more likely than not to buy EuroAir next quarter. Vietnam *might* decrease taxes this year, and they probably aren't going to encourage foreign investment. Indonesia will more likely than not invest in ecotourism this year, but it won't be of much help. Tourism will definitely fall apart completely.
>
> If BI doesn't fire the dissenters and troublemakers who dispute these truths, the firm might as well close...

Is the disagreement all about these three countries?

From: VP, Economic Research, Backwater Investments
To: Head First
Subject: Have these people ever even been to Russia?

While the analytic stuff in the Economic division has continued to flourish and produce quality work on Russian business and government, the rest of BI has shown a shocking ignorance of the internal dynamics of Russia. It's quite unlikely that Russia will puchase EuroAir, and their support of the oil industry next quarter may be the most tentative it's ever been...

Even a top manager is starting to lose his cool!

This guy's writing from the field, where he's doing firsthand research.

From: Junior Researcher, Backwater Investments
To: Head First
Subject: Indonesia

You need to stop listening to the eggheads back at corporate headquarters.

The perspective from the ground is that tourism definitely has a good chance of increasing this year, and Indonesia is all about ecotourism. The eggheads don't know anything, and I'm starting to think that my intel would be better used by a competing firm...

What are the key issues causing the disagreement?

....

....

....

....

The authors each use a bunch of words to describe what they think the likelihoods of various events are. List all the "probability words" they use.

....

....

Sharpen your pencil
Solution

There are a bunch of probability words used in these emails...

What are your impressions of the arguments, now that you've read the analysts' emails?

From: Senior Research Analyst, Backwater Investments
To: Head First
Subject: Rant on Vietnam

For the past six months, I've consistently argued to the staff that the Vietnamese government is probably going to reduce its taxes this year. And everything that we've seen from our people on the ground and in news reports confirms this.

Yet others in the "analytical" community at BI seem to think this is crazy. I'm a dreamer by the higher-ups and told that such a gesture or the part of the government is "highly unlikely." Well, what do they base this assessment on? Clearly the government is encouraging foreign investment. I'll tell you this: if taxes go down, there will be a flood of private

From: Political Analyst, Backwater Investments
To: Head First
Subject: Investing in obscure places: A Manifesto

Russia, Indonesia, Vietnam. The community at BI has become obsessed with these three places. Yet aren't the answers to all our questions abundantly clear? Russia will continue to subsidize oil next quarter like it always has, and they're more likely than not to buy EuroAir next quarter. Vietnam *might* decrease taxes this year, and they probably aren't going to encourage foreign investment. Indonesia will more likely than not invest in ecotourism this year, but it won't be of much help. Tourism will definitely fall apart completely.

If BI doesn't fire the dissenters and troublemakers who dispute these truths, the firm might as well close...

From: VP, Economic Research, Backwater Inve
To: Head First
Subject: Have these people ever even been to R

While the analytic stuff in the Economic divisio continued to flourish and produce quality work Russian business and government, the rest of E shown a shocking ignorance of the internal dyn of Russia. It's quite unlikely that Russia will puc EuroAir, and their support of the oil industry ne quarter may be the most tentative it's ever bee

From: Junior Researcher, Backwater Investments
To: Head First
Subject: Indonesia

You need to stop listening to the eggheads back at corporate headquarters.

The perspective from the ground is that tourism definitely has a good chance of increasing this year, and Indonesia is all about ecotourism. The eggheads don't know anything, and I'm starting to think that my intel would be better used by a competing firm...

What are the key issues causing the disagreement?

There seem to be six areas of disagreement: 1) Will Russia subsidize oil business next quarter?

2) Will Russia purchase EuroAir? 3) Will Vietnam decrease taxes this year? 4) Will Vietnam's

government encourage foreign investment this year? 5) Will Indonesian tourism increase this year? 6)

Will the Indonesian government invest in ecotourism?

The authors use a bunch of words to describe what they think the likelihoods of various events are. List all the "probability words" they use.

The words they use are: probably, highly unlikely, more likely, might, probably aren't, unlikely, may,

definitely, and good chance.

Jim: So we're supposed to come in and tell everyone who's right and who's wrong? That shouldn't be a problem. All we need is to see the data.

Frank: Not so fast. These analysts aren't just regular folks. They're highly trained, highly experienced, serious domain experts when it comes to these countries.

Joe: Yeah. The CEO says they have all the data they could ever hope for. They have access to the best information in the world. They pay for proprietary data, they have people digging through government sources, and they have people on the ground doing firsthand reporting.

Frank: And geopolitics is highly uncertain stuff. They're predicting *single events* that don't have a big trail of numerical frequency data that you can just look at and use to make more predictions. They're aggregating data from a bunch of sources and making very highly educated guesses.

Jim: Then what you're saying is that these guys are smarter than we are, and that there is really nothing we can do to fix these arguments.

Joe: Providing our own data analysis would be just adding more screaming to the argument.

Frank: Actually, all the arguments involve hypotheses about what's going to happen in the various countries, and the analysts really get upset when it comes to those probability words. "Probably?" "Good chance?" What do those expressions even mean?

Jim: So you want to help them find better words to describe their feelings? Gosh, that sounds like a waste of time.

Frank: Maybe not words. We need to find something that will give these judgments more **precision**, even though they're someone's subjective beliefs…

How would you make the probability words more precise?

Subjective probabilities describe expert beliefs

When you assign a numerical probability to your degree of belief in something, you're specifying a **subjective probability**.

Subjective probabilities are a great way to apply discipline to an analysis, especially when you are predicting single events that lack hard data to describe what happened previously under identical conditions.

Everyone talks like this...   **...but what do <u>they</u> really mean?**

Continued Russian support of the oil industry is <u>highly probable</u>.

I believe there is a 60% chance that Russia will continue to support the oil industry.

...there is a 70% chance...

...there is a 80% chance...

...there is a 90% chance...

These are <u>subjective probabilities</u>.

These figures are much more precise than the words the analysts used to describe their beliefs.

Subjective probabilities might show no real disagreement after all

I think it's highly probable.

Fool! It's totally unlikely!

Well, I'd say that there is a 40% chance that it'll happen.

Hmm. Well, I'd say there is a 35% chance it'll happen.

Doesn't seem like we're so far apart after all.

Yeah. Maybe "fool" was a little too strong a word...

Sharpen your pencil

Sketch an outline of a spreadsheet that would contain all the subjective probabilities you need from your analysts. How would you structure it?

Draw a picture of the spreadsheet you want here.

What you want is a subjective probability from each analyst for each of the key areas of dispute.

Sharpen your pencil
Solution

What does the spreadsheet you want from the analysts to describe their subjective probabilities look like?

Russia will subsidize oil business next quarter.

Russia will purchase a European airline next quarter.

Vietnam will decrease taxes this year.

Vietnam's government will encourage foreign investment this year.

Indonesian tourism will increase this year.

Indonesian government will invest in ecotourism.

The table will take each of the six statements and list them at the top.

We can fill in the blanks of what each analyst thinks about each statement here.

Analyst	Statement 1	Statement 2	Statement 3	Statement 4	Statement 5	Statement 6
1						
2						
3						
4						
5						
6						
7						
8						
9						
10						
11						
12						
13						
14						
15						
16						
17						
18						
19						
20						

The analysts responded with their subjective probabilities

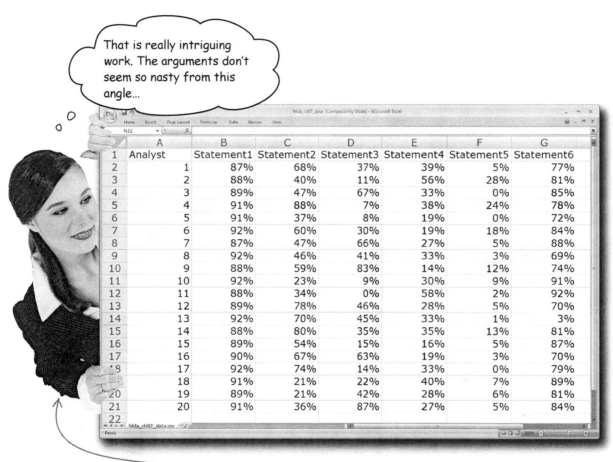

> That is really intriguing work. The arguments don't seem so nasty from this angle...

	A	B	C	D	E	F	G
1	Analyst	Statement1	Statement2	Statement3	Statement4	Statement5	Statement6
2	1	87%	68%	37%	39%	5%	77%
3	2	88%	40%	11%	56%	28%	81%
4	3	89%	47%	67%	33%	0%	85%
5	4	91%	88%	7%	38%	24%	78%
6	5	91%	37%	8%	19%	0%	72%
7	6	92%	60%	30%	19%	18%	84%
8	7	87%	47%	66%	27%	5%	88%
9	8	92%	46%	41%	33%	3%	69%
10	9	88%	59%	83%	14%	12%	74%
11	10	92%	23%	9%	30%	9%	91%
12	11	88%	34%	0%	58%	2%	92%
13	12	89%	78%	46%	28%	5%	70%
14	13	92%	70%	45%	33%	1%	3%
15	14	88%	80%	35%	35%	13%	81%
16	15	89%	54%	15%	16%	5%	87%
17	16	90%	67%	63%	19%	3%	70%
18	17	92%	74%	14%	33%	0%	79%
19	18	91%	21%	22%	40%	7%	89%
20	19	89%	21%	42%	28%	6%	81%
21	20	91%	36%	87%	27%	5%	84%
22							

This analyst from BI is starting to look a little more upbeat!

Now we're getting somewhere.

While you haven't yet figured out how to resolve all their differences, you have definitely succeeded at showing where exactly the disagreements lie.

And from the looks of some of the data, it might not be that there is all that much disagreement after all, at least not on some issues.

Let's see what the CEO has to say about this data...

The CEO doesn't see what you're up to

It appears that he doesn't think these results provide anything that can be used to resolve the disagreements among the analysts.

He doesn't think these figures are of any help.

Ouch! Is he right?

> **From: CEO, Backwater Investments**
> **To: Head First**
> **Subject: Your "subjective probabilities"**
>
> **I'm kind of puzzled by this analysis. What we've asked you to do is resolve the disagreements among our analysts, and this just seems like a fancy way of listing the disagreements.**
>
> **We know what they are. That's not why we brought you on board. What we need you to do is resolve them or at least deal with them in a way that will let us get a better idea of how to structure our investment portfolio in spite of them.**
>
> **You should defend your choice of subjective probabilities as a tool for analysis here. What does it get us?**
>
> **– CEO**

The pressure's on!

You should probably explain and defend your reason for collecting this data to the CEO...

Sharpen your pencil

Is your grid of subjective probabilities…

	A	B	C	D	E	F	G
1	Analyst	Statement1	Statement2	Statement3	Statement4	Statement5	Statement6
2	1	87%	68%	37%	39%	5%	77%
3	2	88%	40%	11%	56%	28%	81%
4	3	89%	47%	67%	33%	0%	85%
5	4	91%	88%	7%	38%	24%	78%
6	5	91%	37%	8%	19%	0%	72%
7	6	92%	60%	30%	19%	18%	84%
8	7	87%	47%	66%	27%	5%	88%
9	8	92%	46%	41%	33%	3%	69%
10	9	88%	59%	83%	14%	12%	74%
11	10	92%	23%	9%	30%	9%	91%
12	11	88%	34%	0%	58%	2%	92%
13	12	89%	78%	46%	28%	5%	70%
14	13	92%	70%	45%	33%	1%	3%
15	14	88%	80%	35%	35%	13%	81%
16	15	89%	54%	15%	16%	5%	87%
17	16	90%	67%	63%	19%	3%	70%
18	17	92%	74%	14%	33%	0%	79%
19	18	91%	21%	22%	40%	7%	89%
20	19	89%	21%	42%	28%	6%	81%
21	20	91%	36%	87%	27%	5%	84%
22							

…any more useful analytically than these angry emails?

From: Political Analyst, Backwater Inve
To: Head First
Subject: Investing in obscure places: A

Russia, Indonesia, Vietnam. The comme
become obsessed with these three plac
the answers to all our questions abunda
Russia will continue to subsidize oil nex
it always has, and they're more likely th
EuroAir next quarter. Vietnam *might* dec
this year, and they probably aren't going
foreign investment. Indonesia will more
invest in ecotourism this year, but it won
help. Tourism will definitely fall apart con

If BI doesn't fire the dissenters and troub
dispute these truths, the firm might as we

From: Senior Research Analyst, Backwater
Investments
To: Head First
Subject: Rant on Vietnam

For the past six months I've consistently
the staff that the Vietnamese governmen
going to reduce its taxes this year. And e
we've seen from our people on the grour
reports confirms this.

Yet others in the "analytical" community
think this is crazy. I'm a dreamer by the h
told that such a gesture or the part of the
is "highly unlikely." Well what do they ba
assessment on? Clearly the government
foreign investment. I'll tell you this: if taxes go down
there will be a flood of private investment, and we need

From: VP, Economic Research, Backwat
To: Head First
Subject: Have these people ever even be

While the analytic stuff in the Economic
continued to flourish and produce quality
Russian business and government, the r
shown a shocking ignorance of the intern
of Russia. It's quite unlikely that Russia w
EuroAir, and their support of the oil indus
quarter may be the most tentative it's ev

From: Junior Researcher, Backwater Investments
To: Head First
Subject: Indonesia

You need to stop listening to the eggheads back at
corporate headquarters.

The perspective from the ground is that tourism
definitely has a good chance of increasing this year,
and Indonesia is all about ecotourism. The eggheads
don't know anything, and I'm starting to think that my
intel would be better used by a competing firm…

Why or why not?

....

....

....

....

Sharpen your pencil
Solution

Is your grid of subjective probabilities...

Any more useful analytically than these angry emails?

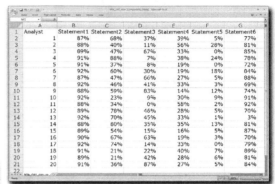

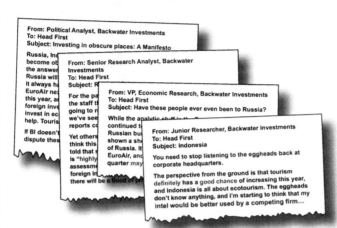

> The subjective probabilities show that some areas are not as contentious as we previously thought.
>
> The subjective probabilities are a precise specification of where there is disagreement and how much
>
> of it there is. The analysts can use them to help them figure out what they should focus on to
>
> solve their problems.

You've bought some time and can continue your work.

From: CEO, Backwater Investments
To: Head First
Subject: Visualization request

OK, you've persuaded me. But I don't want to read a big grid of numbers. Send me a chart that displays this data in a way that is easier for me to understand.

– CEO

Let's make this data visual!

Sharpen your pencil

For each value, plot a dot corresponding to the subjective probability.

	A	B	C	D	E	F	G
1	Analyst	Statement1	Statement2	Statement3	Statement4	Statement5	Statement6
2	1	87%	68%	37%	39%	5%	77%
3	2	88%	40%	11%	56%	28%	81%
4	3	89%	47%	67%	33%	0%	85%
5	4	91%	88%	7%	38%	24%	78%
6	5	91%	37%	8%	19%	0%	72%
7	6	92%	60%	30%	19%	18%	84%
8	7	87%	47%	66%	27%	5%	88%
9	8	92%	46%	41%	33%	3%	69%
10	9	88%	59%	83%	14%	12%	74%
11	10	92%	23%	9%	30%	9%	91%
12	11	88%	34%	0%	58%	2%	92%
13	12	89%	78%	46%	28%	5%	70%
14	13	92%	70%	45%	33%	1%	3%
15	14	88%	80%	35%	35%	13%	81%
16	15	89%	54%	15%	16%	5%	87%
17	16	90%	67%	63%	19%	3%	70%
18	17	92%	74%	14%	33%	0%	79%
19	18	91%	21%	22%	40%	7%	89%
20	19	89%	21%	42%	28%	6%	81%
21	20	91%	36%	87%	27%	5%	84%
22							

The vertical axis doesn't really matter, you can just jitter dots around so you can see them all.

Statement 1
Russia will subsidize oil business next quarter.

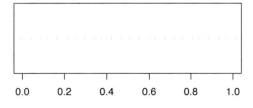

Here's an example.

Statement 2
Russia will purchase a European airline next quarter.

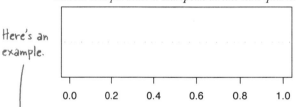

Statement 3
Vietnam will decrease taxes this year.

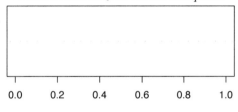

Statement 4
Vietnam's government will encourage foreign investment this year.

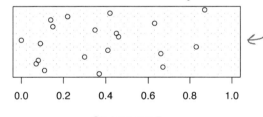

Statement 5
Indonesian tourism will increase this year.

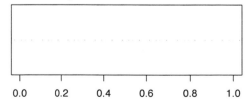

Statement 6
Indonesian government will invest in ecotourism.

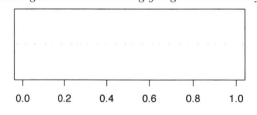

Sharpen your pencil
Solution

How do the spreads of analyst subjective probabilities look on your dot plots?

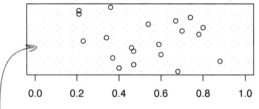

It looks like there is actually some consensus on this statement.

Statement 1
Russia will subsidize oil business next quarter.

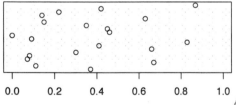

Statement 2
Russia will purchase a European airline next quarter.

The analysts are all over the place on these statements.

Statement 3
Vietnam will decrease taxes this year.

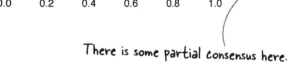

Statement 4
Vietnam's government will encourage foreign investment this year.

There is some partial consensus here.

People are within 20% of each other here, except for one person.

Statement 5
Indonesian tourism will increase this year.

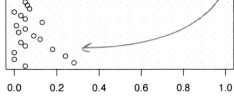

Statement 6
Indonesian government will invest in ecotourism.

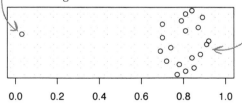

The CEO loves your work

From: CEO, Backwater Investments
To: Head First
Subject: Thank you!

Now this is actually a big help. I can see that there are a few areas where we really should concentrate our resources to get better information. And the stuff that doesn't appear to have real disagreement is just fantastic.

From now on, I don't want to hear anything from my analysts unless it's in the form of a subjective probability (or objective probability, if they can come up with one of those).

Can you rank these questions for me by their level of disagreement? I want to know which ones specifically are the most contentious.– CEO

Subjective probabilities are something that everyone understands but that don't get nearly enough use.

Great data analysts are great communicators, and subjective probabilities are an illuminating way to convey to others exactly what you think and believe.

 BRAIN POWER

What metric would measure disagreement and rank the questions so that the CEO can see the most problematic ones first?

The standard deviation measures how far points are from the average

You want to use the **standard deviation**. The standard deviation measures how far typical points are from the average (or mean) of the data set.

Most of the points in a data set will be within one standard deviation of the mean.

Here's a sample data set.

Most observations in any data set are going to be within one standard deviation of the mean.

Average = 0.5

0.0   0.2   0.4   0.6   0.8   1.0

One standard deviation = 0.1

The unit of the standard deviation is whatever it is that you're measuring. In the case above, one standard deviation from the mean is equal to 0.1 or 10 percent. Most points will be 10 percent above or below the mean, although a handful of points will be two or three standard deviations away.

Standard deviation can be used here to measure disagreement. The larger the standard deviation of subjective probabilities from the mean, the more disagreement there will be among analysts as to the likelihood that each hypothesis is true.

Use the STDEV formula in Excel to calculate the standard deviation.

```
=STDEV(data range)
```

Exercise

For each statement, calculate the standard deviation. Then, sort the list of questions to rank highest the question with the most disagreement.

What formula would you use to calculate the standard deviation for the first statement?

....

This data has been turned on its side so that you can sort the statements once you have the standard deviation.

Load this!

www.headfirstlabs.com/books/hfda/
hfda_ch07_data_transposed.xls

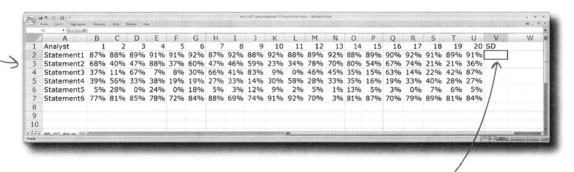

Analyst	1	2	3	4	5	6	7	8	9	10	11	12	13	14	15	16	17	18	19	20	SD
Statement1	87%	88%	89%	91%	91%	92%	87%	92%	88%	92%	88%	89%	92%	88%	89%	90%	92%	91%	89%	91%	
Statement2	68%	40%	47%	88%	37%	60%	47%	46%	59%	23%	34%	78%	70%	80%	54%	67%	74%	21%	21%	36%	
Statement3	37%	11%	67%	7%	8%	30%	66%	41%	83%	9%	0%	46%	45%	35%	15%	63%	14%	22%	42%	87%	
Statement4	39%	56%	33%	38%	19%	19%	27%	33%	14%	30%	58%	28%	33%	35%	16%	19%	33%	40%	28%	27%	
Statement5	5%	28%	0%	24%	0%	18%	5%	3%	12%	9%	2%	5%	1%	13%	5%	3%	0%	7%	6%	5%	
Statement6	77%	81%	85%	78%	72%	84%	88%	69%	74%	91%	92%	70%	3%	81%	87%	70%	79%	89%	81%	84%	

Put your answer here.

Exercise Solution

What standard deviations did you find?

What formula would you use to calculate the standard deviation for the first statement?

$$STDEV(B2:U2)$$

Here's where your function goes.

Copy it for each statement.

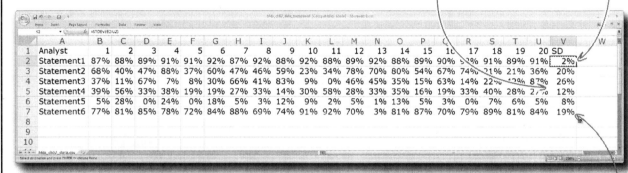

You might need to hit the "%" button on the toolbar to get the right formatting.

Click the Sort Descending button to put the statements in order.

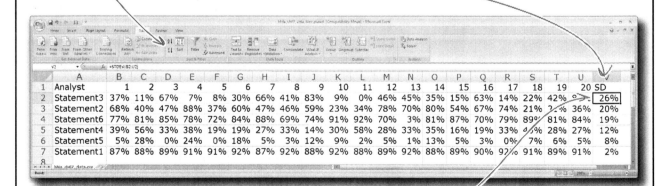

Looks like Statement 3 has the largest standard deviation and the greatest disagreement among analysts.

there are no
Dumb Questions

Q: Aren't subjective probabilities kind of deceptive?

A: Deceptive? They're a lot less deceptive than vague expressions like "really likely." With probability words, the person listening to you can pour all sorts of possible meanings into your words, so specifying the probabilities is actually a much *less* deceptive way to communicate your beliefs.

Q: I mean, isn't it possible or even likely (pardon the expression) that someone looking at these probabilities would get the impression that people are more certain about their beliefs than they actually are?

A: You mean that, since the numbers are in black and white, they might look more certain than they actually are?

Q: That's it.

A: It's a good concern. But the deal with subjective probabilities is the same as any other tool of data analysis: it's easy to bamboozle people with them if what you're trying to do is deceive. But as long as you make sure that your client knows that your probabilities are *subjective*, you're actually doing him a big favor by specifying your beliefs so precisely.

Q: Hey, can Excel do those fancy graphs with the little dots?

A: Yes, but it's a lot of trouble. These graphs were made in a handy little free program called R using the `dotchart` function. You'll get a taste of the power of R in later chapters.

Good work. I'm going to base my trading strategy on this sort of analysis from now on. If it pans out, you'll definitely see a piece of the upside.

The big boss

Russia announces that it will sell all its oil fields, citing loss of confidence in business

In a shocking move, Russian president poo-poohs national industry

"Da, we are finished with oil," said the Russian president to an astonished press corps earlier today in Moscow. "We have simply lost confidence in the industry and are no longer interested in pursuing the resource…"

This is awful! We all predicted that Russia would continue to have confidence in business.

Analyst

You were totally blindsided by this news

The initial reaction of the analysts to this news is great concern. Backwater Investments is heavily invested in Russian oil, largely because of what you found to be a large consensus on oil's prospects for continued support from the government.

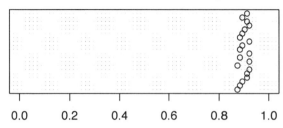

Statement 1
Russia will subsidize oil business next quarter.

But this news could cause the value of these investments to plummet, because people will suddenly expect there to be some huge problem with Russian oil. Then again, this statement could be a stratagem by the Russians, and they might not actually intend to sell their oil fields at all.

Sharpen your pencil

Does this mean that your analysis was wrong?

....

....

....

What should you do with this new information?

....

....

....

Sharpen your pencil
Solution

Were you totally off base?

The analysis definitely wasn't wrong. It accurately reflected beliefs that the analysts made with limited data. The problem is simply that the analysts were wrong. There is no reason to believe that using subjective probabilities guarantees that those probabilities will be right.

What now?

We need to go back and revise all the subjective probabilities. Now that we have more and better information, our subjective probabilities are likely to be more accurate.

We've picked up a lot of analytic tools so far. Maybe one of them could be useful at figuring out how to revise the subjective probabilities.

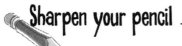 **Sharpen your pencil**

Better pick an analytic tool you can use to incorporate this new information into your subjective probability framework. Why would you or wouldn't you use each of these?

Experimental design?

....

....

....

Optimization?

....

....

....

A nice graphic?

....

....

....

Hypothesis testing?

....

....

....

Bayes' rule?

....

....

....

 **Sharpen your pencil
Solution**

Better pick an analytic tool you can use to incorporate this new information into your subjective probability framework. Why would you or wouldn't you use each of these?

Experimental design?

It's kind of hard to imagine what sort of experiment you could run to get better data. Since all the analysts are evaluating geopolitical events, it seems that every single piece of data they are looking at is observational.

Optimization?

There is no hard numerical data! The optimization tools we've learned presuppose that you have numerical data and a numerical result you want to maximize or minimize. Nothing for optimization here.

A nice graphic?

There's almost always room for a nice data visualization. Once we've revised the subjective probabilities, we'll certainly want a new visualization, but for now, we need a tool that gives us better numbers.

Hypothesis testing?

There is definitely a role for hypothesis testing in problems like this one, and the analysts might use it to derive their beliefs about Russia's behavior. But our job is to figure out specifically how the new data changes people's subjective probabilities, and it's not clear how hypothesis testing would do that.

Bayes' rule?

Now this sounds promising. Using each analyst's first subjective probability as a base rate, maybe we can use Bayes' rule to process this new information.

Bayes' rule is great for revising subjective probabilities

Bayes' rule is not just for lizard flu! It's great for subjective probabilities as well, because it allows you to incorporate *new evidence* into your beliefs about your hypothesis. Try out this more generic version of Bayes' rule, which uses H to refer to your **hypothesis** (or base rate) and E to refer to your **new evidence**.

Here's the formula you used to figure out your chances of having lizard flu.

$$P(L\,|\,+) = \frac{P(L)P(+\,|\,L)}{P(L)P(+\,|\,L) + P(\sim L)P(+\,|\sim L)}$$

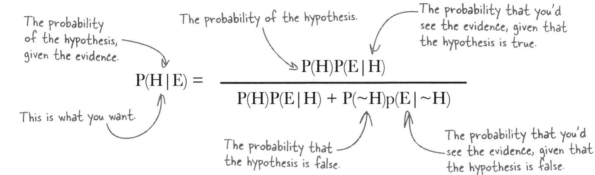

The probability of the hypothesis, given the evidence.

The probability of the hypothesis.

The probability that you'd see the evidence, given that the hypothesis is true.

$$P(H\,|\,E) = \frac{P(H)P(E\,|\,H)}{P(H)P(E\,|\,H) + P(\sim H)p(E\,|\sim H)}$$

This is what you want.

The probability that the hypothesis is false.

The probability that you'd see the evidence, given that the hypothesis is false.

Using Bayes' rule with subjective probabilities is all about asking for **the probability that you'd see the evidence, given that the hypothesis is true**. After you've disciplined yourself to assign a subjective value to this statistic, Bayes' rule can figure out the rest.

Why go to this trouble? Why not just go back to the analysts and ask for new subjective probabilities based on their reaction to the events?

You already have these pieces of data:

You know this.

The subjective probability that Russia will (and won't) continue to subsidize oil

$$P(H) \qquad P(\sim H)$$

You just need to get the analysts to give you these values:

What are these?

The subjective probability that the news report would (or wouldn't) happen, given that Russia will continue to subsidize oil

$$P(E\,|\,H) \qquad P(E\,|\sim H)$$

You could do that. Let's see what that would mean...

Fireside Chats

Tonight's talk: **Bayes' Rule and Gut Instinct smackdown**

Gut Instinct:

I don't see why the analyst wouldn't just ask me for another subjective probability. I delivered like a champ the first time around.

Well, thanks for the vote of confidence. But I still don't appreciate being kicked to the curb once I've given the analyst my first idea.

I still don't get why I can't just give you a new subjective probability to describe the chances that Russia will continue to support the oil industry.

Would anyone ever actually think like this? Sure, I can see why someone would use you when he wanted to calculate the chances he had a disease. But just to deal with subjective beliefs?

I guess I need learn to tell the analyst to use you under the right conditions. I just wish you made a little more intuitive sense.

Not that! Man, that was boring...

Bayes' Rule:

You did indeed, and I can't wait to use your first subjective probability as a base rate.

Oh no! You're still really important, and we need you to provide more subjective probabilities to describe the chances that we'd see the evidence given that the hypothesis is either true or untrue.

Using me to process these probabilities is a rigorous, formal way to incorporate new data into the analyst's framework of beliefs. Plus, it ensures that analysts won't overcompensate their subjective probabilities if they think they had been wrong.

OK, it's true that analysts certainly don't have to use me every single time they learn anything new. But if the stakes are high, they really need me. If you think you might have a disease, or you need to invest a ton of money, you want to use the analytical tools.

If you want, we can draw 1,000 little pictures of Russia like we did in the last chapter...

Exercise

Here's a spreadsheet that lists two new sets of subjective probabilities that have been collected from the analysts.

1) P(E|S1), which is each analyst's subjective probability of Russia announcing that they'd sell their oil fields (E), given the hypothesis that Russia *will* continue to support oil (S1)

2) P(E|~S1), which is each analyst's subjective probability of the announcement (E) given that Russia *won't* continue to support oil (~S1)

This is the probability that the hypothesis is true, given the new evidence.

Write a formula that implements Bayes' rule to give you P(S1|E).

Here are the two new columns of data.

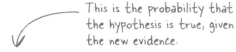

Load this!

www.headfirstlabs.com/books/hfda/
hfda_ch07_new_probs.xls

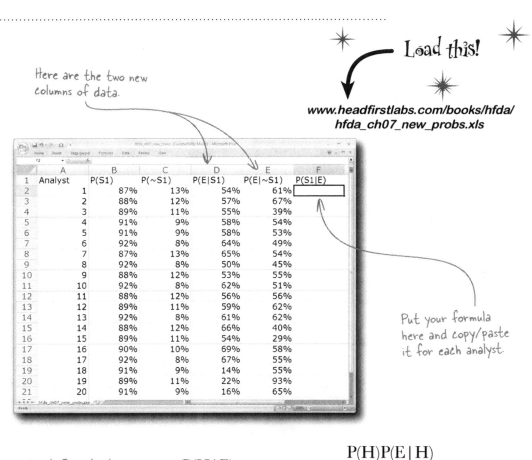

	A	B	C	D	E	F
1	Analyst	P(S1)	P(~S1)	P(E|S1)	P(E|~S1)	P(S1|E)
2	1	87%	13%	54%	61%	
3	2	88%	12%	57%	67%	
4	3	89%	11%	55%	39%	
5	4	91%	9%	58%	54%	
6	5	91%	9%	58%	53%	
7	6	92%	8%	64%	49%	
8	7	87%	13%	65%	54%	
9	8	92%	8%	50%	45%	
10	9	88%	12%	53%	55%	
11	10	92%	8%	62%	51%	
12	11	88%	12%	56%	56%	
13	12	89%	11%	59%	62%	
14	13	92%	8%	61%	62%	
15	14	88%	12%	66%	40%	
16	15	89%	11%	54%	29%	
17	16	90%	10%	69%	58%	
18	17	92%	8%	67%	55%	
19	18	91%	9%	14%	55%	
20	19	89%	11%	22%	93%	
21	20	91%	9%	16%	65%	

Put your formula here and copy/paste it for each analyst.

Here's Bayes' rule again.

$$P(H\,|\,E) = \frac{P(H)P(E\,|\,H)}{P(H)P(E\,|\,H) + P(\sim H)p(E\,|\sim H)}$$

Exercise Solution

What formula did you use to implement Bayes' rule and derive new subjective probabilities for Russia's support of the oil industry?

This formula combines the analysts' base rate with their judgments about the new data to come up with a new assessment.

$$= (B2*D2) / (B2*D2+C2*E2)$$

Here are the results.

	A	B	C	D	E	F
	Analyst	P(S1)	P(~S1)	P(E|S1)	P(E|~S1)	P(S1|E)
2	1	87%	13%	54%	61%	86%
3	2	88%	12%	57%	67%	86%
4	3	89%	11%	55%	39%	92%
5	4	91%	9%	58%	54%	92%
6	5	91%	9%	58%	53%	92%
7	6	92%	8%	64%	49%	94%
8	7	87%	13%	65%	54%	89%
9	8	92%	8%	50%	45%	93%
10	9	88%	12%	53%	55%	88%
11	10	92%	8%	62%	51%	93%
12	11	88%	12%	56%	56%	88%
13	12	89%	11%	59%	62%	89%
14	13	92%	8%	61%	62%	92%
15	14	88%	12%	66%	40%	92%
16	15	89%	11%	54%	29%	94%
17	16	90%	10%	69%	58%	91%
18	17	92%	8%	67%	55%	93%
19	18	91%	9%	14%	55%	72%
20	19	89%	11%	22%	93%	66%
21	20	91%	9%	16%	65%	71%

Those new probabilities look hot! Let's get them plotted and see how they compare to the base rates!

Sharpen your pencil

Using the data on the facing page, plot the new subjective probabilities of each analyst on the chart below.

Make this chart show P(S1|E), your revised probability.

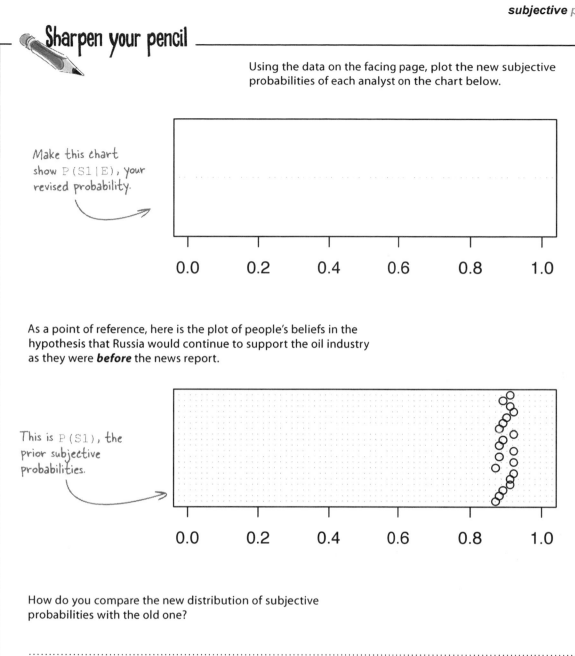

0.0   0.2   0.4   0.6   0.8   1.0

As a point of reference, here is the plot of people's beliefs in the hypothesis that Russia would continue to support the oil industry as they were **before** the news report.

This is P(S1), the prior subjective probabilities.

0.0   0.2   0.4   0.6   0.8   1.0

How do you compare the new distribution of subjective probabilities with the old one?

....

....

....

....

Sharpen your pencil
Solution

How does the distribution of beliefs about Russia's support for the oil industry look now?

Here is the new plot.

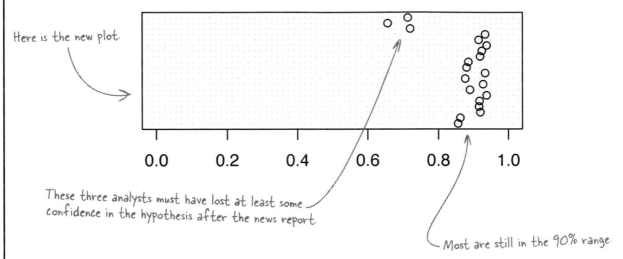

These three analysts must have lost at least some confidence in the hypothesis after the news report.

Most are still in the 90% range.

Here's what people used to think about the hypothesis:

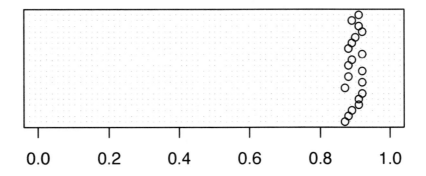

How do you compare the two?

The spread of the new set of subjective probabilities is a little wider, but only three people assign to the hypothesis subjective probabilities that are significantly lower than what they had thought previously. For most people, it still seems around 90% likely that Russia will continue to support oil, even though Russia claims to be selling their oil fields.

The CEO knows exactly what to do with this new information

Everyone is selling their Russia holdings, but this new data on my analysts' beliefs leads me to want to hold on to ours. Let's hope this works!

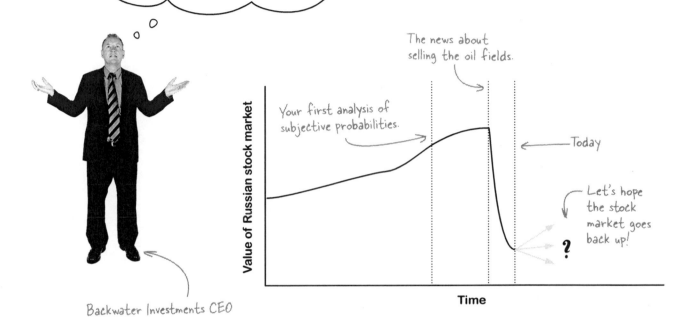

Your first analysis of subjective probabilities.

The news about selling the oil fields.

Today

Let's hope the stock market goes back up!

?

Value of Russian stock market

Time

Backwater Investments CEO

On close inspection, the analysts concluded that the Russian news is likely to report the selling of their oil fields whether it's true that they will stop supporting oil or not.

So the report didn't end up changing their analyses much, and with three exceptions, their new subjective probabilities **[P(S1|E)]** that Russia would support their oil industry were pretty similar to their prior subjective probabilities **[P(S1)]** about the same hypothesis.

But are the analysts right?

Russian stock owners rejoice!

The analysts were right: Russia was bluffing about selling off their oil fields. And the market rally that took place once everyone realized it was very good for Backwater.

Looks like your subjective probabilities kept heads cool at Backwater Investments and resulted in a big payoff for everyone!

The news about selling the oil fields.

Today

Your first analysis of subjective probabilities.

Value of Russian stock market

Your second analysis.

Time

Do a little more work like that, and this will be the start of a long relationship. Don't spend all your earnings in one place!

8 heuristics

Analyze like a human

I have good simple models... inside my brain.

The real world has more variables than you can handle.

There is always going to be data that you can't have. And even when you do have data on most of the things you want to understand, *optimizing* methods are often **elusive** and **time consuming**. Fortunately, most of the actual thinking you do in life is not "rational maximizing"—it's processing incomplete and uncertain information with rules of thumb so that you can make decisions quickly. What is really cool is that these rules can **actually work** and are important (and necessary) tools for data analysts.

LitterGitters submitted their report to the city council

The LitterGitters are a nonprofit group **funded by the Dataville City Council** to run public service announcements to encourage people to stop littering.

They just presented the results of their most recent work to the city council, and the reaction is not what they'd hoped for.

Databurg had a 10% reduction in tonnage!

We want tonnage reduction!

We're cutting your funding in 1 month, unless you can come up with a way to show you've reduced litter tonnage.

That last comment is the one we're really worried about. It's starting to look as if LitterGitters will be in big trouble very soon if you can't persuade the city council that LitterGitters' public outreach programs have been a success relative to the city council's intentions for it.

The LitterGitters have really cleaned up this town

Before the LitterGitters came along, Dataville was a total mess. Some residents didn't respect their home and **polluted it with trash**, damaging Dataville's environment and looks, but all that changed when LitterGitters began their work.

It'd be **terrible** for the city council to cut their funding. They need you to help them get better at communicating why their program is successful so that the city council will continue their support.

> I just know that our program works... help!

Here's what LitterGitters does.

LitterGitters

The LitterGitters director

- Public service announcements
- Clean-up events
- Education in schools
- Publications

If the city council cuts LitterGitters' funding, Dataville will turn back into a big trash dump!

Sharpen your pencil

Brainstorm the metrics you might use to fulfill the mandate. *Where exactly* would litter tonnage reduction data come from?

....

....

....

....

Sharpen your pencil
Solution

How exactly would you collect the data that would show whether the LitterGitters' work had resulted in a reduction in litter tonnage?

We could have garbage men separate litter from normal trash and weigh both repeatedly over time.

Or we could have special collections at places in Dataville that have a reputation for being filled

with litter. Has LitterGitters been making these sort of measurements?

The LitterGitters <u>have been</u> measuring their campaign's effectiveness

LitterGitters have been measuring their results, but they haven't measured the things you imagined in the previous exercise. They've been doing **something else**: surveying the general public. Here are some of their surveys.

Git, litter, git!

Volunteer

Questions for the general public	Your answer
Do you litter in Dataville?	No
Have you heard of the LitterGitters program?	Yes
If you saw someone littering, would you tell them to throw their trash away in a trash can?	Yes
Do you think littering is a problem in Dataville?	Yes
Has LitterGitters helped you better to understand the importance of preventing litter?	Yes
Would you support continued city funding of LitterGitters' educational programs?	Yes

Their tactics, after all, are all about changing people's **behaviors** so that they stop littering. Let's take a look at a summary of their results…

Questions for the general public	Last year	This year
Do you litter in Dataville?	10%	5%
Have you heard of the LitterGitters program?	5%	90%
If you saw someone littering, would you tell them to throw their trash away in a trash can?	2%	25%
Do you think littering is a problem in Dataville?	20%	75%
Has LitterGitters helped you better to understand the importance of preventing litter?	5%	85%
Would you support continued city funding of LitterGitters' educational programs?	20%	81%

These are the percentages of people who responded "yes."

The mandate is to reduce the tonnage of litter

And educating people about why they need to change their behaviors will lead to a reduction in litter tonnage, right? That's the basic premise of LitterGitters, and their survey results do seem to show an increase in public awareness.

But the city council was unimpressed by this report, and you need to help LitterGitters figure out whether they have fulfilled the mandate and then persuade the city council that they have done so.

Sharpen your pencil

Does the LitterGitters' results show or suggest a reduction in the tonnage of litter in Dataville?

....

....

....

Sharpen your pencil
Solution

Does the data show or suggest a litter tonnage reduction because of LitterGitters' work?

It might suggest a reduction, if you believe that people's reported change in beliefs has an impact on litter. But the data itself only discusses public opinion, and there is nothing in it explicitly about litter tonnage.

Tonnage is unfeasible to measure

> Of course we don't measure tonnage. Actually weighing litter is way too expensive and logistically complicated, and everyone in the field considers that Databurg 10% figure bogus. What else are we supposed to do besides survey people?

This could be a problem. The city council is expecting to hear evidence from LitterGitters that demonstrates that the LitterGitters campaign has reduced litter tonnage, but all we provided them is this opinion survey.

If it's true that measuring tonnage directly is logistically unfeasible, then the demand for evidence of tonnage reduction is dooming LitterGitters to failure.

The LitterGitters director

Give people a hard question, and they'll answer an easier one instead

LitterGitters knows that what they are expected to do is reduce litter tonnage, but they decided not to measure tonnage directly because doing so is such an expense.

You're going to need a big scale to weigh all this...

This is complex, expensive, and hard.

They've got trash dumps like this all over Dataville.

Questions for the general public	Your answer
Do you litter in Dataville?	No
Have you heard of the LitterGitters program?	Yes
If you saw someone littering, would you tell them to throw their trash away in a trash can?	Yes
Do you think littering is a problem in Dataville?	Yes
Has LitterGitters helped you better to understand the importance of preventing litter?	Yes
Would you support continued city funding of LitterGitters' educational programs?	Yes

This is fast, easy, and clear. It's just not what the city council wants.

Here are some of the opinion surveys LitterGitters got back from people.

Reacting to difficult questions in this way is actually a very common and very human thing to do. We all face problems that are hard to tackle because they're "expensive" economically—or **cognitively** (more on this in a moment)—and the natural reaction is to answer a different question.

This **simplified** approach might seem like the totally wrong way to go about things, especially for a data analyst, but the irony is that in a lot of situations it *really works*. And, as you're about to see, sometimes it's the **only option**.

Littering in Dataville is a complex system

Here's one of LitterGitters' internal research documents. It describes things you might want to measure in the world of litter.

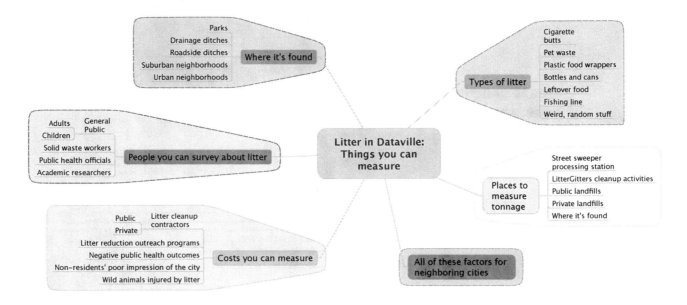

And here is the director's explanation of this big system and the implications that its complexity has for the work of LitterGitters.

> **From: Director, LitterGitters**
> **To: Head First**
> **Subject: Why we can't measure tonnage**
>
> In order to measure tonnage directly, we'd need staff at all the contact points (processing stations, landfills, etc.) at all times. The city workers won't record the data for us, because they already have plenty of work to do.
>
> And staffing the contact points would cost us double what the city already pays us. If we did *nothing* but measure litter tonnage, we still wouldn't have enough money to do it right.
>
> Besides, the city council is all wrong when it focuses on tonnage. Litter in Dataville is actually a complex system. There are lots of people involved, lots of types of litter, and lots of places to find it. To ignore the system and hyper-focus on one variable is a mistake.

You can't build and implement a unified litter-measuring model

Any sort of model you created to try to measure or design an optimal litter control program would have an awful lot of variables to consider.

Not only would you have to come up with a general **quantitative** theory about how all these elements interact, but you'd also have to know how to manipulate *some* of those variables (your **decision variables**) in order to minimize tonnage reduction.

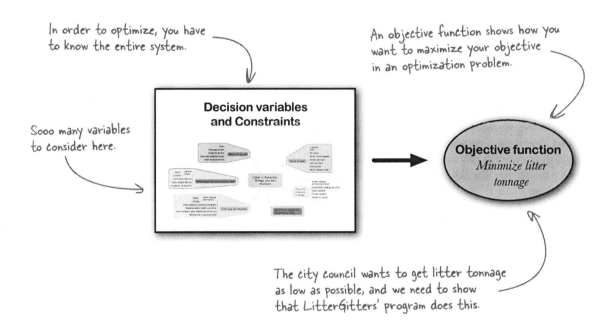

In order to optimize, you have to know the entire system.

An objective function shows how you want to maximize your objective in an optimization problem.

Sooo many variables to consider here.

The city council wants to get litter tonnage as low as possible, and we need to show that LitterGitters' program does this.

This problem would be a **beast** even if you had all the data, but as you've learned getting all the data is too expensive.

Is giving the city council what they want even possible?

Jill: This situation is a mess. We have a city council asking for something we can't give them.

Frank: Yeah. And even if we could provide the tonnage reduction figure, it would not be of much use. The system is too complex.

Joe: Well, that figure would the satisfy city council.

Jill: Yes, we're not here just to satisfy the council. We're here to reduce litter!

Joe: Couldn't we just make something up? Like do our own "estimate" of the tonnage?

Frank: That's an option, but it's pretty dicey. I mean, the city council seems like a really tough group. If we were to make up some subjective metric like that and have it masquerade as a tonnage metric, they might flip out on us.

Jill: Making up something is a sure way to get LitterGitters' funding eliminated. Maybe we could persuade the city council that opinion surveys really are a solid proxy for tonnage reduction?

Frank: LitterGitters already tried that. Didn't you see the city council screaming at them?

Jill: We could come up with an assessment that incorporates *more* variables than just public opinion. Maybe we should try to collect together every variable we can access and just make subjective guesses for *all the other variables*?

Frank: Well, maybe that would work…

Stop! We're making this way too complicated. Why can't we just pick one or two more variables, analyze them too, and leave it at that?

You can indeed go with just a few more variables.

And if you were to assess the effectiveness of LitterGitters by picking one or two variables and using them to draw a conclusion about the whole system, you'd be employing a **heuristic**…

Heuristics are a middle ground between going with your gut and optimization

Do you make decisions impulsively, or with a few well-chosen pieces of key data, or do you make decisions by building a model that incorporates every scrap of relevant data and yields the perfect answer?

Your answer is probably "All of the above," and it's important to realize that these are all different ways of thinking.

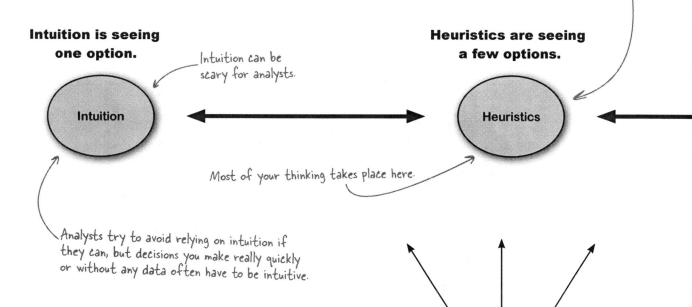

Maybe you don't need to incorporate <u>all</u> the data.

Intuition is seeing one option.

Intuition can be scary for analysts.

Intuition

Heuristics are seeing a few options.

Heuristics

Most of your thinking takes place here.

Analysts try to avoid relying on intuition if they can, but decisions you make really quickly or without any data often have to be intuitive.

If you've solved an optimization problem, you've found *the* answer or answers that represent the maximum or minimum of your objective function.

And for data analysts, optimization is a sort of ideal. It would be elegant and beautiful if all your analytic problems could be definitively solved. **But most of your thinking will be heuristic.**

Which will you use for your data analysis problems?

the Scholar's Corner

Heuristic 1. (Psychological definition.) Substituting a difficult or confusing <u>attribute</u> for a more accessible one. 2. (Computer science definition.) A way of solving a problem that will tend to give you accurate answers but that <u>does not guarantee optimality</u>.

Optimization is seeing *all* the options.

Optimization

Optimization is an ideal for analysts

Is "optimization" even in here?

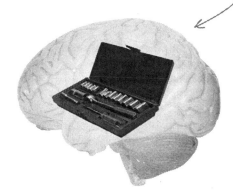

Some psychologists even argue that *all* human reasoning is heuristic and that **optimization is an ideal** that works only when your problems are *ultra-specified*.

But if *anyone's* going to have to deal with an ultra-specified problem, it'll be a **data analyst**, so don't throw away your Solver just yet. Just remember that well-constructed heuristic decision-making protocols need to be part of your analytic toolkit.

there are no
Dumb Questions

Q: It seems weird that you'd have a decision procedure that didn't guarantee a correct answer and call it "data analysis." Shouldn't you call that sort of thing "guesswork"?

A: Now that wouldn't be very nice! Look, data analysis is all about breaking down problems into manageable pieces and fitting mental and statistical models to data to make better judgements. There's no guarantee that you'll always get the right answers.

Q: Can't I just say that I'm always trying to find optimal results? If I've got to dabble in heuristic thinking a little, fine, but my goal is optimality?

A: That's fair to say. You certainly don't want to use heuristic analytical tools when better optimizing tools are available and feasible. But what is important to recognize is that heuristics are a fundamental part of how you think and of the methods of data analysis.

Q: So what's the difference between the psychological and the computer science definition of "heuristics"?

A: They're actually really similar. In computer science, heuristic algorithms have an ability to solve problems without people being able to *prove* that the algorithm will always get the right answer. Many times, heuristic algorithms in computer science can solve problems more quickly and more simply than an algorithm that guarantees the right answer, and often, the only algorithms available for a problem are heuristic.

Q: What does that have to do with psychology?

A: Psychologists have found in experimental research that people use cognitive heuristics all the time. There is just too much data competing for our attention, so we have to use rules of thumb in order to make decisions. There are a number of classic ones that are part of the hard-wiring of our brain, and on the whole, they work really well.

Q: Isn't it kind of obvious that human thinking isn't like optimization?

A: It depends on who you talk to. People who have a strong sense of humans as **rational** creatures might be upset by the notion that we use quick and dirty rules of thumb rather than think through all our sensory input in a more thorough way.

Q: So the fact that a lot of reasoning is heuristic means that I'm irrational?

A: It depends on what you take to be the definition of the word "rational." If rationality is an ability to process every bit of a huge amount of information at lightning speed, to construct perfect models to make sense of that information, and then to have a flawless ability to implement whatever recommendations your models suggest, then yes, you're irrational.

Q: That *is* a pretty strong definition of "rationality."

A: Not if you're a computer.

Q: That's why we let computers do data analysis for us!

A: Computer programs like Solver live in a cognitive world where you determine the inputs. And your choice of inputs is subject to all the limitations of your own mind and your access to data. But within the world of those inputs, Solver acts with perfect rationality.

Q: And since "All models are wrong, but some are useful," even the optimization problems the computer runs look kind of heuristic in the broader context. The data you choose as inputs might never cover every variable that has a relationship to your model; you just have to pick the important ones.

A: Think of it this way: with data analysis, it's all about the **tools**. A good data analyst knows how to use his tools to manipulate the data in the context of solving real problems. There's no reason to get all fatalistic about how you aren't perfectly rational. Learn the tools, use them wisely, and you'll be able to do a lot of great work.

Q: But there is no way of doing data analysis that guarantees correct answers on all your problems.

A: No, there isn't, and if you make the mistake of thinking otherwise, you set yourself up for failure. Analyzing where and how you *expect* reality to deviate from your analytical models is a big part of data analysis, and we'll talk about the fine art of managing error in a few chapters.

Q: So heuristics are hard-wired into my brain, but I can make up my own, too?

A: You bet, and what's really important as a data analyst is that you know it when you're doing it. So let's give it a try...

Use a fast and frugal tree

Here's a heuristic that describes different ways of dealing with the problem of having trash you need to get rid of. It's a really simple rule: if there's a trash can, throw it in the trash can. Otherwise, wait until you see a trash can.

This schematic way of describing a heuristic is called a **fast and frugal tree**. It's fast because it doesn't take long to complete, and it's frugal because it doesn't require a lot of cognitive resources.

What the city council needs is its own heuristic to evaluate the quality of the work that LitterGitters has been doing. Their own heuristic is unfeasible (we'll have to persuade them of that), and they reject LitterGitters' current heuristic.

Can you draw a fast and frugal tree to represent a better heuristic? Let's talk to LitterGitters to see what they think about a more robust decision procedure.

Is there a simpler way to assess LitterGitters' success?

Using a heuristic approach to measure LitterGitters' work would mean picking one or more of these variables and adding them to your analysis. What does the LitterGitters director think would be the best approach?

Which of these variables can you add to your analysis to give a fuller picture of LitterGitters' effectiveness?

Where it's found
- Parks
- Drainage ditches
- Roadside ditches
- Suburban neighborhoods
- Urban neighborhoods

Types of litter
- Cigarette butts
- Pet waste
- Plastic food wrappers
- Bottles and cans
- Leftover food
- Fishing line
- Weird, random stuff

People you can survey about litter
- General Public
- Adults
- Children
- Solid waste workers
- Public health officials
- Academic researchers

Litter in Dataville: Things you can measure

Places to measure tonnage
- Street sweeper processing station
- LitterGitters cleanup activities
- Public landfills
- Private landfills
- Where it's found

Costs you can measure
- Public
- Private
- Litter cleanup contractors
- Litter reduction outreach programs
- Negative public health outcomes
- Non-residents' poor impression of the city
- Wild animals injured by litter

All of these factors for neighboring cities

> You just can't leave out public opinion surveys.
> And, like I've said, there is just no way to weigh all the litter in order to make a good comparison. But maybe you could just poll the solid waste workers. The biggest problem is cigarette butts, and if we periodically poll the street sweepers and landfill workers about how many butts they're seeing, we'd have a not totally complete but still pretty solid grip on what is happening with litter.

Sharpen your pencil

Draw a fast and frugal tree to describe how the city council *should* evaluate the success of LitterGitters. Be sure to include two variables that LitterGitters considers important.

The final judgment should be whether to maintain or eliminate the funding of LitterGitters.

Sharpen your pencil
Solution

What heuristic did you create to evaluate whether LitterGitters has been successful?

While your own tree might be different, here's an example of where you might have ended up.

First, the city council needs to ask whether the public is reacting positively to LitterGitters.

Is LitterGitters increasing people's enthusiasm about stopping litter?

Has the public increased its litter awareness?

Yes   *No*

If not, LitterGitters' funding should be eliminated.

If the public is supportive, do the solid waste workers think there has been a reduction?

Do solid waste workers believe there has been a reduction?   **Kill funding**

Yes   *No*

This attribute is what we're substituting for directly measuring tonnage.

Maintain funding   **Kill funding**

Here's the outcome that LitterGitters wants.

If the solid waste workers don't think there's been any effect, that's the end of funding.

I am looking forward to seeing that report I hear you redid. But I'm expecting you to be like all the other nonprofits that get Dataville money... a bunch of incompetents.

It sounds as if at least one of the city council members has **already made up his mind**. What a jerk. This guy totally has the wrong way of looking at the work of LitterGitters.

City council member

Sharpen your pencil

This city council member is using a heuristic. Draw a diagram to describe his thought process in **forming his expectation** about LitterGitters. You need to understand his reasoning if you are going to be able to persuade this guy that your heuristic assessment ideas are valid.

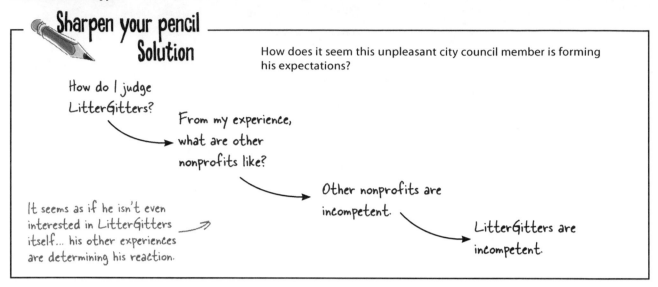

Sharpen your pencil
Solution

How does it seem this unpleasant city council member is forming his expectations?

How do I judge LitterGitters?

From my experience, what are other nonprofits like?

It seems as if he isn't even interested in LitterGitters itself... his other experiences are determining his reaction.

Other nonprofits are incompetent.

LitterGitters are incompetent.

Stereotypes are heuristics

Stereotypes are definitely heuristics: they don't require a lot of energy to process, and they're super-fast. Heck, with a stereotype, you don't even need to collect data on the thing you're making a judgement about. As heuristics, **stereotypes *work***. But in this case, and in a lot of cases, stereotypes lead to poorly reasoned conclusions.

Not all heuristics work well in every case. A fast and frugal rule of thumb might help get answers for some problems while predisposing you to make inadequate judgements in other contexts.

A much better way to judge LitterGitters would be something like this:

Heuristics can be downright dangerous!

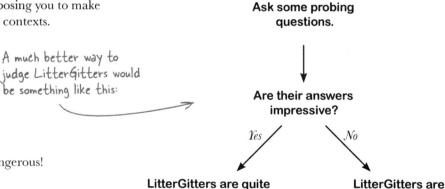

How do I judge LitterGitters?

↓

Ask some probing questions.

↓

Are their answers impressive?

Yes / \ *No*

LitterGitters are quite sharp.

LitterGitters are incompetent.

Maybe we can get some data to describe what the sanitation workers think about what is happening with litter. Then we can present our original analysis along with our decisions heuristic and new data to the city council.

Let's see what those sanitation workers have to say...

Your analysis is ready to present

Between your heuristic and the data you have, including the just-received responses from the sanitation workers below, you're ready to start explaining what you see to the city council.

Here's how you decided the city council should assess the work of LitterGitters.

Has the public increased its litter awareness?

Yes / *No*

Do solid waste workers believe there has been a reduction?   **Kill funding**

Yes / *No*

Maintain funding   **Kill funding**

Here's our original data describing the attitudes of the general public about litter.

Questions for the general public	Last year	This year
Do you litter in Dataville?	10%	5%
Have you heard of the LitterGitters program?	5%	90%
If you saw someone littering, would you tell them to throw their trash away in a trash can?	2%	25%
Do you think littering is a problem in Dataville?	20%	75%
Has LitterGitters helped you better to understand the importance of preventing litter?	5%	85%
Would you support continued city funding of LitterGitters' educational programs?	20%	81%

Here's some new data describing the sanitation workers' impressions of litter in Dataville since LitterGitters began their program.

Questions for the sanitation workers	This year
Have you noticed a reduction in litter coming into Dataville landfills since LitterGitters began their work?	75%
Are there fewer cigarette butts being collected off the streets since LitterGitters began their work?	90%
Have high-litter areas (downtown, city parks, etc.) seen a reduction in litter since LitterGitters began their work?	30%
Is littering still a significant problem in Dataville?	82%

We can't compare this figure to last year, because we just started collecting data for this report.

These numbers represent the percentage of people who answered "yes."

Sharpen your pencil

Answer the following questions from the city council about your work with LitterGitters.

Why can't you measure tonnage directly?

....

....

....

Can you prove that the campaign had an effect?

....

....

....

Can you guarantee that your tactics will continue to work?

....

....

....

Why not spend money on cleanup rather than education?

....

....

....

You guys are just as incompetent as the others.

....

....

....

Sharpen your pencil
Solution

How did you respond to the city council?

Why can't you measure tonnage directly?

We can measure tonnage directly. The problem with doing it, though, is that it'd be too expensive.

It'd cost twice the amount of money you actually pay LitterGitters to do their work. So the best

course of action is to use this heuristic to assess performance. It's simple but in our belief accurate.

Can you prove that the campaign had an effect?

All the data is observational, so we can't prove that the increase in awareness of the general public

about litter and the reduction that sanitation workers believe has taken place is the result of

LitterGitters. But we have good reasons to believe that our program was the cause of these results.

Can you guarantee that your tactics will continue to work?

There are never guarantees in life, but as long as we can sustain

the improved public awareness that came out of our outreach

program, it's hard to imagine that people will suddenly resume littering more.

> Hmmm. It's like you actually know what you're talking about.

Why not spend money on cleanup rather than education?

But in that case, your objective wouldn't be to reduce litter, because you'd

be doing nothing to get people to stop littering. The objective would be to

clean it up as fast as you can, and that's not what LitterGitters does.

You guys are just as incompetent as the others.

We can't speak for other nonprofits, but we have a crystal clear idea of

what we're doing and how to measure the results, so we're definitely not

incompetent. When did you say you were up for reelection?

Looks like your analysis impressed the city council members

Memorandum
Re: LitterGitters and litter in Dataville

The city council is pleased to renew the contract of LitterGitters, thanks to the excellent work from the Head First data analyst. We recognize that our previous assessment of the work of LitterGitters did not adequately treat the whole issue of litter in Dataville, and we discounted the importance of public opinion and behavior. The new decision procedure you provided is excellently designed, and we hope the LitterGitters continue to live up to the high bar they have set for themselves. LitterGitters will receive increased funding from the Dataville City Council this year, which we expect will help…

Thanks so much for your help. Now there is so much more we'll be able to do to get the word out about stopping litter in Dataville. You really saved LitterGitters!

Dataville will stay clean because of your analysis.

Thanks to your hard work and subtle insight into these analytical problems, you can pat yourself on the back for keeping Dataville neat and tidy.

9 histograms

The shape of numbers

Most of the action in this city concentrates right here. That's why I'm so tall.

So what? The important work is done in this area. If you understood the landscape, you'd see why!

How much can a bar graph tell you?

There are about a zillion ways of **showing data with pictures**, but one of them is special. **Histograms**, which are kind of similar to bar graphs, are a super-fast and easy way to summarize data. You're about to use these powerful little charts to measure your data's **spread, variability, central tendency**, and more. No matter how large your data set is, if you draw a histogram with it, you'll be able to "see" what's happening inside of it. And you're about to do it with a new, free, crazy-powerful **software tool**.

Your annual review is coming up

You've been doing some really excellent analytical work lately, and it's high time you got what's coming to you.

The powers that be want to know what you think about your own performance.

Oh boy, a self evaluation.

Starbuzz Analyst Self-review

Thank you for filling out our self-review! This document is important for our files and will help determine your future at Starbuzz.

Date   _____

Analyst Name   _____

Circle the number that represents how well-developed you consider your abilities to be. A low score means you think you need some help, and a high score means you think your work is excellent.

The overall quality of your analytical work.

    1   2   3   4   5

Your ability to interpret the meaning and importance of past events.

    1   2   3   4   5

Your ability to make level-headed judgements about the future.

    1   2   3   4   5

Quality of written and oral communication.

    1   2   3   4   5

Your ability to keep your client well-informed and making good choices.

    1   2   3   4   5

Bet you'd score higher now than you would have in chapter 1!

Your work is totally solid.

You deserve a pat on the back.

Not a literal pat on the back, though… something more. Some sort of *real* recognition. But what kind of recognition? And how do you go about actually getting it?

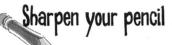

Sharpen your pencil

You'd better brainstorm about strategies to get recognized. Write down how you'd respond to each of these questions.

Should you just say thanks to your boss and hope for the best? If your boss really believes you've been valuable, he'll reward you, right?

....

....

....

....

Should you give yourself super-positive feedback, and maybe even exaggerate your talents a little? Then demand a **big raise?**

....

....

....

....

Can you envision a data-based way of deciding on how to deal with this situation?

....

....

....

....

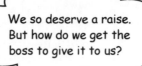

However you answered the questions on the last page, we think you should go for more money. You're not doing this hard work for your health, after all.

Going for more cash could play out in a bunch of different ways

People can be skittish about trying to get more money from their bosses. And who can blame them? There are lots of **possible outcomes**, and not all of them are good.

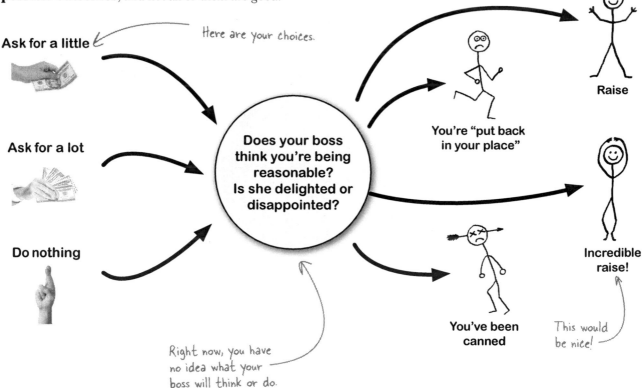

Anything could happen.

Here are your choices.

Ask for a little

Ask for a lot

Do nothing

Does your boss think you're being reasonable? Is she delighted or disappointed?

You're "put back in your place"

Raise

Incredible raise!

This would be nice!

You've been canned

Right now, you have no idea what your boss will think or do.

Could research help you predict the outcomes?

Even though your case is unique to you, it still might make sense to get an idea of your boss's **baseline expectations**.

Here's some data on raises

Because you're so plugged in to Starbuzz's data, you have access to some sweet numbers: Human Resource's records about raises for the past three years.

Load this!

www.headfirstlabs.com/books/hfda/
hfda_ch09_employees.csv

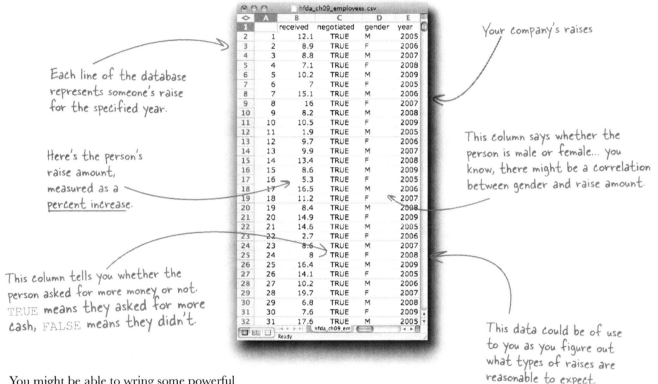

Your company's raises

Each line of the database represents someone's raise for the specified year.

Here's the person's raise amount, measured as a percent increase.

This column says whether the person is male or female... you know, there might be a correlation between gender and raise amount.

This column tells you whether the person asked for more money or not. `TRUE` means they asked for more cash, `FALSE` means they didn't.

This data could be of use to you as you figure out what types of raises are reasonable to expect.

You might be able to wring some powerful insights out of this data. If you assume that your boss will act in a similar way to how previous bosses acted, this data could tell you what to expect.

Problem is, with approximately 3,000 employees, the data set is pretty **big**.

You're going to need to do something to make the data useful.

How would you deal with this data? Could you manage it to make it more useful?

Jim: We should forget about the data and just go for as much as we can get. Nothing in there will tell us what they think we're worth. There's a range of numbers in the boss's head, and we need to figure out how to get the upper end of that range.

Joe: I agree that most of the data is useless to tell us what they think *we* are worth, and I don't see how we find out. The data will tell us the average raise, and we can't go wrong shooting for the average.

Jim: The **average**? You've got to be joking. Why go for the middle? Aim higher!

Frank: I think a more subtle analysis is in order. There's some rich information here, and who knows what it'll tell us?

Joe: We need to stay risk-averse and follow the herd. The middle is where we find safety. Just average the `Raise` column and ask for that amount.

Jim: That's a complete cop-out!

Frank: Look, the data shows whether people negotiated, the year of the raise, and people's genders. All this information can be useful to us if we just massage it into the right format.

Jim: OK, smarty pants. *Show me.*

Frank: Not a problem. First we have to figure out how to collapse all these numbers into figures that make more sense…

Better summarize the data. There's just too much of it to read and understand all at once, and until you've summarized the data you don't really know what's in it.

Start by breaking the data down into its basic constituent pieces. Once you have those pieces, then you can look at averages or whatever other summary statistic you consider useful.

Where will you begin your summary of this data?

Sharpen your pencil

As you know, much of analysis consists of taking information and breaking it down into smaller, more manageable pieces.

Draw a picture to describe how you would break these data fields down into smaller elements.

Draw pictures here to represent how you'd split the data into smaller pieces.

Here are some examples.

Raises of 6–8%

Women

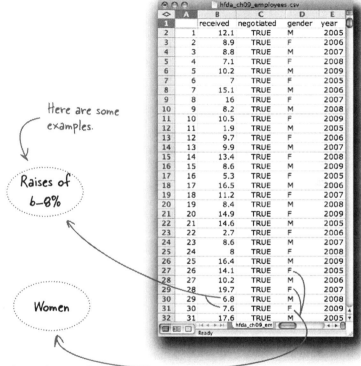

What statistics could you use to summarize these elements? Sketch some tables that incorporate your data fields with summary statistics.

Sharpen your pencil
Solution

What sort of pieces would you break your data into?

Here are some examples... your answers might be a little different.

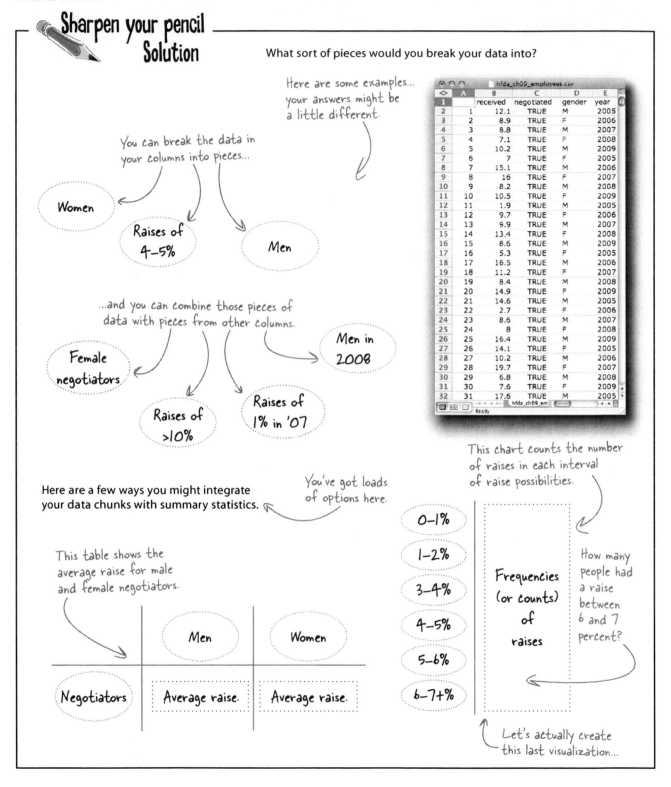

You can break the data in your columns into pieces...

Women

Raises of 4-5%

Men

...and you can combine those pieces of data with pieces from other columns.

Female negotiators

Men in 2008

Raises of >10%

Raises of 1% in '07

Here are a few ways you might integrate your data chunks with summary statistics.

You've got loads of options here.

This table shows the average raise for male and female negotiators.

	Men	Women
Negotiators	Average raise.	Average raise.

This chart counts the number of raises in each interval of raise possibilities.

0-1%

1-2%

3-4%

4-5%

5-6%

6-7+%

Frequencies (or counts) of raises

How many people had a raise between 6 and 7 percent?

Let's actually create this last visualization...

It sure is fun to imagine summarizing these pieces of the data, but here's a thought. How about we actually do it?

Using the groupings of data you imagined, you're ready to start summarizing.

When you need to slice, dice, and summarize a complex data set, you want to use your best software tools to do the dirty work. So let's dive in and make your software reveal just what's going on with all these raises.

TEST DRIVE

A visualization of the number of people who fall in each category of raises will enable you to *see* the whole data set at once.

So let's create that summary… or even better, let's do it **graphically**.

1 Open the Data Analysis dialogue box.

> With your data open in Excel, click the Data Analysis button under the Data tab.

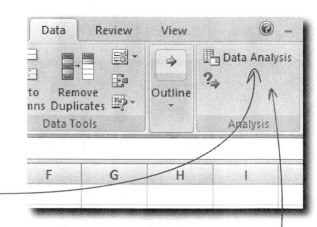

> If you don't see the Data Analysis button, see Appendix iii for how to install it.

In OpenOffice and older versions of Excel, you can find Data Analysis under the Tools menu.

> Here it is!

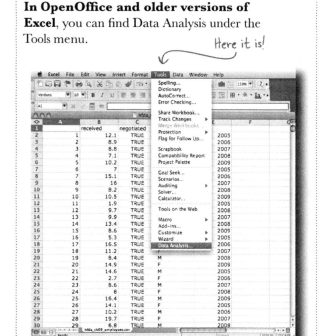

2 Select Histogram.

> In the pop-up window, tell Excel that you want to create a histogram.

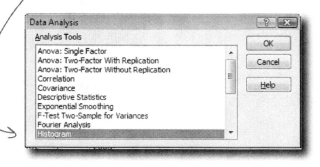

3 Select your data.

Select all your raise data under the `received` column.

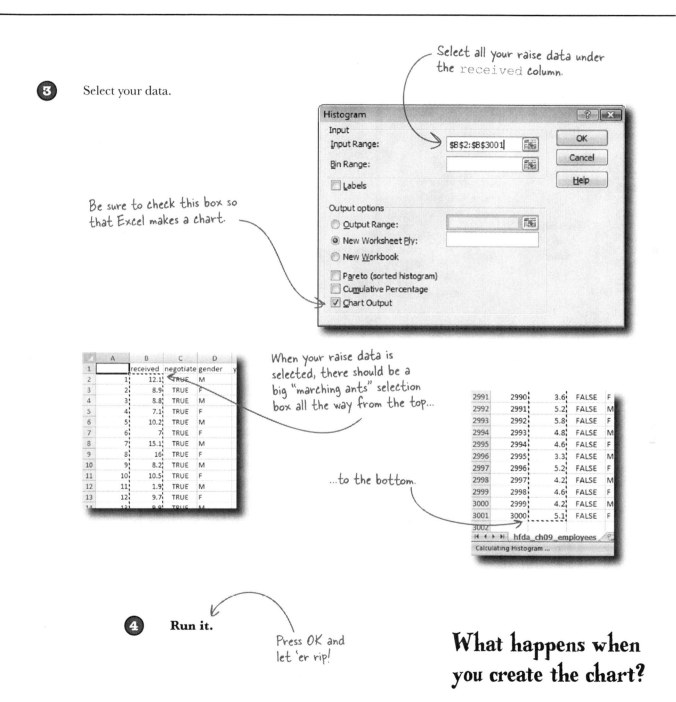

Histogram		
Input		OK
Input Range:	$B$2:$B$3001	Cancel
Bin Range:		Help

☐ Labels

Output options

Be sure to check this box so that Excel makes a chart.

○ Output Range:
◉ New Worksheet Ply:
○ New Workbook

☐ Pareto (sorted histogram)
☐ Cumulative Percentage
☑ Chart Output

	A	B	C	D
1		received	negotiate	gender
2	1	12.1	TRUE	M
3	2	8.9	TRUE	F
4	3	8.8	TRUE	M
5	4	7.1	TRUE	F
6	5	10.2	TRUE	M
7	6	7	TRUE	F
8	7	15.1	TRUE	M
9	8	16	TRUE	F
10	9	8.2	TRUE	M
11	10	10.5	TRUE	F
12	11	1.9	TRUE	M
13	12	9.7	TRUE	F
14	13	9.9	TRUE	M

When your raise data is selected, there should be a big "marching ants" selection box all the way from the top...

...to the bottom.

2991	2990	3.6	FALSE	F
2992	2991	5.2	FALSE	M
2993	2992	5.8	FALSE	F
2994	2993	4.8	FALSE	M
2995	2994	4.6	FALSE	F
2996	2995	3.3	FALSE	M
2997	2996	5.2	FALSE	F
2998	2997	4.2	FALSE	M
2999	2998	4.6	FALSE	F
3000	2999	4.2	FALSE	M
3001	3000	5.1	FALSE	F
3002				

hfda_ch09_employees

Calculating Histogram ...

4 Run it.

Press OK and let 'er rip!

What happens when you create the chart?

Histograms show frequencies of groups of numbers

Histograms are a powerful visualization because, no matter how large your data set is, they show you the **distribution** of data points across their range of values.

For example, the table you envisioned in the last exercise would have told you how many people received raises at about 5 percent.

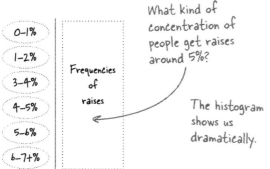

What kind of concentration of people get raises around 5%?

The histogram shows us dramatically.

This histogram shows graphically how many people fall into each raise category, and it concisely shows you what people are getting across the spectrum of raises.

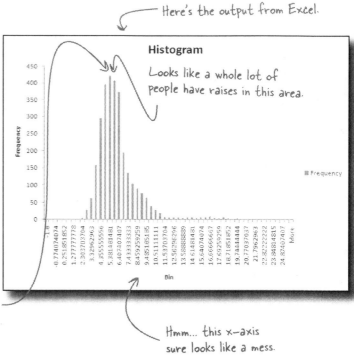

Here's the output from Excel.

Looks like a whole lot of people have raises in this area.

Hmm... this x-axis sure looks like a mess.

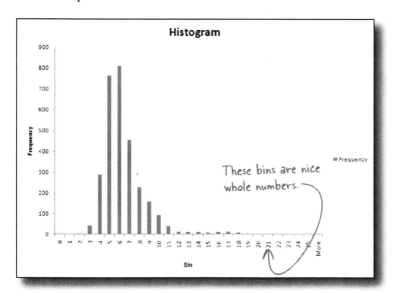

These bins are nice whole numbers.

On the other hand, there are some problems with what Excel did for you. The default settings for the **bins** (or "class intervals") end up producing messy, noisy x-axis values. The graph would be easier to read with plain integers (rather than long decimals) on the x-axis to represent the bins.

Sure, you *can* tweak the settings to get those bins looking more like the data table you initially envisioned.

But even this histogram has a serious problem. Can you spot it?

Gaps between bars in a histogram mean gaps among the data points

In histograms, gaps mean that there is data missing between certain ranges. If, say, no one got a raise between 5.75 percent and 6.25 percent, there might be a gap. If the histogram showed that, it might really be worth investigating.

In fact, there will always be gaps if there are more bins than data points (unless your data set is the same number repeated over and over).

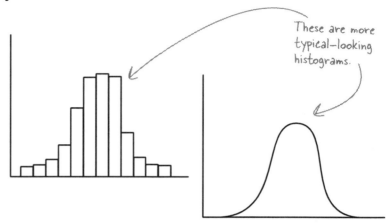

These are more typical-looking histograms.

Histograms Up Close

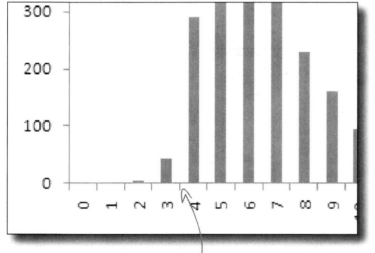

Does this gap mean that there are no people who got raises between 3.3% and 3.8%?

That's exactly what the gap *should* mean, at least if the histogram is written correctly. If you assumed this histogram was correct, and that there were gaps between these values, you'd get the totally wrong idea. You need a software tool to create a better histogram.

The problem with Excel's function is that it creates these messy, artificial breaks that are really deceptive.

And there's a technical workaround for the issues (with Excel, there's almost always a workaround if you have the time to write code using Microsoft's proprietary language).

But it's chapter 9, and you've been kicking serious butt. You're ready for a **software tool** with more power than Excel to manage and manipulate statistics.

The software you need is called **R**. It's a free, open source program that might be the future of statistical computing, and you're about to dive into it!

Install and run R

Head on over to ***www.r-project.org*** to download R. You should have no problem finding a mirror near you that serves R for Windows, Mac, and Linux.

Click this download link.

Once you've fired up the program, you'll see a window that looks like this.

This little cursor here represents the command prompt and is where you'll be entering your commands into R.

The command prompt is your friend.

Relax

Working from the command prompt is something you get the hang of quickly, even though it requires you to think a little harder at first. And you can always pull up a spreadsheet-style visualization of your data by typing edit(*yourdata*).

Load data into R

For your first R command, try loading the *Head First Data Analysis* script using the `source` command:

Load this!

```
source("http://www.headfirstlabs.com/books/hfda/hfda.R")
```

That command will load the raise data you need for R. You'll need to be connected to the Internet for it to work. If you want to save your R session so that you can come back to the *Head First* data when you're not connected to the Internet you can type `save.image()`.

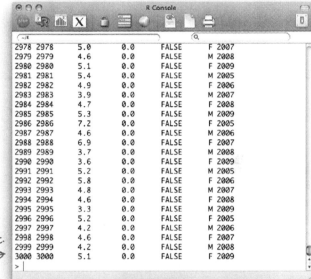

So what did you download? First, take a look at the **data frame** from your download called "Employees." Just type this command and press Enter:

```
employees
```

Type the name of the data frame to get R to display it.

The output you see on the right is what R gives you in response.

The command returns a listing of all the rows in the data frame.

Exercise

Generate a histogram in R by typing this command:

```
hist(employees$received, breaks=50)
```

What does this mean?

What do you think the various elements of the command mean? Annotate your response.

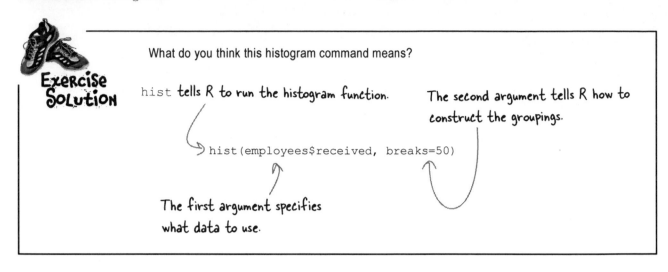

What do you think this histogram command means?

`hist` tells R to run the histogram function.

The second argument tells R how to construct the groupings.

`hist(employees$received, breaks=50)`

The first argument specifies what data to use.

R creates beautiful histograms

With histograms, the areas under the bars don't just measure the count (or **frequency**) of the thing being measured; they also show the percentage of the entire data set being represented by individual segments.

When you run the command, a window pops up showing this.

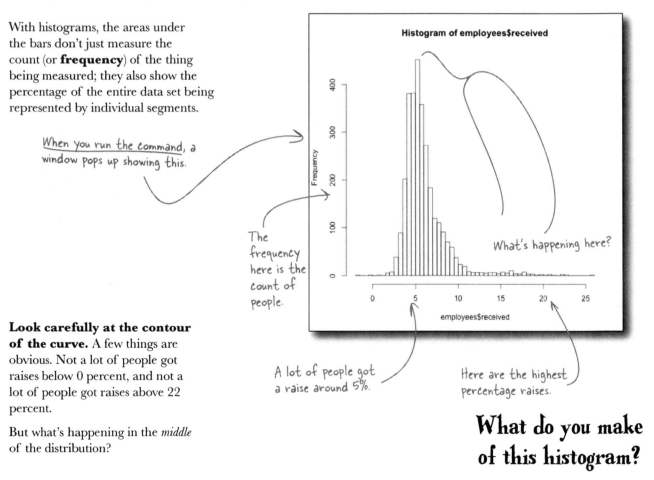

The frequency here is the count of people.

What's happening here?

A lot of people got a raise around 5%.

Here are the highest percentage raises.

Look carefully at the contour of the curve. A few things are obvious. Not a lot of people got raises below 0 percent, and not a lot of people got raises above 22 percent.

But what's happening in the *middle* of the distribution?

What do you make of this histogram?

Exercise

These commands will tell you a little more about your data set and **what people's raises look like**. What happens when you run the commands?

sd(employees$received)

Why do you think R responds to each of these the way it does?

summary(employees$received)

Type help(sd) *and* help(summary) *to find out what the commands do.*

What do the two commands do?

....

....

....

Look closely at the histogram. How does what you see on the histogram compare with what R tells you from these two commands?

....

....

....

Exercise Solution

You just ran some commands to illustrate the summary statistics for your data set about raises. What do you think these commands did?

What do the two commands do?

The sd command returns the standard

deviation of the data range you specify,

and the summary() command shows you

summary statistics about the received

column.

On average, the raises are 2.43 percentage points from the mean.

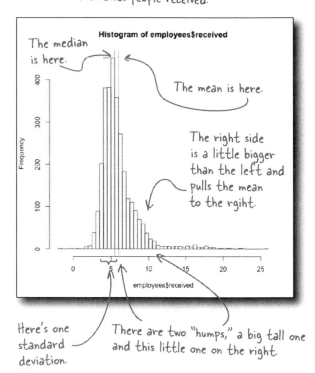

```
> sd(employees$received)
[1] 2.432138
> summary(employees$received)
   Min. 1st Qu.  Median    Mean 3rd Qu.    Max.
 -1.800   4.600   5.500   6.028   6.700  25.900
> |
```

summary() gives you some basic summary stats for the raises people received.

Look closely at the histogram. How does what you see on the histogram compare with what R tells you from these two commands?

The histogram does a good job of visually

showing mean, median, and standard

deviation. Looking at it, you can't see the

exact figures, but you can get a sense of

those numbers by looking at the shape of the

curve.

Histogram of employees$received

The median is here.

The mean is here.

The right side is a little bigger than the left and pulls the mean to the rgiht.

Here's one standard deviation.

There are two "humps," a big tall one and this little one on the right.

Joe: If the histogram were symmetrical, the mean and median would be in the same place—in the dead center.

Frank: Right. But in this case, the small hump on the right side is pulling the mean away from the center of the larger hump, where most of the observations are.

Joe: I'm struggling with those two humps. What do they **mean**?

Frank: Maybe we should take another look at those pieces of data we identified earlier and see if they have any relevance to the histogram.

Joe: Good idea.

Female negotiators

Raises of 4–5%

Raises of 1% in '07

Men

Men in 2008

Women

Raises of >10%

The data groupings you imagined earlier.

Sharpen your pencil

Can you think of any ways that the groups you identified earlier might explain the two humps on the histogram?

....

....

....

Sharpen your pencil
Solution

How might the groupings of data you identified earlier account for the two humps on your histogram?

There could be variation among years: for example, raises in 2007 could be on average much higher than raises from 2006. And there could be gender variation, too: men could, on average, get higher raises than women, or vice versa. Of course, all the data is observational, so any relationships you discover won't necessarily be as strong as what experimental data would show.

there are no
Dumb Questions

Q: So it seems like we have a lot of flexibility when it comes to how the histograms look.

A: It's true. You should think of the very act of creating a histogram as an interpretation, not something you do *before* interpretation.

Q: Are the defaults that R uses for creating a histogram generally good?

A: Generally, yes. R tries to figure out the number of breaks and the scale that will best represent the data, but R doesn't *understand* the meaning of the data it's plotting. Just as with the summary functions, there's nothing wrong with running a quick and dirty histogram to see what's there, but before you draw any big conclusions about what you see, you need to use the histogram (and redraw the histogram) in a way that remains mindful of what you're looking at and what you hope to gain from your analysis.

Q: Are either of those humps the "bell curve?"

A: That's a great question. Usually, when we think of bell curves, we're talking about the normal or Gaussian distribution. But there are other types of bell-shaped distributions, and a lot of other types of distributions that aren't shaped like a bell.

Q: Then what's the big deal about the normal distribution?

A: A lot of powerful and simple statistics can come into play if your data is normally distributed, and a lot of natural and business data follows a natural distribution (or can be "transformed" in a way that makes it naturally distributed).

Q: So is our data normally distributed?

A: The histogram you've been evaluating is definitely not normally distributed. As long as there's more than one hump, there's no way you can call the distribution bell-shaped.

Q: But there are definitely two humps in the data that look like bells!

A: And that shape must have some sort of meaning. The question is, why is the distribution shaped that way? How will you find out?

Q: Can you draw histograms to represent small portions of the data to evaluate individually? If we do that, we might be able to figure out why there are two humps.

A: That's the right intuition. Give it a shot!

Can you break the raise data down in a way that isolates the two humps and explains why they exist?

Make histograms from subsets of your data

You can make a histogram out of your entire data set, but you can also split up the data into subsets to make other histograms.

Inside your data are subsets of data that represent different groups.

If you plot the raise *values for each subset, you might get a bunch of different shapes.*

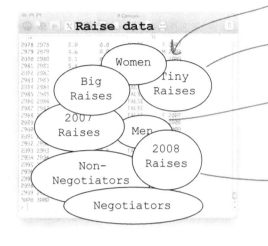

Raise data

Women
Big Raises
Tiny Raises
2007 Raises
Men
2008 Raises
Non-Negotiators
Negotiators

The shape of men's raises, for example, might tell you something by itself or in comparison to the shape of women's raises.

Exercise

Let's make a bunch of histograms that describe subsets of the raise data. Maybe looking at these other histograms will help you figure out what the two humps on the raise histogram mean. Is there a group of people who are earning more in raises than the rest?

1) To start, look at this histogram command and annotate its syntax. What do you think its components mean?

```
hist(employees$received[employees$year == 2007], breaks = 50)
```

Write down here what you think each piece means.

2) Run the above command each of these commands. What do you see? The results are on the next page, where you'll write down your interpretations.

```
hist(employees$received[employees$year == 2008], breaks = 50)
hist(employees$received[employees$gender == "F"], breaks = 50)
hist(employees$received[employees$gender == "M"], breaks = 50)
hist(employees$received[employees$negotiated == FALSE], breaks = 50)
hist(employees$received[employees$negotiated == TRUE], breaks = 50)
```

LONG EXERCISE

These histograms represent the raises for different subgroups of your employee population. What do they tell you?

The `hist()` command makes a histogram.

`received` is the set of values you want plotted in the histogram.

Breaks are the number of bars in the histogram.

```
hist(employees$received[employees$year == 2007], breaks = 50)
```

These brackets are the subset operator, which extracts a subset of your data.

In this case, you're extracting records where the year is 2007.

Histogram of employees$received[employees$year == 2007]

....

....

....

....

```
hist(employees$received[employees$year == 2008],
 breaks = 50)
```

Histogram of employees$received[employees$year == 2008]

....

....

....

....

```
hist(employees$received[employees$gender == "F"],
 breaks = 50)
```

Histogram of employees$received[employees$gender == "F"]

....

....

....

....

```
hist(employees$received[employees$gender == "M"],
 breaks = 50)
```

Histogram of employees$received[employees$gender == "M"]

....

....

....

....

```
hist(employees$received[employees$negotiated == FALSE],
 breaks = 50)
```

Histogram of employees$received[employees$negotiated == FALSE]

....

....

....

....

```
hist(employees$received[employees$negotiated == TRUE],
 breaks = 50)
```

Histogram of employees$received[employees$negotiated == TRUE]

....

....

....

....

Long Exercise
Solution

You looked at the different histograms in search of answers to help you understand who is getting what raises. What did you see?

```
hist(employees$received[employees$year == 2007],
  breaks = 50)
```

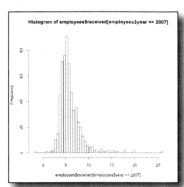

This histogram selects only raises for 2007 and has the same basic shape as the original histogram. The scale is different—e.g., only 8 people are in the largest break here. But the shape is the same, and the 2007 group might have the same characteristics as the overall group.

```
hist(employees$received[employees$year == 2008],
  breaks = 50)
```

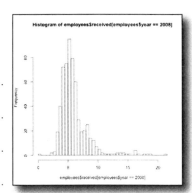

There's the exact same thing going on here as we see with the 2007 data. R even chose to plot the data using the exact same scale. At least as far as this data is concerned, 2007 and 2008 are pretty similar.

```
hist(employees$received[employees$gender == "F"],
  breaks = 50)
```

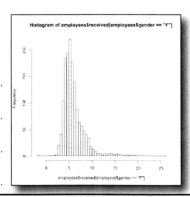

Once again, we see the big hump and the little hump attached on the right, although the scale is different on this histogram. This graph shows raises earned by women by all the years represented in the data, so there's a lot of them.

```
hist(employees$received[employees$gender == "M"],
 breaks = 50)
```

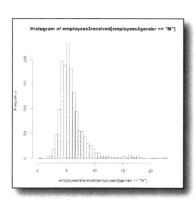

This looks a lot like the histogram for females. The scale is different, but when you count the bars, it looks like there are roughly the same number of men as women in the different categories. As usual, there are two humps.

```
hist(employees$received[employees$negotiated == FALSE],
 breaks = 50)
```

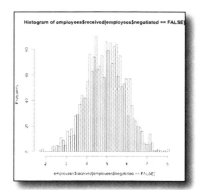

Now here's something interesting: just one hump. And the horizontal scale shows that these people—the ones who did not negotiate their raises—are on the low end of the raise range. And there are a lot of them, as you can see from the vertical scale.

```
hist(employees$received[employees$negotiated == TRUE],
 breaks = 50)
```

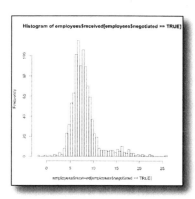

It looks like splitting those who did and did not negotiate neatly separates the two humps. Here we see people earning a lot more in raises, and there are far fewer people. It looks like negotiating for a raise gives people a completely different outcome distribution.

Negotiation pays

Your analysis of histograms of different subsets of the raise data shows that getting a larger raise is all about *negotiation*.

People have a different **spread of outcomes** depending on their choice of whether to negotiate. If they do, their whole histogram shifts to the right.

Don't negotiate

Negotiate

Non-negotiators tend to get lower raises.

Negotiation outcomes are higher.

If you run the summary statistics on your negotiation subsets, the results are just as dramatic as what you see with the two curves.

This is the function that calculates the standard deviation.

The mean and median are about the same within each distribution.

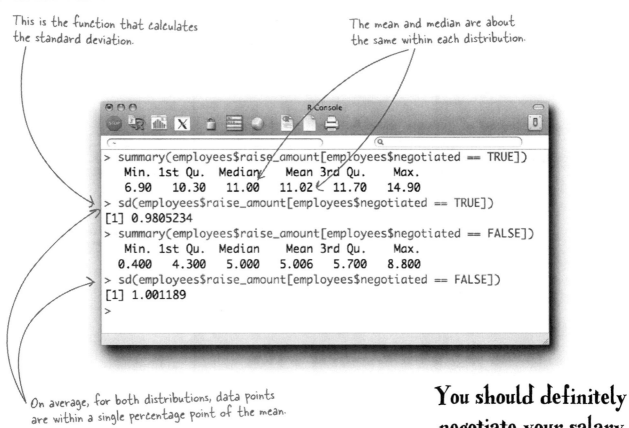

```
> summary(employees$raise_amount[employees$negotiated == TRUE])
   Min. 1st Qu.  Median   Mean 3rd Qu.    Max.
   6.90   10.30   11.00  11.02   11.70   14.90
> sd(employees$raise_amount[employees$negotiated == TRUE])
[1] 0.9805234
> summary(employees$raise_amount[employees$negotiated == FALSE])
   Min. 1st Qu.  Median   Mean 3rd Qu.    Max.
  0.400   4.300   5.000  5.006   5.700   8.800
> sd(employees$raise_amount[employees$negotiated == FALSE])
[1] 1.001189
>
```

On average, for both distributions, data points are within a single percentage point of the mean.

You should definitely negotiate your salary.

What will negotiation mean for you?

Now that you've analyzed the raise data, it should be pretty clear which strategies will have the best results.

The data suggest that negotiation will tend to create these outcomes.

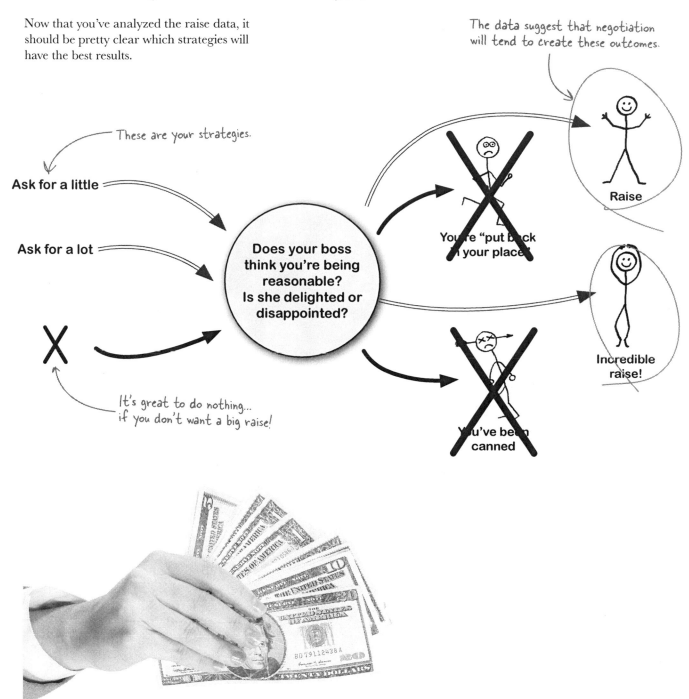

These are your strategies.

Ask for a little

Ask for a lot

Does your boss think you're being reasonable? Is she delighted or disappointed?

It's great to do nothing... if you don't want a big raise!

You're "put back in your place"

You've been canned

Raise

Incredible raise!

10 regression

Prediction

I've got all this data, but I really need it to tell me what will happen in the future. How can I do that?

Predict it.

Regression is an incredibly powerful statistical tool that, when used correctly, has the ability to help you predict certain values. When used with a controlled experiment, regression can actually help you predict the future. Businesses use it like crazy to help them build models to explain customer behavior. You're about to see that the judicious use of regression can be very profitable indeed.

What are you going to do with all this money?

Your quest for a raise paid off. With your histograms, you figured out that people who chose to negotiate their salaries got consistently higher outcomes. So when you went into your boss's office, you had the confidence that you were pursuing a strategy that tended to pay off, and it did!

These are the histograms you looked at in the final exercises of the previous chapter, except they've been redrawn to show the same scale and bin size.

Nice work!

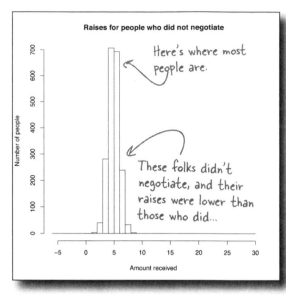

Here's where most people are.

These folks didn't negotiate, and their raises were lower than those who did...

Your boss was impressed that you negotiated and gave you 15%.

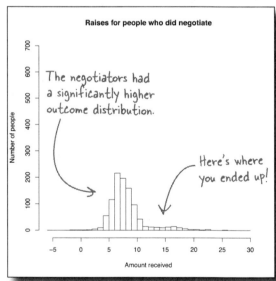

The negotiators had a significantly higher outcome distribution.

Here's where you ended up!

No point in stopping now.

Lots of people could benefit from your insight about how to get better raises. Few of your colleagues took the savvy approach your did, and you have a lot to offer those who didn't.

You should set up a business that specializes in getting people raises!

Sharpen your pencil

Here are a few questions to get you thinking about data-based ways of creating a business around your insights in salary negotiations.

What do you think your clients would want from a business that helps them understand how to negotiate raises?

....

....

....

....

....

....

If you ran such a business, what would be a fair way to compensate you for your knowledge?

....

....

....

....

....

....

Sharpen your pencil
Solution

What sort of data-based compensation consulting business do you envision?

What do you think your clients would want from a business that helps them understand how to negotiate raises?

There are all sorts of ways that people negotiating for a raise could be helped: they might want to know how to dress, how to think about the issue from the perspective of their boss, what words will soften people up, and so forth. But one question is fundamental: how much do I ask for?

If you ran such a business, what would be a fair way to compensate you for your knowledge?

Clients will want you to have an incentive to make sure that their experience works out well. So why not charge them a percentage of what they actually get when they use your advice? That way, your incentive is to get them the biggest raise you can get them, not to waste their time.

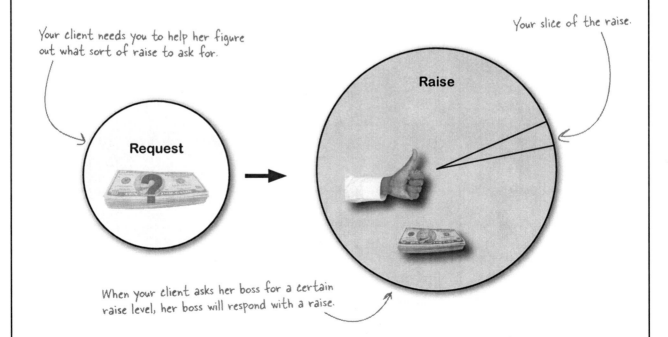

Your client needs you to help her figure out what sort of raise to ask for.

Request

Raise

Your slice of the raise.

When your client asks her boss for a certain raise level, her boss will respond with a raise.

An analysis that tells people what to ask for could be huge

What amount of money is reasonable to ask for? How will a request for a raise translate into an actual raise? Most people just don't know.

I have no idea where to start.

I want more, but I don't know what to ask for.

BRAIN POWER

You need a basic outline of your service so you know what you're shooting for. What will your product look like?

Behold... the Raise Reckoner!

People want to know what to ask for. And they want to know what they'll get, given what they've asked for.

You need an **algorithm**.

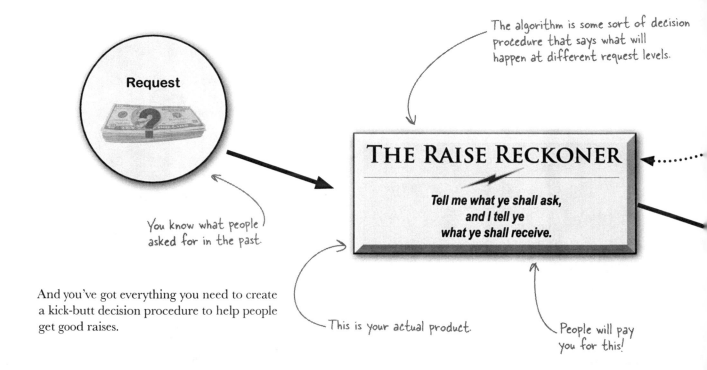

The algorithm is some sort of decision procedure that says what will happen at different request levels.

Request

You know what people asked for in the past.

THE RAISE RECKONER

Tell me what ye shall ask, and I tell ye what ye shall receive.

And you've got everything you need to create a kick-butt decision procedure to help people get good raises.

This is your actual product.

People will pay you for this!

the Scholar's Corner

Algorithm Any procedure you follow to complete a calculation. Here, you'll take the input to the algorithm, the Amount Requested, and perform some steps in order to predict the Amount rewarded. But what steps?

What goes inside this thing?

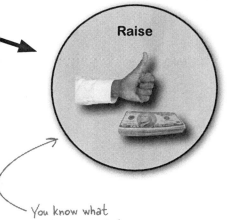

Raise

You know what people received, too.

What happens inside the algorithm?

It's all well and good to draw a pretty picture like this, but in order for you to have something that people are willing to pay for—and, just as important, in order for you to have something that *works*—you're going to need to do a serious analysis.

So what do you think goes inside?

Inside the algorithm will be a method <u>to predict</u> raises

Prediction is a big deal for data analysis. Some would argue that, speaking generally, **hypothesis testing** and **prediction** together are the *definition* of data analysis.

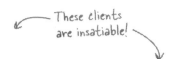

These clients are insatiable!

We need your predictions now!

BULLET POINTS

Things you might need to predict:

- People's actions
- Market movements
- Important events
- Experimental results
- Stuff that's not in your data

Questions you should always ask:

- Do I have enough data to predict?
- How good is my prediction?
- Is it qualitative or quantitative?
- Is my client using the prediction well?
- What are the limits of my prediction?

Let's take a look at some data about what negotiators asked for. Can you **predict** what sort of raise you'll get at various levels of requests?

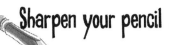

Sharpen your pencil

The histograms below describe the amount of money the negotiators received and the amount of money they **requested**.

Do the histograms tell you what people *should* request in order to get a big raise? Explain how comparing the two histograms might illuminate the relationship between these two variables, so that you might be able to predict how much you would receive for any given request.

....

....

....

....

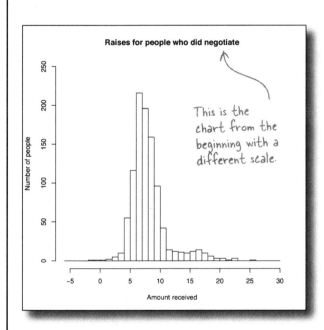

This is the chart from the beginning with a different scale.

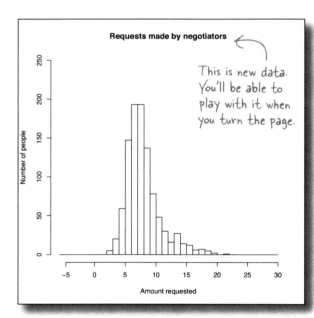

This is new data. You'll be able to play with it when you turn the page.

Sharpen your pencil
Solution

Can you tell from looking at these two histograms how much someone should request in order to get the biggest raise?

No. The histograms show spreads of single variables, but they don't actually compare them. In order to know how these two variables relate to each other, we'd have to see where single individuals fall on both the `requested` and `received` distributions.

A small request could get a big raise...

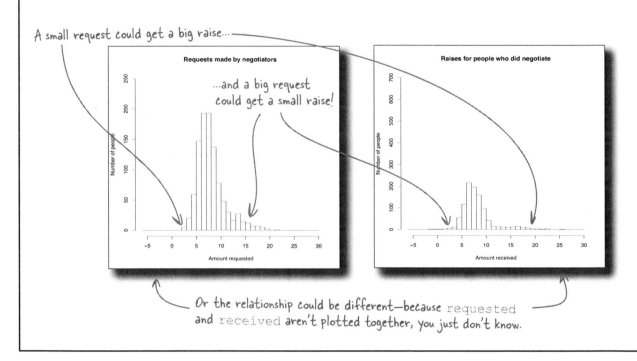

...and a big request could get a small raise!

Or the relationship could be different—because `requested` and `received` aren't plotted together, you just don't know.

there are no
Dumb Questions

Q: Can't I just overlay two histograms onto the same grid?

A: You totally can. But in order to make a good comparison, the two histograms need to describe **the same thing**. You made a bunch of histograms in the previous chapter using subsets of the same data, for example, and comparing those subsets to each other made sense.

Q: But Amount Received and Amount Requested are really similar, aren't they?

A: Sure, they're similar in the sense that they are measured using the same metric: percentage points of one's salary. But what you want to know is not so much the distribution of either variable but how, for a single person, one variable relates to the other.

Q: I get it. So once we have that information, how will we make use of it?

A: Good question. You should stay focused on the end result of your analysis, which is some sort of intellectual "product" that you can sell to your customers. What do you need? What will the product look like? But first, you need a visualization that **compares these two variables**.

Scatterplot Magnets

Remember scatterplots from chapter 4? They're a great visualization for looking at two variables together. In this exercise, take the data from these three people and use it to place them on the graph.

You'll need to use other magnets to draw your scale and your axis labels.

Bob   Fannie   Julia

Bob requested 5% and received 5%.

Fannie requested 10% and received 8%.

Julia requested 2% and received 10%.

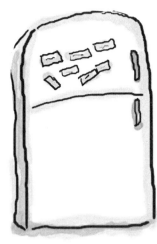

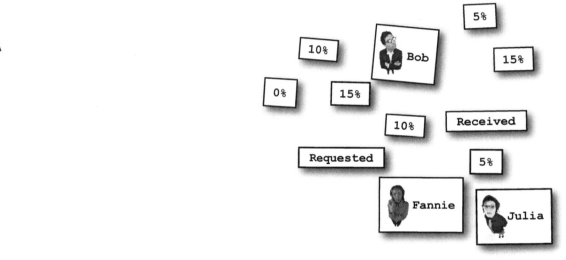

Use this x–y axis to plot Bob, Fannie, and Julia.

Scatterplot Magnets

You just plotted Bob, Fannie, and Julia on the axis to create a scatterplot. What did you find?

Bob requested 5% and received 5%.

Fannie requested 10% and received 8%.

Julia requested 2% and received 10%.

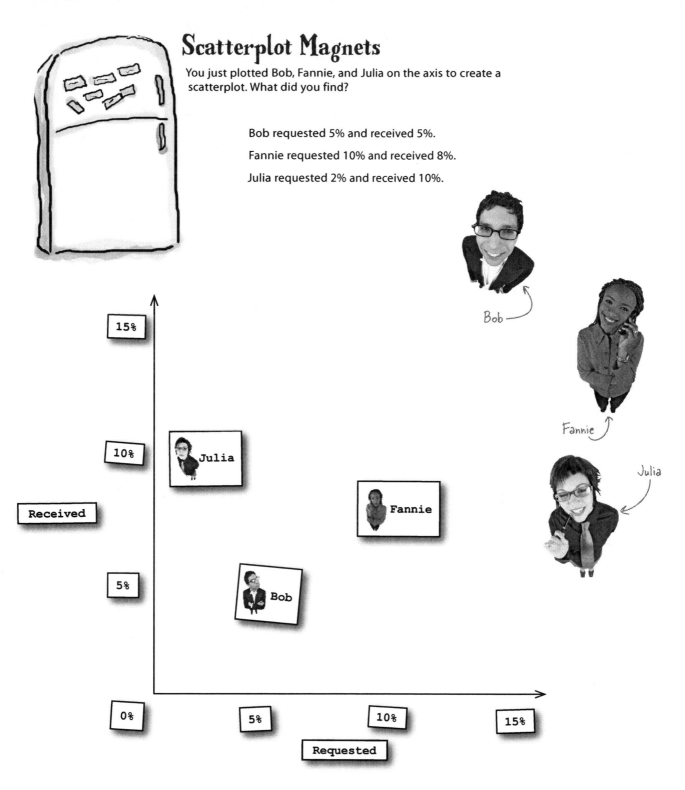

there are no Dumb Questions

Q: When can I use scatterplots?

A: Try to use them as frequently as you can. They're a quick way to show rich patterns in your data. Any time you have data with observations of two variables, you should think about using a scatterplot.

Q: So any two variables can be put together in a scatterplot?

A: As long as the two variables are in pairs that describe the same underlying thing or person. In this case, each line of our database represents an instance of an employee asking for a raise, and for each employee, we have a received and a requested value.

Q: What should I look for when I see them?

A: For an analyst, scatterplots are ultimately all about looking for causal relationships between variables. If high requests cause low raises, for example, you'll see an association between the two variables on the scatterplot. The scatterplot by itself only shows *association*, and to demonstrate causation you'll need more (for starters, you'd need an explanation of *why* one variable might follow from the other).

Q: What if I want to compare *three* pieces of data?

A: You can totally create visualizations in R that make a comparison among more than two variables. For this chapter, we're going to stick with two, but you can plot three variables using 3D scatterplots and multi-panel lattice visualizations. If you'd like a taste of multidimensional scatterplots, copy and run some of the examples of the cloud function that can be found in the help file at help(cloud).

Q: So when do we get to look at the 2D scatterplot for the raise data?

A: Right now. Here's some ready bake code that will grab some new, more detailed data for you and give you a handy scatterplot. Go for it!

Ready Bake Code

Run these commands inside of R to generate a **scatterplot** that shows **what people requested** and **what they received**.

Make sure you're connected to the Internet when you run this command, because it pulls data off the Web.

```
employees <- read.csv("http://www.headfirstlabs.com/books/hfda/
        hfda_ch10_employees.csv", header=TRUE)

head(employees,n=30)

plot(employees$requested[employees$negotiated==TRUE],
      employees$received[employees$negotiated==TRUE])
```

This command loads some new data and doesn't display any results.

This command displays the scatterplot.

This command will show you what's in the data... always a good idea to take a look.

What happens when you run these commands?

Scatterplots compare two variables

Each one of the points on this **scatterplot** represents a single observation: a single person.

Like histograms, scatterplots are another quick and elegant way to show data, and they show the spread of data. But unlike histograms, scatterplots show **two** variables. Scatterplots show *how* the observations are paired to each other, and a good scatterplot can be part of how you demonstrate **causes**.

This dude asked for 7% but got 20%. He must be important.

The `plot` command produced the scatterplot on the right.

Ready Bake Code

```
head(employees,n=30)

plot(employees$requested[employees$negotiated==TRUE],
    employees$received[employees$negotiated==TRUE])
```

This gentleman asked for 8% and received 8%.

The `head` command shows you the data below.

Here's the output of the `head` command.

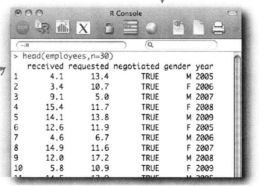

```
> head(employees,n=30)
   received requested negotiated gender year
1      4.1      13.4       TRUE      M 2005
2      3.4      10.7       TRUE      F 2006
3      9.1       5.0       TRUE      M 2007
4     15.4      11.7       TRUE      F 2008
5     14.1      13.8       TRUE      M 2009
6     12.6      11.9       TRUE      F 2005
7      4.6       6.7       TRUE      M 2006
8     14.9      11.6       TRUE      F 2007
9     12.0      17.2       TRUE      M 2008
10     5.8      10.9       TRUE      F 2009
```

This guy asked for 12% but had a 3% pay cut!

These three people and more are all inside this data set.

The `head` command is a quick way to peek inside any new data you load.

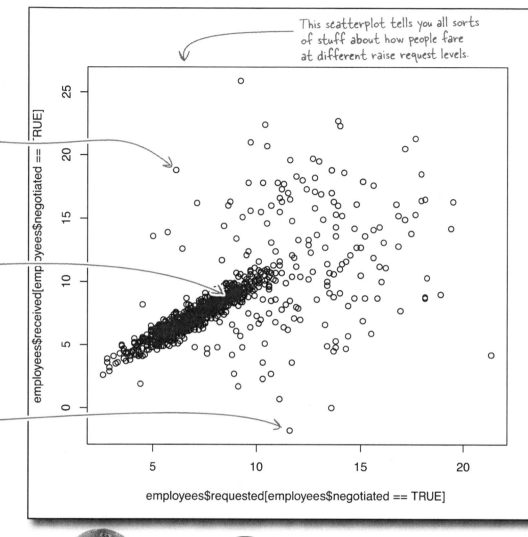

This scatterplot tells you all sorts of stuff about how people fare at different raise request levels.

Together, these dots represent all the negotiators in the database.

Can I draw a line through the dots?

Of course you *can*, but why would you? Remember, you're trying to build an algorithm here.

What would a line through the data do for you?

....

....

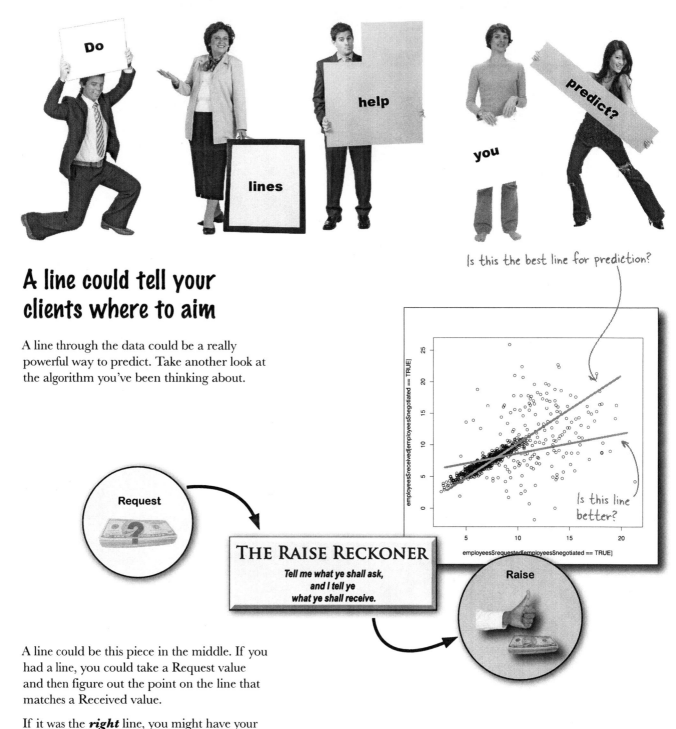

Do

lines

help

you

predict?

Is this the best line for prediction?

A line could tell your clients where to aim

A line through the data could be a really powerful way to predict. Take another look at the algorithm you've been thinking about.

Request

THE RAISE RECKONER

Tell me what ye shall ask, and I tell ye what ye shall receive.

Raise

Is this line better?

A line could be this piece in the middle. If you had a line, you could take a Request value and then figure out the point on the line that matches a Received value.

If it was the **right** line, you might have your missing piece of the algorithm.

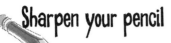

Sharpen your pencil

In order to figure out how to get the right line, why not just try answering a specific question about a single raise with your scatterplot? Here's an example:

If someone asks for a 8 percent raise, what is he likely to receive in return? See if looking at this scatterplot can tell you what sort of results people got from asking for 8 percent.

Take a good look at the scatterplot to answer this question.

....

....

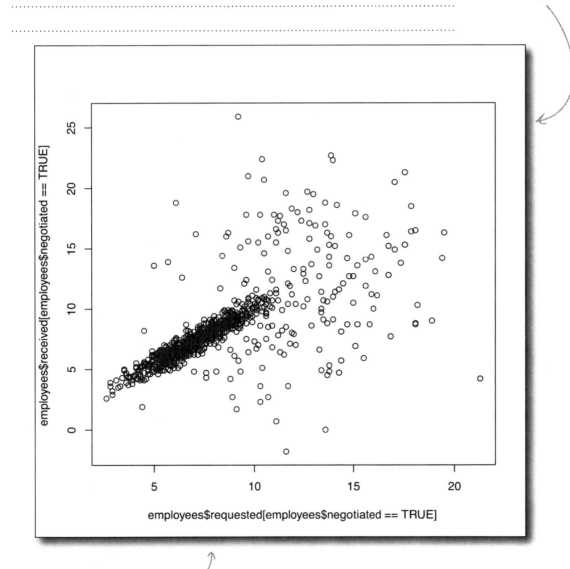

Hint: look at the dots in the 8% requested range!

Sharpen your pencil
Solution

Using the scatterplot, how do you determine what an 8% raise request is likely to get you?

Just take the average amount received for dots around the range of amount requested you're

looking at. If you look around 8% on the x-axis (the amount requested), it looks like the

corresponding dots on the y-axis are about 8%, too. Take a look at the graph below.

Here is the employee who's asking for 8%.

This strip is the dots that have x-axis values of between 7.5% and 8.5%.

Almost everyone who asks for 8% gets around 8%.

This is the y-axis value for receiving an 8% raise.

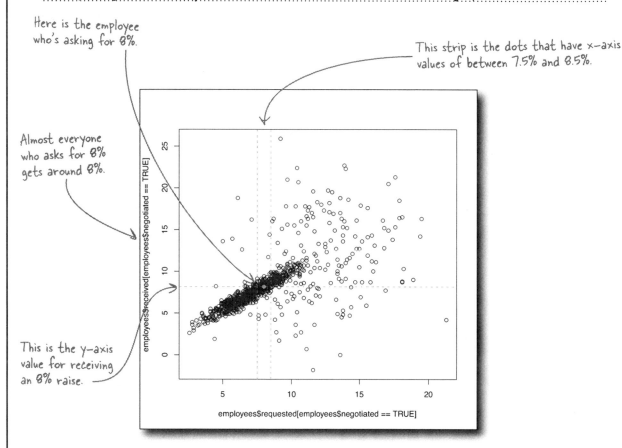

If you take the **mean** of the Amount Received scores for dots in the 8 percent range (or **strip**), you get around 8 percent. On average, if you ask for 8 percent, you get 8 percent.

So you've solved the raise question for one group of people: those who ask for 8 percent. But other people will ask for different amounts.

What happens if you look at the average amount received for all the x-axis strips?

Predict values in each strip with the graph of averages

The **graph of averages** is a scatterplot that shows the predicted y-axis value for **each strip on the x-axis**. This graph of averages shows us what people get, on average, when they request each different level of raise.

The graph of averages is a lot more powerful than just taking the overall average. The overall average raise amount, as you know, is 4 percent. But this graph shows you a much more subtle representation of how it all shakes out.

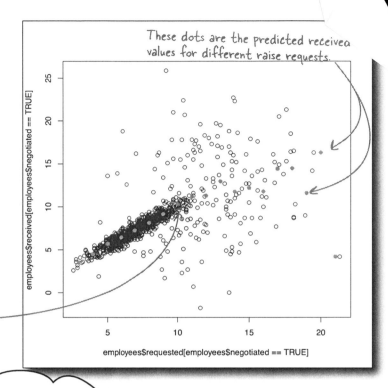

These dots are the predicted received values for different raise requests.

Here's the point we created to predict the likely value from an 8% raise request.

Man, I wanted to draw a line through the first scatterplot. I'm **dying** to draw a line through the graph of averages!

You've hit on the right line.

Seriously. Draw a line through the points on the graph of averages.

Because that line is the one you're looking for, the line that you can use to **predict raises for everybody**.

he regression line predicts what raises people will receive

Here you have it, the fascinating regression line.

The regression line is just **the line that best fits the points on the graph of averages**. As you're about to see, you don't just have to draw them on your graphs.

You can represent them with a simple equation that will allow you to predict the y variable for any x variable in your range.

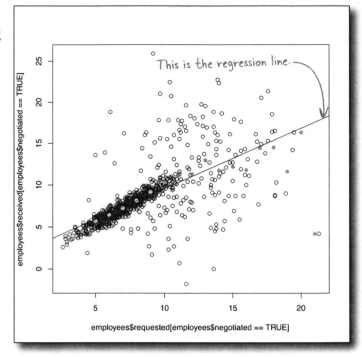

This is the regression line.

there are no
Dumb Questions

Q: **Why is it called a regression?**

A: The guy who discovered the method, Sir Francis Galton (1822-1911), was studying how the height of fathers predicted the height of their sons. His data showed that, on average, short fathers had taller sons, and tall fathers had shorter sons. He called this phenomenon "regression to mediocrity."

Q: **Sounds kind of snooty and elitist. It seems that the word "regression" has more to do with how Galton felt about numbers on boys and their dads than anything statistical.**

A: That's right. The word "regression" is more a historical artifact than something analytically illuminating.

Q: **We've been predicting raise amount from raise request. Can I predict raise request from raise amount? Can I predict the x-axis from the y-axis?**

A: Sure, but in that case, you'd be predicting the value of a past event. If someone came to you with a raise she received, you'd predict the raise she had requested. What's important is that you always do a reality check and make sure you keep track of the *meaning* of whatever it is that you're studying. Does the prediction **make sense?**

Q: **Would I use the same line to predict the x-axis from the y-axis?**

A: Nope. There are **two regression lines**, one for x given y and one for y given x. Think about it. There are two different graphs of averages: one for each of the two variables.

Q: **Does the line have to be straight?**

A: It doesn't have to be straight, as long as the regression makes sense. **Nonlinear regression** is a cool field that's a lot more complicated and is beyond the scope of this book.

You're forgetting something. Are you <u>sure</u> the line is actually useful? I mean, what's it doing for ya?

Make sure your line is actually useful.

There are **a lot of different ways the scatterplot could look**, and a lot of different regression lines.

The question is how useful is the line in *your* scatterplot. Here are a few different scatterplots. Are the lines for each one going to be about as useful as the lines for any other? Or do some regression lines seem more powerful?

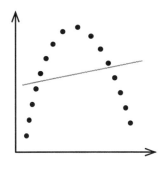

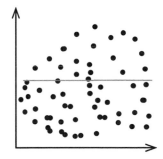

The line is useful if your data shows a linear correlation

A **correlation** is a linear association between two variables, and for an association to be linear, the scatterplot points need to roughly follow a line.

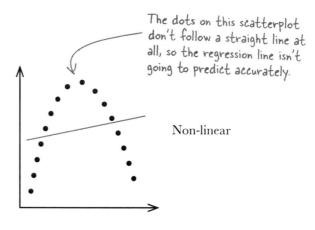

The dots on this scatterplot don't follow a straight line at all, so the regression line isn't going to predict accurately.

Non-linear

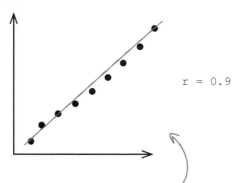

r = 0.9

These two scatterplots show tight, strong correlations, and their regression lines will give you good predictions.

These dots are all over the place, so the regression line might not be of much use here either.

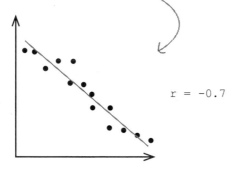

r = -0.7

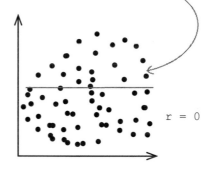

r = 0

You can have strong or weak correlations, and they're measured by a **correlation coefficient**, which is also known as r (not to be confused with [big] R, the software program). In order for your regression line to be useful, data must show a strong linear correlation.

r ranges from -1 to 1, where 0 means *no association* and 1 or -1 means a *perfect* association between the two variables.

Does your raise data show a linear correlation?

Ready Bake
R Code

Try using R (the program) to calculate **r** (the correlation
coefficient) on your data raise. Type and execute this function:

```
cor(employees$requested[employees$negotiated==TRUE],
        employees$received[employees$negotiated==TRUE])
```

Annotate the elements of the function. What do you think they mean?

How does the output of the correlation function square with your scatterplot? Does the
value match what you believe the association between these two variables to be?

....

....

....

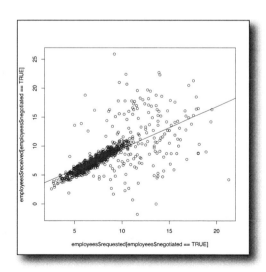

Ready Bake R Code

You just told R to give you the correlation coefficient of your two variables. What did you learn?

The cor *function tells R to return the correlation of the two variables.*

These are the two variables you want to test for correlation.

You can see a linear association by looking at the chart.

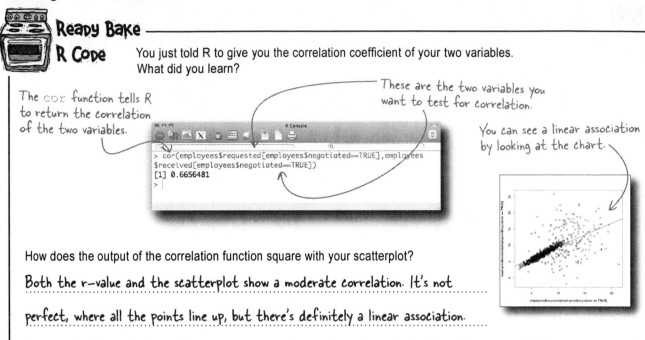

```
> cor(employees$requested[employees$negotiated==TRUE],employees
$received[employees$negotiated==TRUE])
[1] 0.6656481
>
```

How does the output of the correlation function square with your scatterplot?

Both the r-value and the scatterplot show a moderate correlation. It's not

perfect, where all the points line up, but there's definitely a linear association.

Correlation Up Close

How do you get the correlation coefficient? The actual calculation to get the correlation coefficient is simple but tedious.

Here's one of the algorithms that can be used to calculate the correlation coefficient:

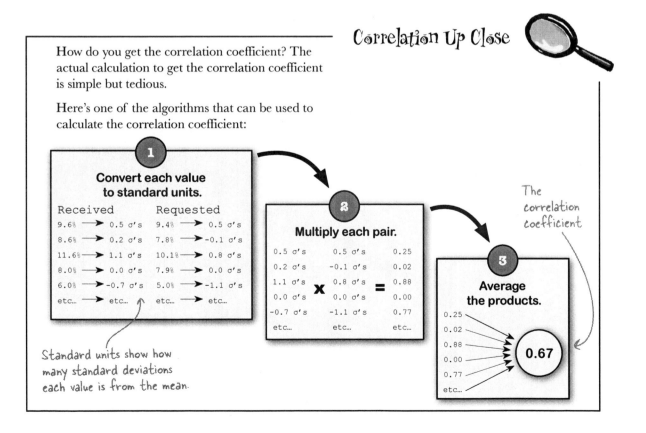

1

Convert each value to standard units.

Received		Requested	
9.6%	→ 0.5 σ's	9.4%	→ 0.5 σ's
8.6%	→ 0.2 σ's	7.8%	→ -0.1 σ's
11.6%	→ 1.1 σ's	10.1%	→ 0.8 σ's
8.0%	→ 0.0 σ's	7.9%	→ 0.0 σ's
6.0%	→ -0.7 σ's	5.0%	→ -1.1 σ's
etc...	→ etc...	etc...	→ etc...

Standard units show how many standard deviations each value is from the mean.

2

Multiply each pair.

0.5 σ's	0.5 σ's	0.25
0.2 σ's	-0.1 σ's	0.02
1.1 σ's **×**	0.8 σ's **=**	0.88
0.0 σ's	0.0 σ's	0.00
-0.7 σ's	-1.1 σ's	0.77
etc...	etc...	etc...

3

Average the products.

```
0.25
0.02
0.88        0.67
0.00
0.77
etc...
```

The correlation coefficient

there are no Dumb Questions

Q: I can see that a correlation of 1 or -1 is strong enough to enable me to use a regression line. But how low of a correlation is too low?

A: You just need to use your best judgment on the context. When you use the regression line, your judgments should always be qualified by the correlation coefficient.

Q: But how will I know how low of a correlation coefficient is too low?

A: As in all questions in statistics and data analysis, think about whether the regression **makes sense**. No statistical tool will get you the precisely correct answer all the time, but if you use those tools well, you will know how close they will get you on average. Use

your best judgment to ask, "Is this correlation coefficient large enough to justify decisions I make from the regression line?"

Q: How can I tell for sure whether my distribution is linear?

A: You should know that there are fancy statistical tools you can use to quantify the linearity of your scatterplot. But usually you're safe eyeballing it.

Q: If I show a linear relationship between two things, am I proving scientifically that relationship?

A: Probably not. You're specifying a relationship in a really useful mathematical sense, but whether that relationship *couldn't be otherwise* is a different matter. Is your data quality really high? Have other people replicated your results over and over again?

Do you have a strong qualitative theory to explain what you're seeing? If these elements are all in place, you can say you've demonstrated something in a rigorous analytic way, but "proof" might be too strong a word.

Q: How many records will fit onto a scatterplot?

A: Like the histogram, a scatterplot is a really high-resolution display. With the right formatting, you can fit thousands and thousands of dots on it. The high-res nature of the scatterplot is one of its virtues.

OK, OK, the regression line is useful. But here's a question: how do I <u>use</u> it? I want to calculate specific raises precisely.

You're going to need a **mathematical function** in order to get your predictions precise…

You need an equation to make your predictions precise

Straight lines can be described algebraically using the **linear equation**.

y is the y-axis value, which in this case in the thing we're trying to predict: raise received.

x is the x-axis value, which in this case in the thing we know: the raise amount requested.

$$y = a + bx$$

Your regression line can be represented by this linear equation. If you knew what yours was, you'd be able to plug any raise request you like into the x variable and get a prediction of what raise that request would elicit.

You just need to find the numerical values for a and b, which are values called the **coefficients**.

a represents the y-axis intercept

The first variable of the right side of the linear equation represents the y-axis **intercept**, where your line passes the y-axis.

Here's is the y-axis intercept.

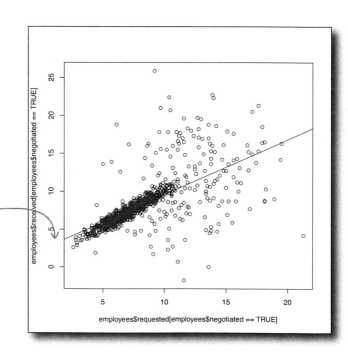

If you happen to have dots on your scatterplot that are around x=0, you can just find the point of averages for that strip. We're not so lucky, so finding the intercept might be a little trickier.

b represents the slope

The **slope** of a line is a measure of its angle. A line with a steep slope will have a large b value, and one with a relatively flat slope will have a b value close to zero. To calculate slope, measure how quickly a line rises (its "rise," or change in y-value) for every unit on the x-axis (its run).

$$\text{slope} = \frac{\text{rise}}{\text{run}} = b$$

Once you know the slope and y-axis intercept of a line, you can easily fill those values into your linear equation to get your line.

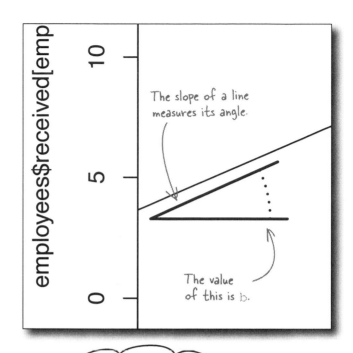

The slope of a line measures its angle.

The value of this is b.

Wouldn't it be dreamy if R would just find the slope and intercept for me?

Tell R to create a regression object

If you give R the variable you want to predict on the basis of another variable, R will generate a regression for you in a snap.

The basic function to use for this is `lm`, which stands for **linear model**. When you create a linear model, R creates an **object** in memory that has a long list of properties, and among those properties are your coefficients for the regression equation.

Here's a list of all the properties R creates inside your linear model.

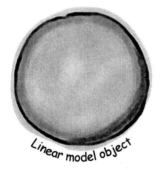

Linear model object

Watch it!

No software can tell you whether your regression makes sense.

R and your spreadsheet program can generate regressions like nobody's business, but it's up to you to make sure that it makes sense to try to predict one variable from another. It's easy to create useless, meaningless regressions.

Try creating your linear regression inside of R.

1 Run the formulas that create a linear model to describe your data and display the coefficients of the regression line.

```
myLm <- lm(received[negotiated==TRUE]~requested[negotiated==TRUE],
       data=employees)
myLm$coefficients
```

2 Using the numerical coefficients that R finds for you, write the regression equation for your data.

....

y = a + bx

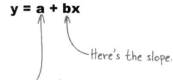

Here's the slope.

Here's the intercept.

Exercise Solution

What formula did you create using the coefficients that R calculated?

1 Run the formulas that create a linear model to describe your data and display the coefficients of the regression line.

```
> myLm <- lm(received[negotiated==TRUE]~requested[negotiated==TRUE],data=employees)
> myLm$coefficients
                  (Intercept) requested[negotiated == TRUE]
                    2.3121277                     0.7250664
>
```

2 Using the coefficients that R found for you, you can write your regression equation like this.

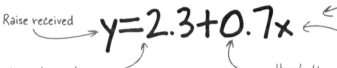

Raise received →

$$y = 2.3 + 0.7x$$

— This is your regression formula!

Raise requested

Here's the intercept. ———

———Here's the slope.

Geek Bits

How did R calculate the slope? It turns out that the slope of the regression line is equal to the correlation coefficient multiplied by the standard deviation of y divided by the standard deviation of x.

$$b = r * \sigma_y / \sigma_x$$

This equation calculates the slope of the regression line.

Here's your slope!

$$b = .67 * 3.1 / 2.8 = 0.7$$

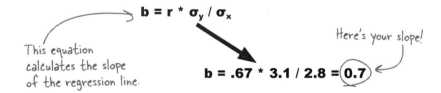

Ugh. Let's just say that calculating the slope of a regression line is one of those tasks that should make us all happy we have computers to do our dirty work. These are pretty elaborate calculations. But what's important to remember is this:

As long as you can see a solid association between your two variables, and as long as your regression *makes sense*, you can trust your software to deal with the coefficients.

The regression equation goes hand in hand with your scatterplot

Take the example of the person who wanted to know what sort of raise he'd receive if he asked for 8 percent. A few pages back, you made a prediction just by looking at the scatterplot and the vertical strip around 8 percent on the x-axis.

Here's the guy who might ask for 8%.

The regression equation your found with the help of the `lm` function gives you the same result.

$$y = 2.3 + 0.7x$$
$$= 2.3 + 0.7 * 8$$
$$= 7.9$$

Here's what the regression equation predicts he'll receive.

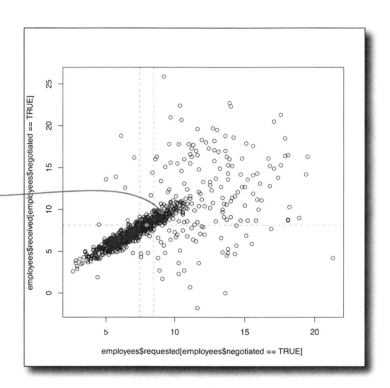

So what *is* the Raise Reckoner?

You've done a lot of neat work crafting a regression of the raise data. Does your regression equation help you create a product that will provide crafty compensating consulting for your friends and colleagues?

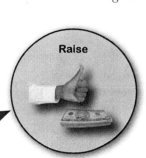

Request

THE RAISE RECKONER

Tell me what ye shall ask, and I tell ye what ye shall receive.

Raise

You still haven't filled in this part of your algorithm.

The regression equation is the Raise Reckoner algorithm

By taking a hard look at how people in the past have fared at different negotiation levels for their salaries, you identified a **regression equation** that can be used to predict raises given a certain level of request.

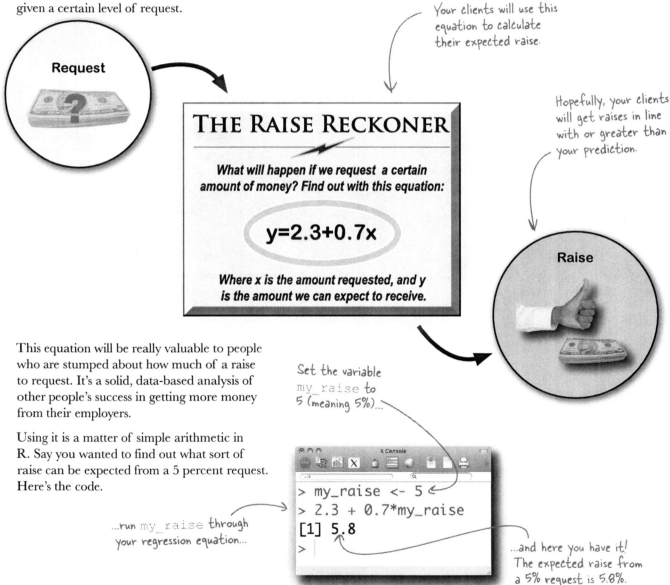

Your clients will use this equation to calculate their expected raise.

Request

THE RAISE RECKONER

What will happen if we request a certain amount of money? Find out with this equation:

$$y=2.3+0.7x$$

Where x is the amount requested, and y is the amount we can expect to receive.

Hopefully, your clients will get raises in line with or greater than your prediction.

Raise

This equation will be really valuable to people who are stumped about how much of a raise to request. It's a solid, data-based analysis of other people's success in getting more money from their employers.

Using it is a matter of simple arithmetic in R. Say you wanted to find out what sort of raise can be expected from a 5 percent request. Here's the code.

Set the variable `my_raise` to 5 (meaning 5%)...

...run `my_raise` through your regression equation...

```
> my_raise <- 5
> 2.3 + 0.7*my_raise
[1] 5.8
>
```

...and here you have it! The expected raise from a 5% request is 5.8%.

there are no
Dumb Questions

Q: How do I know that what people ask for tomorrow will be like they received today?

A: That's one of the big questions in regression analysis. Not only "Will tomorrow be like today?" but "What happens to my business if tomorrow is different?" The answer is that you don't know whether tomorrow will be like today. It **always** might be different, and sometimes completely different. The likelihood of change and its implications depend on your problem domain.

Q: How so?

A: Well, compare medical data versus consumer preferences. How likely is it that the human body, tomorrow, will suddenly change the way it works? It's possible, especially if the environment changes in a big way, but unlikely. How likely is it that consumer preferences will change tomorrow? You can bet that consumer preferences will change, in a big way.

Q: So why bother even trying to predict behavior?

A: In the online world, for example, a good regression analysis can be very profitable for a period of time, even it stops producing good predictions tomorrow. Think about your own behaviors. To an online bookseller, you're just a set of data points.

Q: That's kind of depressing.

A: Not really—it means the bookseller knows how to get you what you want. You're a set of data points that the bookseller runs a regression on to predict which books you'll want to buy. And that prediction will work until your tastes change. When they do, and you start buying different books, the bookseller will run the regression again to accommodate the new information.

Q: So when the world changes and the regression doesn't work any more, I should update the it?

A: Again, it depends on your problem domain. If you have good qualitative reasons to believe that your regression is accurate, you might never have to change it. But if your data is constantly changing, you should be running regressions constantly and using them in a way that enables you to benefit if the regressions are correct but that doesn't destroy your business if reality changes and the regressions fail.

Q: Shouldn't people ask for the raise they think they *deserve* rather than the raise they see other people getting?

A: That's an excellent question. The question is really part of your mental model, and statistics won't tell you whether what you're doing is the right or fair approach. That's a qualitative question that you, the analyst, need to use your best judgment in evaluating. (But the short answer is: you deserve a *big raise!*)

Exercise

Meet your first clients! Write down what sort of raise you think is appropriate for them to request, given their feelings about asking, and use R to calculate what they can expect.

I'm scared to ask for anything. Just give me a low number. Something modest.

I'm ready to go all out. I want a double-digit raise!

Exercise Solution

What did you recommend to your first two clients, and what did R calculate their expected raises to be?

I'm scared to ask for anything. Just give me a low number. Something modest.

I'm ready to go all out. I want a double digit raise!

Why not ask for 3%? That's on the low end of the scale.

You might have picked different numbers than these.

A more aggressive raise request would be for 15%.

A low raise request might be 3%.

A higher raise request might be 15%.

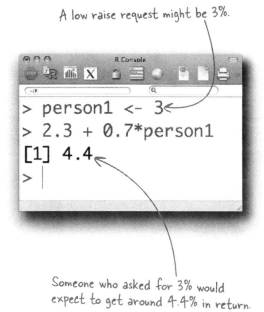

```
> person1 <- 3
> 2.3 + 0.7*person1
[1] 4.4
>
```

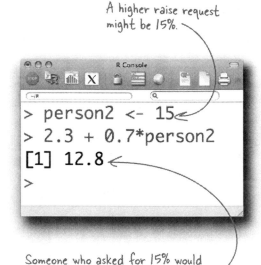

```
> person2 <- 15
> 2.3 + 0.7*person2
[1] 12.8
>
```

Someone who asked for 15% would expect to get around 12.8% in return.

Someone who asked for 3% would expect to get around 4.4% in return.

Let's see what happened...

Your raise predictor didn't work out as planned...

People were falling all over themselves to get your advice, and you got off your first round of recommendations smoothly.

But then the **phone started ringing**. Some of your clients were pleased as punch about the results, but others were not so happy!

I got 5%! I'm definitely satisfied. Good for you. The check's in the mail!

12.8%? Man, I got 0.0%. Hope you know a good lawyer!

Looks like this one did just fine!

This guy's request didn't pan out so well for him.

Did this thing misfire?

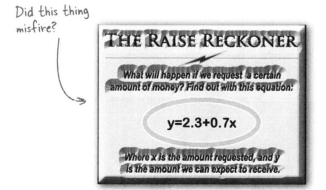

THE RAISE RECKONER

What will happen if we request a certain amount of money? Find out with this equation:

$$y = 2.3 + 0.7x$$

Where x is the amount requested, and y is the amount we can expect to receive.

What did your clients **do** with your advice? What went wrong for those who came back unhappy?

You'll have to get to the bottom of this situation in the **next chapter**…

11 error

The world is messy.

So it should be no surprise that your predictions rarely hit the target squarely. But if you offer a prediction with an error range, you and your clients will know not only the average predicted value, but also how far you expect typical deviations from that error to be. Every time you express error, you offer a much richer perspective on your predictions and beliefs. And with the tools in this chapter, you'll also learn about how to get error under control, getting it as low as possible to increase confidence.

Your clients are pretty ticked off

In the previous chapter, you created a linear regression to predict what sort of raises people could expect depending on what they requested.

Lots of customers are using the raise algorithm. Let's see what they have to say.

I got a 4.5% raise. It was a good raise. I think that's the sort of raise I deserved. I was so nervous in the meeting that I can't even remember what I asked for.

I can't believe it! I got a 5.0% bigger raise than the algorithm predicted! My negotiation must have scared my boss, and he just started throwing money at me!

Yeah, I got **no raise**. Did you hear that? **0.0%** I have some ideas for you about what you can do with your algorithm.

I'm pretty pleased. My raise was 0.5% lower than expected, but it's still a solid raise. I'm pretty sure I wouldn't have gotten it if I hadn't negotiated.

Bull's-eye! I got the exact raise the algorithm predicted. I'm telling you, it's incredible. You must be some sort of genius. You rock my world.

What did your raise prediction algorithm <u>do</u>?

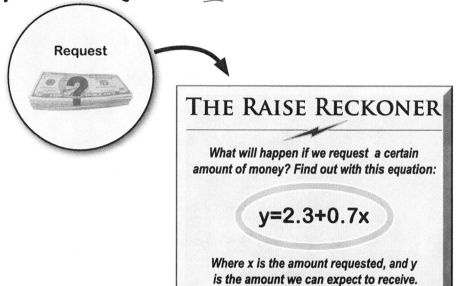

Request

THE RAISE RECKONER

What will happen if we request a certain amount of money? Find out with this equation:

$$y = 2.3 + 0.7x$$

Where x is the amount requested, and y is the amount we can expect to receive.

Raise

Everyone used the same formula, which was based on solid empirical data.

But it looks like people had a bunch of different experiences.

What happened?

Sharpen your pencil

The statements on the facing page are qualitative data about the effectiveness of your regression.

How would you **categorize** the statements?

....

....

....

....

Sharpen your pencil
Solution

You looked closely at your customers' qualitative responses to your raise prediction algorithm. What did you find?

The statements.

Bull's-eye! I got the exact raise the algorithm predicted. I'm telling you, it's incredible. You must be some sort of genius. You rock my world.

This one's spot on!

I'm pretty pleased. My raise was 0.3% lower than expected, but it's still a solid raise. I'm pretty sure I wouldn't have gotten it if I hadn't negotiated.

This one got a raise that was close but not exactly what you predicted.

Yeah, I got no raise. Did you hear that? **0.0%** I have some ideas for you about what you can do with your algorithm.

I can't believe it! I got a 5.0% bigger raise than the algorithm predicted! My negotiation must have scared my boss, and he just started throwing money at me!

These two appear to be way off.

It looks like there are basically three types of response, qualitatively speaking. One of them got exactly what the algorithm predicted. Another received a raise that was a little off, but still close to the prediction. Two of them got raises that were way off. And the last one, well, unless there's a trend of people who can't remember what they requested there's probably not much you can make of it.

This one's just weird. It's kind of hard to draw any conclusion off a statement like this.

I got a 4.5% raise. It was a good raise. I think that's the sort of raise I deserved. I was so nervous in the meeting that I can't even remembered what I asked for.

The segments of customers

Remember, the regression equation predicts what people will hit **on average**. Obviously, not everyone is going to be exactly at the average.

Your responses

off but ok

way off!

spot on

Exercise

Let's take a few more responses from your clients. The ones below are a little more specific than the previous ones.

Draw arrows to point where each of these people would end up if you plotted their request/raise experiences on your scatterplot.

I demanded 5% and got 10%.

I requested 8%, and I got 7%.

Draw arrows to show where each of these people would show up on the scatterplot.

I asked for 25% and got 0.0%... because I was fired!

Payoffs for negotiators

Received

Requested

Do you notice anything *weird*?

....

....

....

EXERCISE SOLUTION

You just added new dots to your scatterplot to describe where three of your customers would be shown. What did you learn?

I demanded 5% and got 10%.

I requested 8%, and I got 7%.

This person would show up right in the middle of the biggest clump of observations.

This person shows up above the regression line on the far left of the chart.

This person doesn't show up on the scatterplot at all.

I asked for 25% and got 0.0%... because I was fired!

He's off the chart!

Payoffs for negotiators

Received

Requested

The guy who asked for 25% went outside the model

Using a regression equation to predict a value outside your range of data is called **extrapolation**. Beware extrapolation!

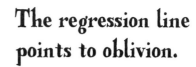

The regression line points to oblivion.

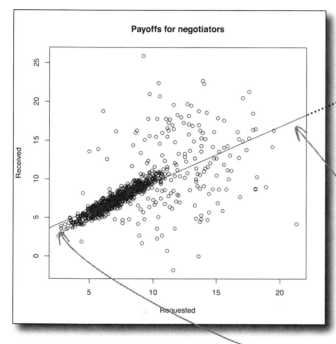

Extrapolating is predicting out here.

Interpolating is just making a prediction within these bounds.

You don't know what's going on out here. Maybe if you had more data, you could use your equation to predict what a bigger request would get.

But you'd definitely have to run your regression again on the new data to make sure you're using the right line.

Extrapolation is different from **interpolation**, where you are predicting points within your range of data, which is what regression is designed to do. Interpolation is fine, but you should be leery of extrapolation.

People extrapolate all the time. But if you're going to do it, you need to **specify additional assumptions** that make explicit your ignorance about what happens outside the data range.

What would you say to a client who is wondering what he should expect if he requested a 30% raise?

How to handle the client who wants a prediction outside the data range

You've basically got two options when your clients want a prediction outside your data range: say nothing at all, or introduce an assumption that you can use to find a prediction.

Say nothing:

No comment. If you ask for 25%, I have no idea what will happen.

You

Use an assumption to make a prediction:

The data won't really tell us, but this has been a lucrative year, so a 30% request is reasonable. I think it'll get you 20% or so.

Here's an assumption you might use to make the prediction.

You may or may not have good reason to believe this assumption!

Which of these responses would be more **beneficial to your client?** The second one might satisfy your client's desire to have a specific prediction, but a **crummy prediction might be worse than no prediction.**

there are no Dumb Questions

Q: So what exactly might happen outside the data range that's such a problem?

A: There might not even be data outside the range you're using. And if there is, the data could look totally different. It might even be nonlinear.

Q: I won't necessarily have all the points *within* my data range, though.

A: You're right, and that's a data quality and sampling issue. If you don't have all the data points—if you're using a sample—you want to make sure that the sample is representative of the overall data set and is therefore something you can build a model around.

Q: Isn't there something to be said for thinking about what would happen under different hypothetical, purely speculative situations?

A: Yes, and you should definitely do it. But it takes discipline to make sure your ideas about hypothetical worlds don't spill over into your ideas (and actions) regarding the real world. People abuse extrapolation.

Q: Isn't any sort of prediction about the *future* a type of extrapolation?

A: Yes, but whether that's a problem depends on what you're studying. Is what you're looking at the sort of thing that could totally change its behavior in the future, or is it something that is pretty stable? The physical laws of the universe probably aren't going to change much next week, but the associations that apparently explain the stock market might. These considerations should help you know how to use your model.

Always keep an eye on your model assumptions.

Watch it! *And when you're looking at anyone else's models, always think about how reasonable their assumptions are and whether they might have forgotten to mention any. Bad assumptions can make your model completely useless at best and dangerously deceptive at worst.*

BE the model
Look at this list of possible assumptions for the Raise Reckoner. How might each of these change your model, if it were true?

Economic performance has been about the same for all years in the data range, but this year we made a lot less money.

....

One boss administered all the raises in the company for the data we have, but he's left the company and been replaced by another boss.

....

How you ask makes a big difference in what kind of raise you get.

....

The spread of dots in the 20-50 percent range looks just like the spread of dots in the 10-20 percent range.

....

Only tall people ask for raises.

....

BE the model
Look at this list of possible assumptions for the Raise Reckoner. How might each of these change your model, if it were true?

Economic performance has been about the same for all years in the data range, but this year we made a lot less money.

This year's raises could be down, on average. The model might not work.

One boss administered all the raises in the company for the data we have, but he's left the company and been replaced by another boss.

The new guy might think differently and break the model.

Yikes! That'd be the end of your business, at least until you have data on the new guy!

How you ask makes a big difference in what kind of raise you get.

This is surely true, and the data reflects the variation, so the model's OK.

You don't have data on how to ask for money... the model just says what you'll get on average at different requests.

The spread of dots in the 20-50 percent range looks just like the spread of dots in the 10-20 percent range.

If this were true, you'd be able to extrapolate the regression equation.

Only tall people have asked for raises in the past.

If this were true, the model wouldn't apply to shorter people.

Shorter people might do better or worse than taller people.

Now that you've thought through how your assumptions affect your model, you need to change your algorithm **so that people know how to deal with extrapolation**.

Sharpen your pencil

You need to tweak your algorithm to instruct your clients to avoid the trap of extrapolation. What would you add?

Request

THE RAISE RECKONER

What will happen if we request a certain amount of money? Find out with this equation:

$$y = 2.3 + 0.7x$$

Where x is the amount requested, and y is the amount we can expect to receive.

Write your caveat about extrapolation here.

Raise

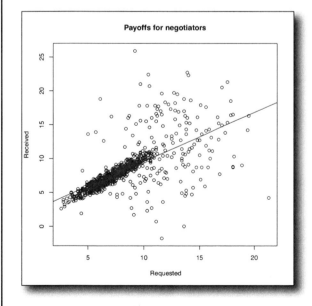

How would you **explain to your clients** that they need to avoid extrapolation?

Sharpen your pencil
Solution

How did you modify your compensation algorithm to ensure that your clients don't extrapolate beyond the data range?

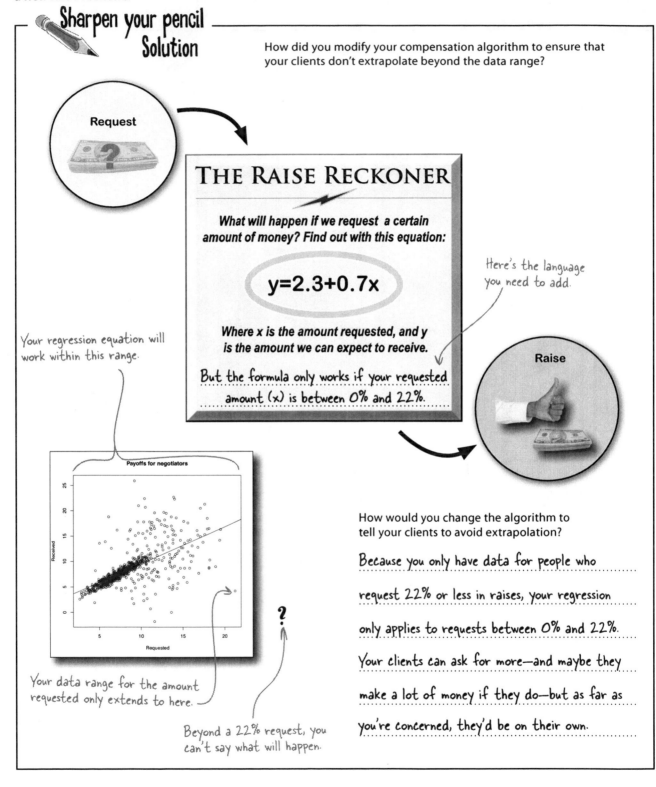

Request

THE RAISE RECKONER

What will happen if we request a certain amount of money? Find out with this equation:

$$y=2.3+0.7x$$

Where x is the amount requested, and y is the amount we can expect to receive.

But the formula only works if your requested amount (x) is between 0% and 22%.

Here's the language you need to add.

Your regression equation will work within this range.

Raise

Payoffs for negotiators

Your data range for the amount requested only extends to here.

Beyond a 22% request, you can't say what will happen.

How would you change the algorithm to tell your clients to avoid extrapolation?

Because you only have data for people who request 22% or less in raises, your regression only applies to requests between 0% and 22%. Your clients can ask for more—and maybe they make a lot of money if they do—but as far as you're concerned, they'd be on their own.

The guy who got fired because of extrapolation has cooled off

Well, at least you're fixing your analysis as you go along. That's integrity. I'll still hit you up for advice next time I'm up for a raise.

With your new-and-improved regression formula, fewer clients will run with it into the **land of statistical unknowns**.

So does that mean you're finished?

You've only solved part of the problem

There are still lots of people who got screwy outcomes, even though they requested raise amounts that were inside your data range.

What will you do about those folks?

I requested 8%, and I got 7%.

This guy got more than he asked for by a pretty big margin.

I demanded 5% and got 10%.

She asked for a common amount and got just a little bit less than she requested.

Why do you think he got 10% rather than 5%?

What does the data for the screwy outcomes look like?

Take another look at your visualization and regression line. Why don't people just get what they ask for?

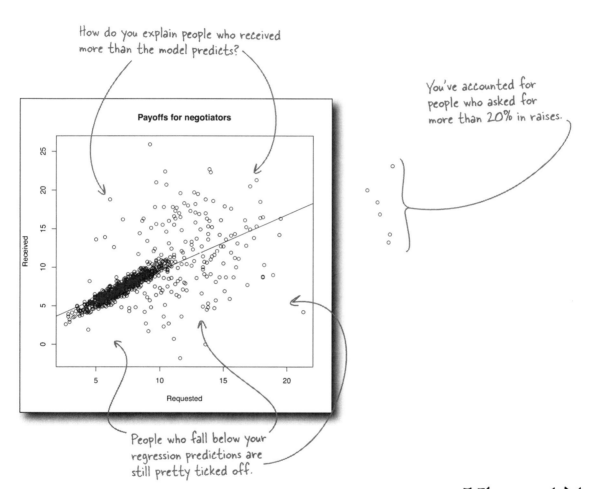

How do you explain people who received more than the model predicts?

You've accounted for people who asked for more than 20% in raises.

People who fall below your regression predictions are still pretty ticked off.

Payoffs for negotiators

Received

Requested

What could be causing these deviations from your prediction?

Chance errors are deviations from what your model predicts

You're always going to be making predictions of one sort or another, whether you do a full-blown regression or not. Those predictions are rarely going to be *exactly* correct, and the amount by which the outcomes deviate from your prediction is called **chance error**.

In statistics, chance errors are also called **residuals**, and the analysis of residuals is at the heart of good statistical modeling.

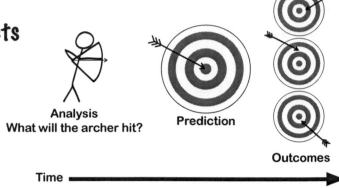

Analysis
What will the archer hit?

Prediction

Outcomes

Time ➡

While you might never have a good explanation for why individuals residuals deviate from the model, you should always look carefully at the residuals on scatterplots.

If you interpret residuals correctly, you'll better understand your data and the use of your model.

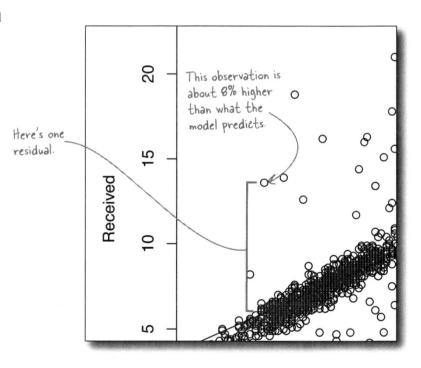

Here's one residual.

This observation is about 8% higher than what the model predicts.

You'll always have chance errors in your predictions, and you might never learn why they're in your data.

Sharpen your pencil

Better refine your algorithm some more: this time, you should probably say something about error.

Here are some possible provisions to your algorithm about chance error. Which one would you add to the algorithm?

"You probably won't get what the model predicts because of chance error."

....
....
....
....

"Your results may vary by a margin of 20 percent more or less than your predicted outcome."

....
....
....
....

"Only actual results that fit the model results are guaranteed."

....
....
....
....

"Please note that your own results may vary from the prediction because of chance error."

....
....
....
....

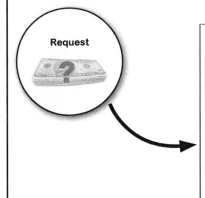

The provision you prefer will go here.

THE RAISE RECKONER

What will happen if we request a certain amount of money? Find out with this equation:

$$y = 2.3 + 0.7x$$

Where x is the amount requested, and y is the amount we can expect to receive.

But the formula only works if your requested amount (x) is between 0% and 22%.

....
....

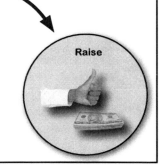

Sharpen your pencil
Solution

You refined the algorithm to incorporate chance errors. What does it say now?

"You probably won't get what the model predicts because of chance error."

This is true. Probably only a few people

will get exactly what the equation

returns. But it won't be a very satisfying

explanation for the client.

"Your results may vary by a margin of 20 percent more or less than your predicted outcome."

It's good to specify error quantitatively.

But what reason do you have to believe

the 20% figure? And if it's true,

wouldn't you want less error than that?

"Only actual results that fit the model results are guaranteed."

This is just important-sounding nonsense.

Your results are only guaranteed if they

fit the model prediction? Well what if

they don't? That's just silly.

"Please note that your own results may vary from the prediction because of chance error."

True, not terribly satisfying. Until we have

some more powerful tools, this statement

will have to do.

Request

Here's the caveat about chance error.

THE RAISE RECKONER

What will happen if we request a certain amount of money? Find out with this equation:

$$y = 2.3 + 0.7x$$

Where x is the amount requested, and y is the amount we can expect to receive.

But the formula only works if your requested amount (x) is between 0% and 22%.

Please note that your own results may vary from the prediction because of chance error.

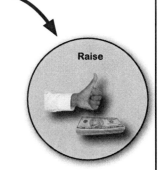

Raise

You just lost all your clients.

Hate to break it to ya, but your whole business has just fallen apart. That last line on your compensation algorithm was the difference between people feeling like you were helping them and people feeling like your product was worthless.

How are you going to fix your product?

Error is good for you and your client

The more forthcoming you are about the chance error that your clients should expect in your predictions, the better off both of you will be.

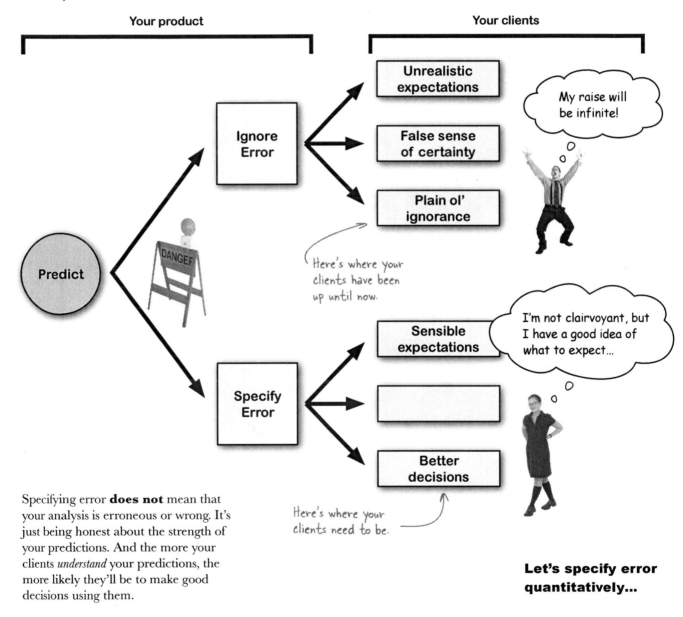

Your product

Your clients

Predict

Ignore Error

DANGER

Unrealistic expectations

False sense of certainty

Plain ol' ignorance

My raise will be infinite!

Here's where your clients have been up until now.

Specify Error

Sensible expectations

Better decisions

I'm not clairvoyant, but I have a good idea of what to expect...

Here's where your clients need to be.

Specifying error **does not** mean that your analysis is erroneous or wrong. It's just being honest about the strength of your predictions. And the more your clients *understand* your predictions, the more likely they'll be to make good decisions using them.

Let's specify error quantitatively...

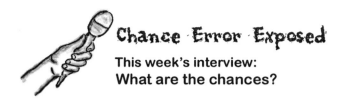

Chance Error Exposed

**This week's interview:
What are the chances?**

Head First: Man, you're a pain in the butt.

Chance Error: Excuse me?

Head First: It's just that, because of you, regression will never really be able to make good predictions.

Chance Error: *What?* I'm an indispensable part of regression in particular and any sort of measurement generally.

Head First: Well, how can anyone trust a regression prediction as long as you're a possibility? If our clients want to know how much money they'll get when they request a raise, they don't want to hear from us that it's always possible (or even likely!) that what they get will be different from what the model predicts.

Chance Error: You've got me all wrong. Think of me as someone who's always there but who isn't so scary if you just know how to talk about me.

Head First: So "error" isn't necessarily a bad word.

Chance Error: Not at all! There are so many contexts where error specification is useful. In fact, the world would be a better place if people did a better job expressing error often.

Head First: OK, so here's what I'm saying to clients right now. Say someone wants to know what they'll get if they ask for 7 percent in a raise. I say, "The model predicts 7 percent, but chance error means that you probably will get something different from it."

Chance Error: How about you say it like this. If you ask for 7 percent, you'll *probably* get between 6 percent and 8 percent. Doesn't that sound better?

Head First: That doesn't sound so scary at all! Is it really that simple?

Chance Error: Yes! Well, sort of. In fact, getting

control of error is a really big deal, and there's a huge range of statistical tools you can use to analyze and describe error. But the most important thing for you to know is that specifying a **range** for your prediction is a heck of a lot more useful (and *truthful*) than just specifying a single number.

Head First: Can I use error ranges to describe subjective probabilities?

Chance Error: You can, and you really, really should. To take another example, which of these guys is the more thoughtful analyst: one who says he believes a stock price will go up 10 percent next year, or one who says he thinks it'll go up between 0–20 percent next year?

Head First: That's a no-brainer. The first guy can't seriously mean he thinks a stock will go up *exactly* 10 percent. The other guy is more reasonable.

Chance Error: You got it.

Head First: Say, where did you say you came from?

Chance Error: OK, the news might not be so good here. A lot of times you'll have no idea where chance error comes from, especially for a single observation.

Head First: Seriously, you mean it's impossible to explain why observations deviate from model predictions?

Chance Error: Sometimes you can explain some of the deviation. For example, you might be able to group some data points together and reduce the chance error. But I'll always be there on some level.

Head First: So should it be my job to reduce you as much as possible?

Chance Error: It should be your job to make your models and analyses have as much explanatory and predictive power as you can get. And that means accounting for me intelligently, not getting rid of me.

Specify error quantitatively

It's a happy coincidence if your observed outcome is exactly what your predicted outcome is, but the real question is what is the spread of the chance error (the **residual distribution**).

What you need is a statistic that shows how far typical points or observations are, *on average*, from your regression line.

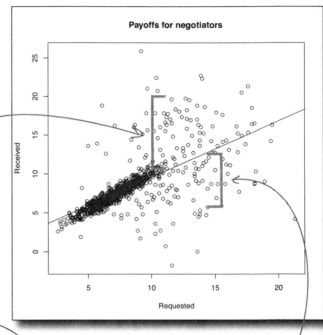

The spread or distribution of residuals around the regression line says a lot about your model.

Hey, that sounds like the standard deviation. The standard deviation describes how far typical points are from the mean observation.

The tighter your observations are around your regression line, the more powerful your line will be.

Definitely. The distribution of chance error, or R.M.S. error, around a regression line is a metric you can use just like the standard deviation around a mean.

If you have the value of the R.M.S. error for your regression line, you'll be able to use it to explain to your clients **how far away from the prediction typical outcomes will be**.

Quantify your residual distribution with Root Mean Squared error

Remember the units that you use for standard deviation? They're the same as whatever's being measured: if your standard deviation of raises received is 5 percent, then typical observations will be 5 percent away from the mean.

It's the same deal with R.M.S. error. If, say, your R.M.S. error for predicting Received from Requested is 5 percent, then the typical observation will be 5 percent away from whatever value the regression equation predicts.

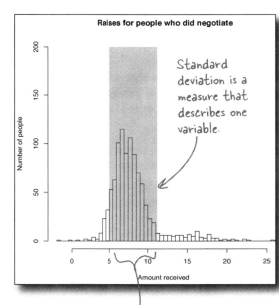

Standard deviation is a measure that describes one variable.

The standard deviation describes the spread around the mean.

The R.M.S. error describes the spread from the regression line.

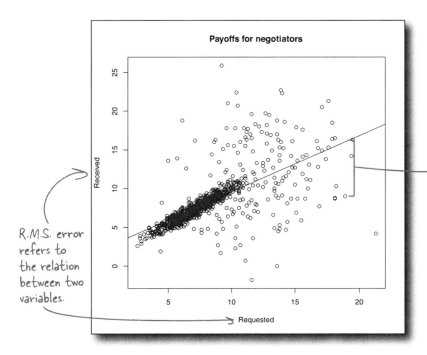

R.M.S. error refers to the relation between two variables.

So how do you calculate the R.M.S. error?

Your model in R already knows the R.M.S. error

The linear model object your created inside of R in the last chapter doesn't just know the y-axis intercept and slope of your regression line.

It has a handle on all sorts of statistics pertaining to your model, including the R.M.S. error. If you don't still have the myLm object you created in R, type in this function before the next exercise:

Make sure you have the most current data loaded.

```
employees <- read.csv("http://www.headfirstlabs.com/books/hfda/
    hfda_ch10_employees.csv", header=TRUE)

myLm <- lm(received[negotiated==TRUE]~
    requested[negotiated==TRUE], data=employees)
```

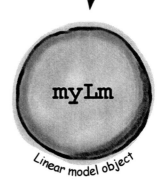

myLm

Linear model object

Under the hood, R is using this formula to calculate the R.M.S. error:

$$\sigma_y * \sqrt{1-r^2}$$

The standard deviation of y.

The correlation coefficient.

there are no Dumb Questions

Q: Do I need to memorize that formula?

A: As you'll see in just a second, it's pretty easy to calculate the R.M.S. error inside of R or any other statistical software package. What's most important for you to know is that error can be described and used quantitatively, and that you should always be able to describe the error of your predictions.

Q: Do all types of regression use this same formula to describe error?

A: If you get into nonlinear or multiple regression, you'll use different formulas to specify error. In fact, even within linear regression there are more ways of describing variation than R.M.S. error. There are all sorts of statistical tools available to measure error, depending on what you need to know specifically.

Test Drive

Instead of filling in the algebraic equation to get the R.M.S. error, let's have R do it for us.

Take a look at R's summary of your model by entering this command:

```
summary(myLm)
```

Your R.M.S. error will be in the output, but you can also type this to see the error:

```
summary(myLm)$sigma
```

The R.M.S. error is also called "sigma" or "residual standard error."

Next, color in an error band across your entire regression line to represent your R.M.S. error.

The error band should follow along the regression line and the thickness above and below the line should be equal to one R.M.S. error.

Start your error band here.

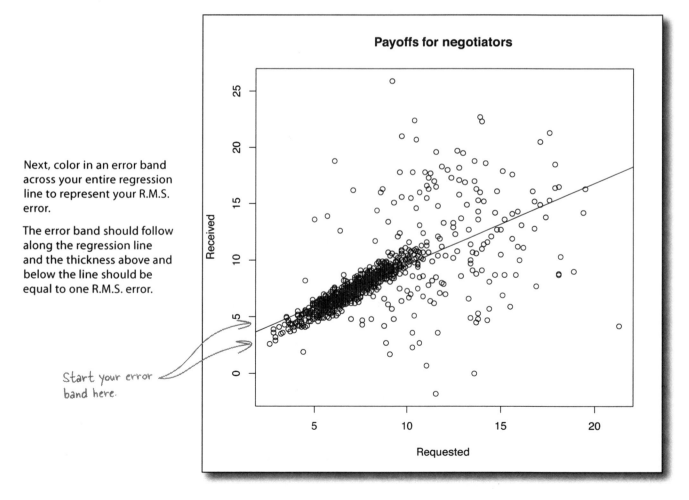

R's summary of your linear model shows your R.M.S. error

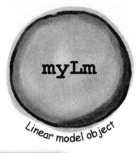

When you ask R to summarize your linear model object, it gives you a bunch of information about what's inside the object.

Here's a summary of your model.

```
> summary(myLm)

Call:
lm(formula = received[negotiated == TRUE] ~ requested[negotiated ==
    TRUE], data = employees)

Residuals:
    Min      1Q   Median      3Q      Max
-13.5560 -0.5914 -0.0601  0.3879  16.9173

Coefficients:
                                Estimate Std. Error t value Pr(>|t|)
(Intercept)                      2.31213    0.21775   10.62   <2e-16 ***
requested[negotiated == TRUE]    0.72507    0.02573   28.18   <2e-16 ***
---
Signif. codes:  0 '***' 0.001 '**' 0.01 '*' 0.05 '.' 0.1 ' ' 1

Residual standard error: 2.298 on 998 degrees of freedom
Multiple R-squared: 0.443,  Adjusted R-squared: 0.4425
F-statistic:   794 on 1 and 998 DF,  p-value: < 2.2e-16

>
```

R has all sorts of things to tell you about your linear model.

These are the slope and intercept of your regression line.

Not only do you see your regression coefficients, like you saw in the previous chapter, but you also see the R.M.S. error and a bunch of other statistics to describe the model.

And here's your R.M.S. error!

If you draw a band that's about 2.3 percentage points above and below your regression line, you get a spread that looks like this.

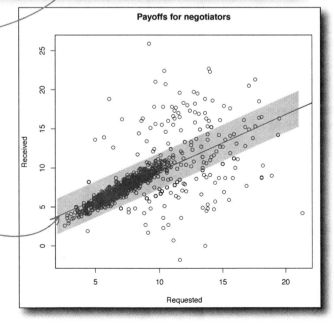

Sharpen your pencil

You're ready to have another go at your compensation algorithm.
Can you incorporate a more nuanced conception of chance error?

How would you change this algorithm to incorporate your R.M.S. error? Write
your answer inside the Raise Reckoner.

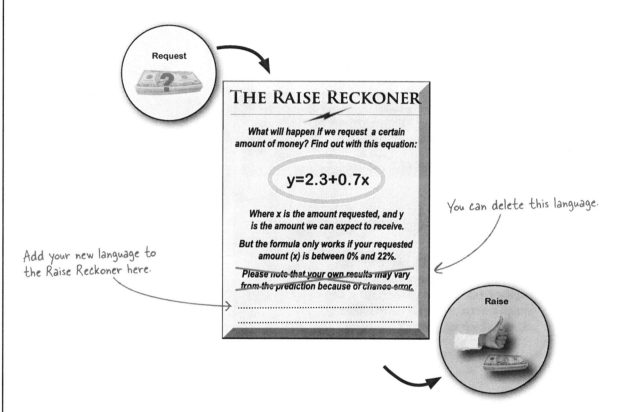

Request

THE RAISE RECKONER

*What will happen if we request a certain
amount of money? Find out with this equation:*

$$y=2.3+0.7x$$

*Where x is the amount requested, and y
is the amount we can expect to receive.*

*But the formula only works if your requested
amount (x) is between 0% and 22%.*

~~Please note that your own results may vary
from the prediction because of chance error.~~

You can delete this language.

Add your new language to
the Raise Reckoner here.

....

....

Raise

```
Signif. codes:  0 '***' 0.001

Residual standard error: 2.298
Multiple R-squared: 0.4431,  Ad
```

Use the R.M.S. error to
improve your algorithm.

Sharpen your pencil
Solution

Let's take a look at your new algorithm, complete with R.M.S. error for your regression.

Request

THE RAISE RECKONER

What will happen if we request a certain amount of money? Find out with this equation:

$$y = 2.3 + 0.7x$$

Where x is the amount requested, and y is the amount we can expect to receive.

But the formula only works if your requested amount (x) is between 0% and 22%.

Most but not all raises will be within a range of 2.5% more or less than the prediction.

Here's your new language, which incorporates the R.M.S. error.

This statement tells your clients the range they should expect their own raise to be inside of.

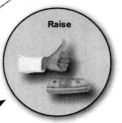

Raise

So if I ask for 7%, I'll get 4.5—9.5% back? I just need more than that if you want me to take you seriously. Can you give me a prediction with a lower amount of error, please?

She has a point.

Is there anything you can do to make this regression more useful? Can you look at your data in a way that reduces the error?

Exercise

Look at different strips on your scatterplot. Is the R.M.S. error different at the various strips along the regression line?

For each strip on the scatterplot, color in what you think the error is within that strip.

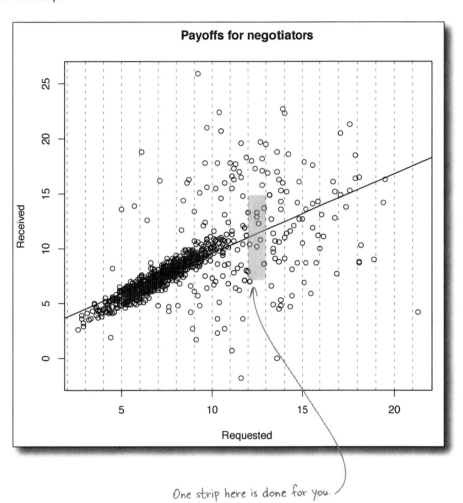

One strip here is done for you.

Do you see **segments** where the residuals are fundamentally different?

You've looked at the R.M.S. error for each strip. What did you find?

Exercise Solution

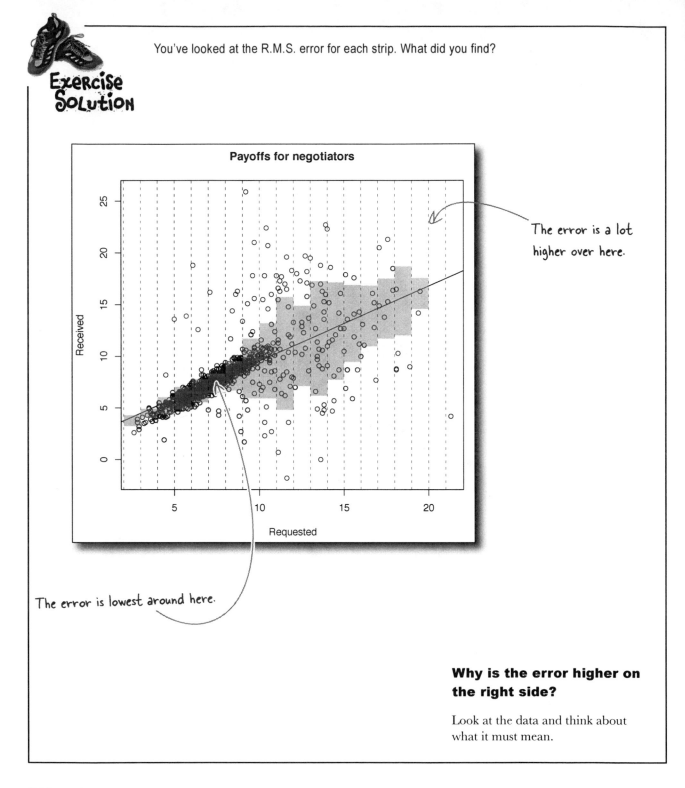

The error is a lot higher over here.

The error is lowest around here.

Why is the error higher on the right side?

Look at the data and think about what it must mean.

Jim: Oh man, that's nuts! It looks like there's a different spread of predictions for every strip along the scatterplot!

Joe: Yeah, that's crazy. Seriously. How in the world do we explain that to our customers?

Jim: They'll never buy it. If we say to them, your error is looking relatively low at 7–8 percent, but at 10–11 percent the error is through the roof, they just won't get it.

Frank: Hey, relax you guys. Maybe we should ask *why* the error bands look the way they do. It might help us understand what's happening with all these raises.

Jim: [*Scoff*] There you go being all circumspect again.

Frank: Well, we're *analysts*, right?

Joe: Fine. Let's look at what people are asking for. At the start of the scale, there's kind of a big spread that narrows as soon as we hit 5 percent or so.

Jim: Yeah, and there are only 3 people who asked for less than 5 percent, so maybe we shouldn't put too much stock in that error from 4–5 percent.

Frank: Excellent! So now we're looking at the range from 5 percent all the way up to about 10 percent. The error is lowest there.

Joe: Well, people are being conservative about what they're asking for. And their bosses are reacting, well, conservatively.

Frank: But then you get over 10 percent…

Jim: And who knows what'll happen to you. Think about it. 15 percent is a big raise. I wouldn't have the guts to request that. Who knows what my boss would do?

Frank: Interesting hypothesis. Your boss might reward you for being so bold, or she might kick your butt for being so audacious.

Jim: Once you start asking for a *lot* of money, anything can happen.

Joe: You know, guys, I think we've got two different groups of people in this data. In fact, I think we may even have two different **models**.

What would your analysis look like if you split your data?

Segmentation is all about managing error

Splitting data into groups is called **segmentation**, and you do it when having multiple predictive models for subgroups will result in less error over all than one model.

On a single model, the error estimate for people who ask for 10 percent or less is ***too high***, and the error estimate for people who ask for more than 10 percent is ***too low***!

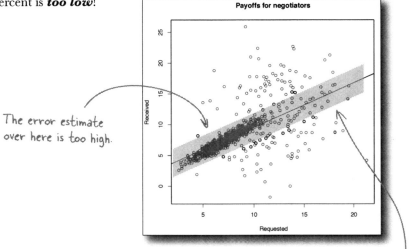

The error estimate over here is too high.

This error estimate is too low.

When we looked at the strips, we saw that the error in the two regions is quite different. In fact, segmenting the data into two groups, giving each a model, would provide a more realistic explanation of what's going on.

Segmenting your data into two groups will help you **manage error** by providing more sensible statistics to describe what happens in each region.

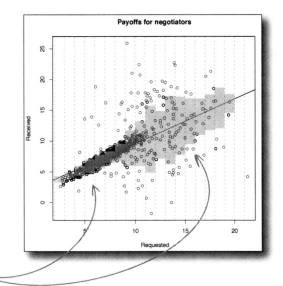

These error estimates are more realistic.

Sharpen your pencil

If you segment your data between people who requested less than 10 percent and people who requested more than 10 percent, chances are, your regression lines will look different.

Here's the split data. Draw what you think the regression lines are for these two sets of data.

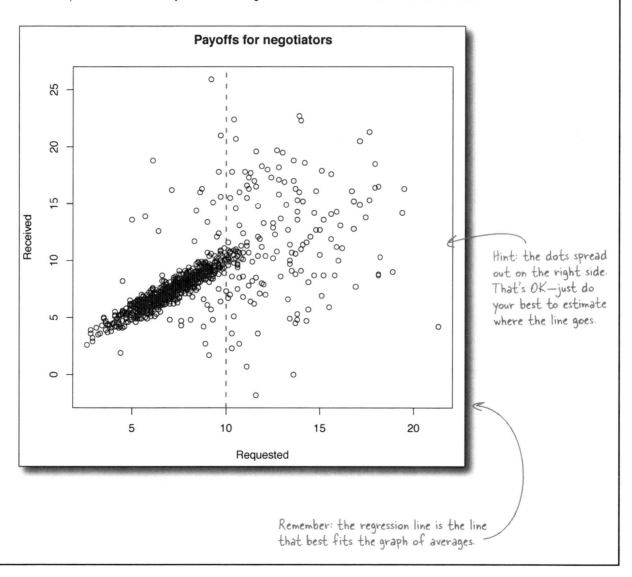

Hint: the dots spread out on the right side. That's OK—just do your best to estimate where the line goes.

Remember: the regression line is the line that best fits the graph of averages.

Sharpen your pencil
Solution

You've created two regression lines—two separate models!

What do they look like?

This line through the people who make low requests should fit the data much better than the original model.

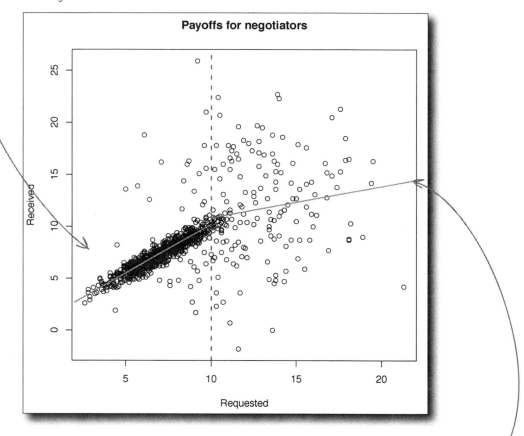

Here's your original model.

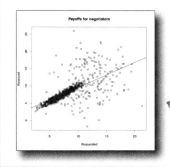

The regression line through the more aggressive negotiators should have a different slope from the other line.

Two regression lines, huh? Why not twenty? I could draw a separate regression line for each strip... how would you like that?!?

BRAIN BARBELL

This is a good one. Why stop at two regression lines? Would having more lines—a *lot* more, say—make your model more useful?

Good regressions balance explanation and prediction

Two segments in your raise regression will let you fit the data without going to the extreme of too much explanation or too much prediction. As a result, your model will be **useful**.

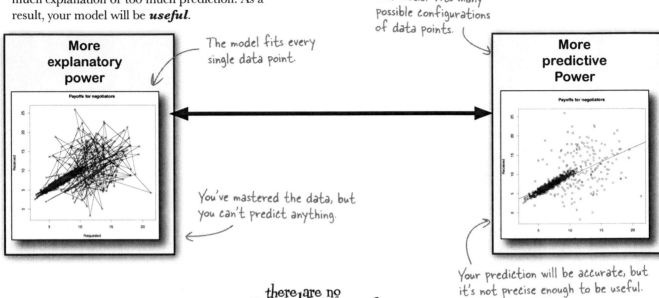

The model fits many possible configurations of data points.

The model fits every single data point.

You've mastered the data, but you can't predict anything.

Your prediction will be accurate, but it's not precise enough to be useful.

there are no
Dumb Questions

Q: **Why would I stop at splitting the data into 2 groups? Why not split them into 5 groups?**

A: If you've got a good *reason* to do it, then go right ahead.

Q: **I could go nuts and split the data into 3,000 groups. That's as many "segments" as there are data points.**

A: You certainly could. And if you did, how powerful do you think your 3,000 regressions would be at predicting people's raises?

Q: **Ummm...**

A: If you did that, you'd be able to **explain** everything. All your data points would be accounted for, and the R.M.S. error of your regression equations would all be zero. But your models would have lost all ability to **predict** anything.

Q: **So what would an analysis look like that had a whole lot of predictive power but not a lot of explanatory power?**

A: It'd look something like your first model. Say your model was this: "No matter what you ask for, you'll receive somewhere between -1,000 percent and 1,000 percent in raises."

Q: **That just sounds dumb.**

A: Sure, but it's a model that has *incredible* predictive power. The chances are that no one you ever meet will be outside that range. But the model doesn't *explain* anything. With a model like that, you sacrifice explanatory power to get predictive power.

Q: **So that's what zero error looks like: no ability to predict anything.**

A: That's it! Your analysis should be somewhere between having complete explanatory power and complete predictive power. And where you fall between those two extremes has to do with your best judgemnt as an analyst. What sort of model does your client need?

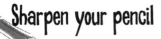 Sharpen your pencil

For each of these two models, color in bands that represent R.M.S. error.

Draw bands to describe the distribution of residuals for each model.

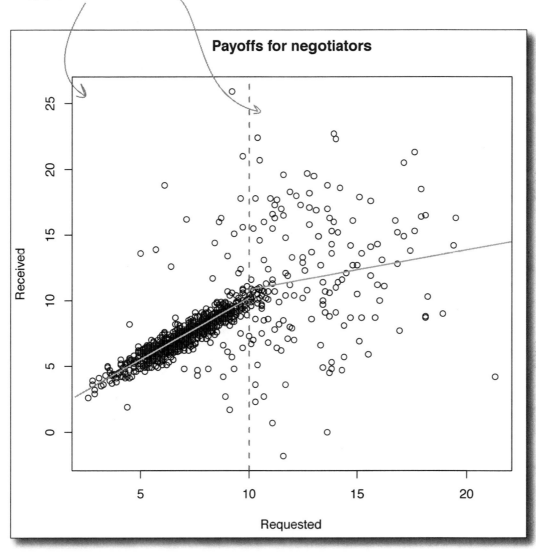

Payoffs for negotiators

Received

Requested

Your segmented models manage error better than the original model

They're more powerful because they do a better job of describing what's actually happening when people ask for raises.

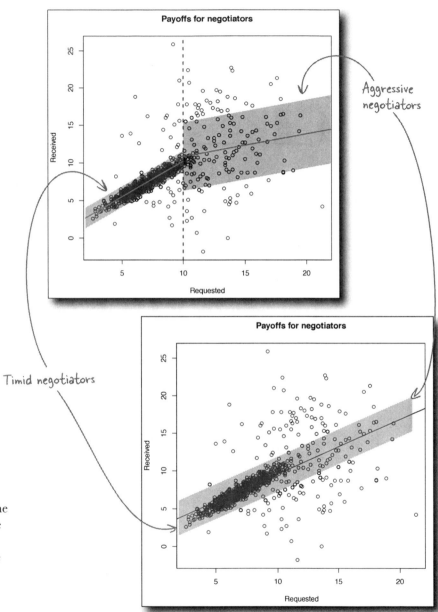

Your new model for **timid negotiators** does a better job fitting the data.

The slope of the regression line is more on target, and the R.M.S. error is lower.

Your new model for **aggressive negotiators** is a better fit, too.

The slope is more on target, and the R.M.S. error is higher, which more accurately represents what people experience when they ask for more than 10 percent.

Let's implement these models in R...

Exercise

It's time to implement those new models and segments in R. Once you have the models created, you'll be able to use the coefficients to refine your raise prediction algorithm.

Create new linear model objects that correspond to your two segments by typing the following at the command line:

This code tells R to look only at the data in your database for negotiators...

```
myLmBig <- lm(received[negotiated==TRUE & requested > 10]~
        requested[negotiated==TRUE & requested > 10],
        data=employees)
myLmSmall <- lm(received[negotiated==TRUE & requested <= 10]~
        requested[negotiated==TRUE & requested <= 10],
        data=employees)
```

...and to split the segments at the 10% raise request range.

Look at the summaries of both linear model objects using these versions of the summary() function. Annotate these commands to show what each one does:

```
summary(myLmSmall)$coefficients
summary(myLmSmall)$sigma
summary(myLmBig)$coefficients
summary(myLmBig)$sigma
```

These results will make your algorithm much more powerful.

Exercise Solution

You just ran two new regressions on segmented data. What did you find?

When you tell R to create the new models, R doesn't display anything in the console.

But quite a lot happens behind the scenes!

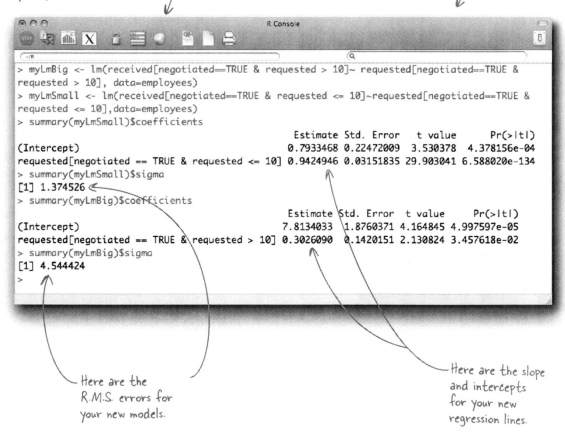

```
> myLmBig <- lm(received[negotiated==TRUE & requested > 10]~ requested[negotiated==TRUE &
requested > 10], data=employees)
> myLmSmall <- lm(received[negotiated==TRUE & requested <= 10]~requested[negotiated==TRUE &
requested <= 10],data=employees)
> summary(myLmSmall)$coefficients
                                                Estimate Std. Error  t value      Pr(>|t|)
(Intercept)                                    0.7933468 0.22472009  3.530378  4.378156e-04
requested[negotiated == TRUE & requested <= 10] 0.9424946 0.03151835 29.903041 6.588020e-134
> summary(myLmSmall)$sigma
[1] 1.374526
> summary(myLmBig)$coefficients
                                                Estimate Std. Error  t value     Pr(>|t|)
(Intercept)                                    7.8134033  1.8760371 4.164845 4.997597e-05
requested[negotiated == TRUE & requested > 10] 0.3026090  0.1420151 2.130824 3.457618e-02
> summary(myLmBig)$sigma
[1] 4.544424
>
```

Here are the R.M.S. errors for your new models.

Here are the slope and intercepts for your new regression lines.

Sharpen your pencil

You now have everything you need to create a much more powerful algorithm that will help your customers understand what to expect no matter what level of raise they request. Time to toss out the old algorithm and incorporate everything you've learned into the new one.

Using the slopes and intercepts of your new models, write the equations to describe both of them.

....

....

For what levels of raises does each model apply? ⟵   *Don't forget about avoiding extrapolation!*

....

....

How close to the prediction should your client expect her own raise to be, depending on which model she uses?   *Think about the R.M.S. error.*

....

....

Request

THE RAISE RECKONER

What will happen if we request a certain amount of money?

?

Your answers will be your new algorithm.

Raise

Sharpen your pencil
Solution

What is your final compensation algorithm?

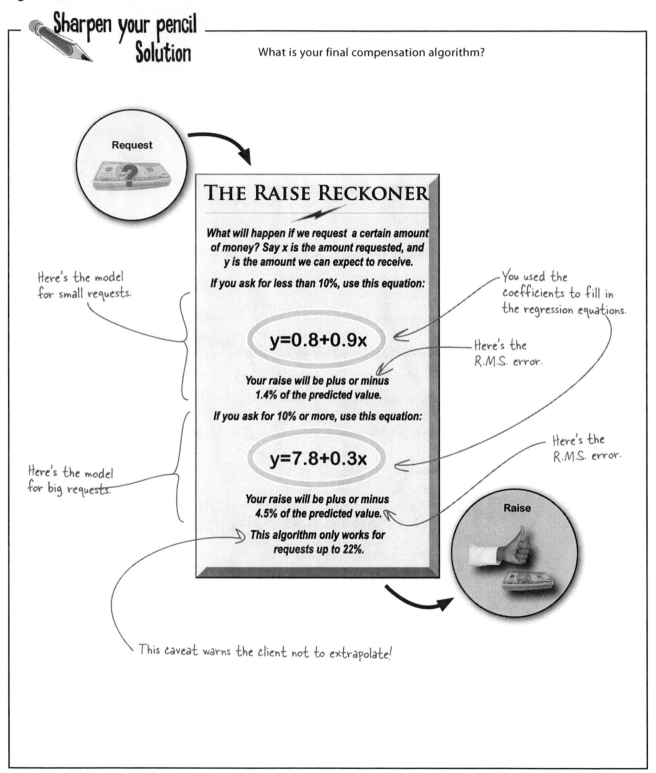

Request

Here's the model for small requests.

You used the coefficients to fill in the regression equations.

THE RAISE RECKONER

What will happen if we request a certain amount of money? Say x is the amount requested, and y is the amount we can expect to receive.

If you ask for less than 10%, use this equation:

$$y=0.8+0.9x$$

Here's the R.M.S. error.

Your raise will be plus or minus 1.4% of the predicted value.

If you ask for 10% or more, use this equation:

$$y=7.8+0.3x$$

Here's the R.M.S. error.

Here's the model for big requests.

Your raise will be plus or minus 4.5% of the predicted value.

This algorithm only works for requests up to 22%.

Raise

This caveat warns the client not to extrapolate!

Your clients are returning in droves

Your new algorithm is really starting to pay off, and everyone's excited about it.

Now people can decide whether they want to take the riskier strategy of asking for a lot of money or just would rather play it safe and ask for less.

The people who want to play it safe are getting what they want, and the risk-takers understand what they're getting into when they ask for a lot.

12 relational databases

Can you relate?

There is just one of me, but so many of them...

How do you structure really, really multivariate data?

A spreadsheet has only *two dimensions*: rows and columns. And if you have a bunch of dimensions of data, the **tabular format** gets old really quickly. In this chapter, you're about to see firsthand where spreadsheets make it really hard to manage multivariate data and learn **how relational database management systems** make it easy to store and retrieve countless permutations of multivariate data.

The Dataville Dispatch wants to analyze sales

The *Dataville Dispatch* is a popular news magazine, read by most of Dataville's residents. And the *Dispatch* has a very specific question for you: they want to tie the number of articles per issue to sales of their magazine and find an optimum number of articles to write.

They want each issue be as cost effective as possible. If putting a hundred articles in each issue doesn't get them any more sales than putting fifty articles in each issue, they don't want to do it. On the other hand, if fifty article issues correlate to *more* sales than ten article issues, they'll want to go with the fifty articles.

They'll give you **free advertising** for your analytics business for a year if you can give them a thorough analysis of these variables.

Here's the data they keep to track their operations

The *Dispatch* has sent you the data they use to manage their operations as four separate spreadsheet files. The files all relate to each other in **some way**, and in order to analyze them, you'll need to figure out how.

Looks like they keep track of a lot of stuff.

How do these data tables relate to each other?

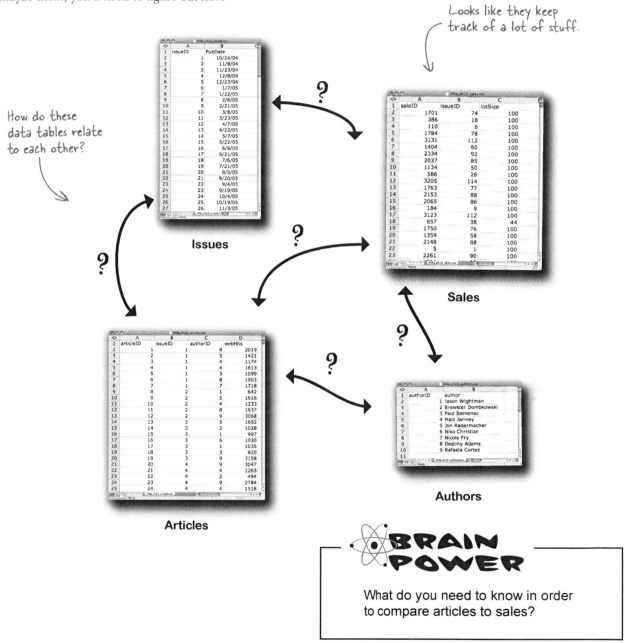

Issues

Sales

Articles

Authors

⚛ **BRAIN POWER**

What do you need to know in order to compare articles to sales?

You need to know how the data tables relate to each other

The table or tables you create to get the answers that the *Dispatch* wants will tie **article count** to **sales**.

So you need to know *how* all these tables relate to each other. What specific data fields tie them together? And beyond that, what is the **meaning** of the relationships?

Here is what the Dispatch has to say about how they maintain their data.

From: Dataville Dispatch

To: Head First

Subject: About our data

Well, each issue of the magazine has a bunch of articles, and each article has an author, so in our data we tie the authors to the articles. When we have an issue ready, we call our list of wholesalers. They place orders for each issue, which we record in our sales table. The "lot size" in the table you're looking at counts the number of copies of that issue that we sell—usually in denominations of 100, but sometimes we sell less. Does that help?

— DD

They have a lot of stuff to record, which is why they need all these spreadsheets.

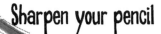
Sharpen your pencil

Draw arrows and use words to describe the relationship between the things being recorded in each spreadsheet.

Sales

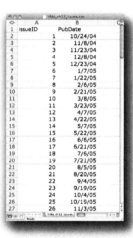

Issues

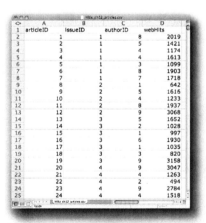

Articles

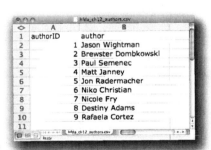

Authors

Draw arrows between the tables and describe how each relates to the other.

Sharpen your pencil
Solution

What relationships did you discover among the spreadsheets that the *Dataville Dispatch* keeps?

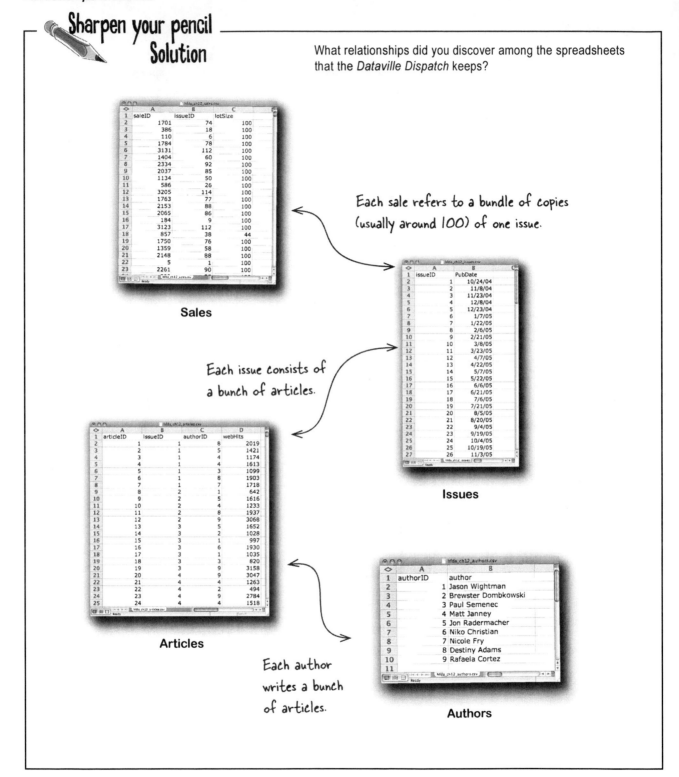

Sales

Each sale refers to a bundle of copies (usually around 100) of one issue.

Issues

Each issue consists of a bunch of articles.

Articles

Each author writes a bunch of articles.

Authors

A database is a collection of data with well-specified relations to each other

A **database** is a table or collection of tables that manage data in a way that makes these relationships explicit to each other. Database software manages these tables, and you have a lot of different choices of database software.

For organizations that collect the same type of data, out-of-the-box databases specifically manage that sort of data.

Out-of-the-box implementation

There's a ton of different kinds of database software out there.

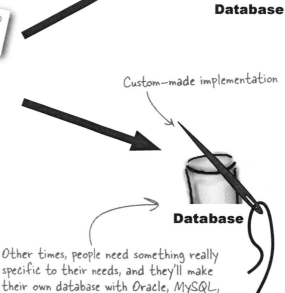

Database

Database software

Custom-made implementation

Other times, people need something really specific to their needs, and they'll make their own database with Oracle, MySQL, or something else under the hood.

Database

What's really important is that you **know the relationships** within the software of the data you want to record.

Here's the big question.

So how do you use this knowledge to calculate article <u>count</u> and sales <u>total</u> for each issue?

Trace a path through the relations to make the comparison you need

When you have a bunch of tables that are separate but linked through their data, and you have a question you want to answer that involves multiple tables, you need to trace the paths among the tables that are relevant.

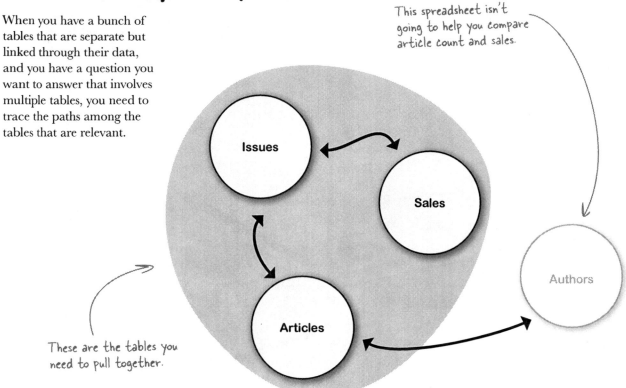

This spreadsheet isn't going to help you compare article count and sales.

These are the tables you need to pull together.

Create a spreadsheet that goes across that path

Once you know which tables you need, then you can come up with a plan to tie the data together with formulas.

Here, you need a table that compares article count and sales for each issue. You'll need to write formulas to calculate those values.

In the next exercise, you'll calculate these values.

Issue	Article count	Sales Total
1	5	1250
2	7	1800
3	8	1500
4	6	1000

You'll need formulas for these.

Exercise

Let's create a spreadsheet like the one in the facing page and start by calculating the "Article count" for each issue of the *Dispatch*.

1 Open the *hfda_ch12_issues.csv* file and save a copy for your work. Remember, you don't want to mess up an original file! Call your new file "dispatch analysis.xls".

Save this file under a new name, so you don't destroy the original data.

Load these!

www.headfirstlabs.com/books/hfda/
hfda_ch12_issues.csv

www.headfirstlabs.com/books/hfda/
hfda_ch12_articles.csv

hfda_ch12_issues.csv   dispatch analysis.xls

2 Open *hfda_ch12_articles.csv* and right-click an the tab that list the file name at the bottom of the sheet. Tell your spreadsheet to move the file to your *dispatch analysis.xls* document.

Copy your articles sheet to your new document.

3 Create a column for Article count on your issue sheet. Write a COUNTIF formula to count the number of articles for that issue, and copy and paste that formula for each issue.

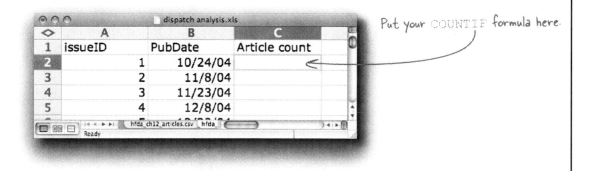

Put your COUNTIF *formula here.*

	A	B	C
1	issueID	PubDate	Article count
2	1	10/24/04	
3	2	11/8/04	
4	3	11/23/04	
5	4	12/8/04	

Exercise Solution

What sort of article count did you find each issue to have?

1 Open the **hfda_ch12_issues.csv** file and save a copy for your work. Remember, you don't want to mess up an original file! Call your new file "dispatch analysis.xls".

2 Open **hfda_ch12_articles.csv** and right-click an the tab that list the file name at the bottom of the sheet. Tell your spreadsheet to move the file to your **dispatch analysis.xls** document.

3 Create a column for Article count on your issue sheet. Write a COUNTIF formula to count the number of articles for that issue, and copy and paste that formula for each issue.

The formula looks at the "articles" tab in your spreadsheet.

=COUNTIF(hfda_ch12_articles.csv!B:B,hfda_ch12_issues.csv!A2)

It counts the number of times each issue shows up in the list of articles.

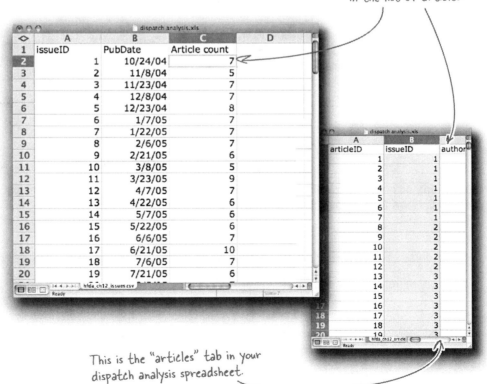

This is the "articles" tab in your dispatch analysis spreadsheet.

Cool! When you add the sales figures to your spreadsheet, keep in mind that the numbers just refer to units of the magazine, not dollars. I really just need you to measure sales in terms of the number of magazines sold, not in dollar terms.

Here's the Dispatch's managing editor.

Sounds good... let's add sales to this list!

Exercise

Load this!

Add a field for sales totals to the spreadsheet you are creating.

www.headfirstlabs.com/books/hfda/
hfda_ch12_sales.csv

1 Copy the **hfda_ch12_sales.csv** file as a new tab in your **dispatch analysis.xls**. Create a new column for Sales on the same sheet you used to count the articles.

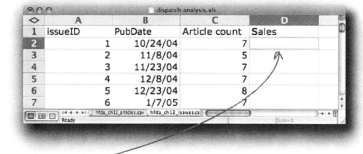

Add this column and put your new formulas here.

	A	B	C	D
1	issueID	PubDate	Article count	Sales
2		1	10/24/04	7
3		2	11/8/04	5
4		3	11/23/04	7
5		4	12/8/04	7
6		5	12/23/04	8
7		6	1/7/05	7

2 Use the SUMIF formula to tally the sales figures for issueID #1, putting the formula in cell C2. Copy that formula and then paste it for each of the other issues.

Exercise Solution

What formula did you use to add sales to your spreadsheet?

This formula shows that issue #1 sold 2,227 units.

The first argument of the SUMIF formula looks at the issues.

=SUMIF(hfda_ch12_sales.csv!B:B, hfda_ch12_issues.csv!A2, hfda_ch12_sales.csv!C:C)

dispatch analysis.xls

	A	B	C	D	E
1	issueID	PubDate	Article count	Sales	
2	1	10/24/04	7	2227	
3	2	11/8/04	5	703	
4	3	11/23/04	7	2252	
5	4	12/8/04	7	2180	
6	5	12/23/04	8	2894	
7	6	1/7/05	7	2006	
8	7	1/22/05	7	2140	
9	8	2/6/05	7	2308	
10	9	2/21/05	6	1711	
11	10	3/8/05	5	1227	
12	11	3/23/05	9	3642	
13	12	4/7/05	7	2153	
14	13	4/22/05	6	1826	
15	14	5/7/05	6	1531	
16	15	5/22/05	6	1406	
17	16	6/6/05	7	2219	
18	17	6/21/05	10	4035	

The second argument looks at the specific issue whose sales you want to count.

	A	B	C	D	E
1	saleID	issueID	lotSize		
2	1701	74	100		
3	386	18	100		
4	110	6	100		
5	1784	78	100		
6	3131	112	100		
7	1404	60	100		
8	2334	92	100		
9	2037	85	100		
10	1134	50	100		
11	586	26	100		
12	3205	114	100		
13	1763	77	100		
14	2153	88	100		
15	2065	86	100		
16	184	9	100		
17	3123	112	100		
18	857	38	100		

The third argument points to the actual sales figures you want to sum.

Your summary ties article count and sales together

This is exactly the spreadsheet you need to tell you whether there is a relationship between the number of articles that the *Dataville Dispatch* publishes every issue and their sales.

> This seems nice. But it'd be a little easier to understand if it were made into a scatterplot. Have you ever heard of scatterplots?

Definitely! Let's let him have it...

Sharpen your pencil

1 Open R and type the `getwd()` command to figure out where R keeps its data files. Then, in your spreadsheet, go to File > Save As... and save your data as a CSV into that directory.

Execute this command to load your data into R:

```
dispatch <- read.csv("dispatch analysis.csv",
      header=TRUE)
```

Name your file dispatch analysis.csv.

This function tells you R's working directory, where it looks for files.

Save your spreadsheet data as a CSV in R's working directory.

2 Once you have your data loaded, execute this function. Do you see an optimal value?

```
plot(Sales~jitter(Article.count),data=dispatch)
```

You'll see how `jitter` works in a second...

Sharpen your pencil
Solution

Did you find an optimal value in the data you loaded?

The optimum appears to be around 10 articles.

Use this command to load your CSV into R.

The `head` command shows you what you have just loaded... it's always good to check.

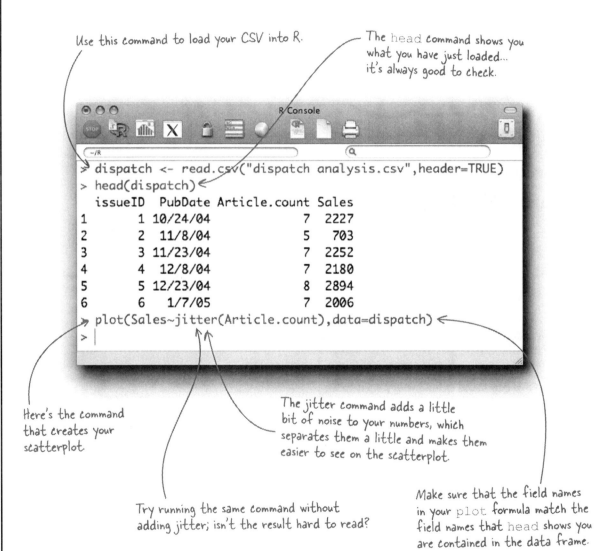

```
> dispatch <- read.csv("dispatch analysis.csv",header=TRUE)
> head(dispatch)
  issueID  PubDate Article.count Sales
1       1 10/24/04             7  2227
2       2  11/8/04             5   703
3       3 11/23/04             7  2252
4       4  12/8/04             7  2180
5       5 12/23/04             8  2894
6       6   1/7/05             7  2006
> plot(Sales~jitter(Article.count),data=dispatch)
>
```

Here's the command that creates your scatterplot.

The jitter command adds a little bit of noise to your numbers, which separates them a little and makes them easier to see on the scatterplot.

Try running the same command without adding jitter; isn't the result hard to read?

Make sure that the field names in your `plot` formula match the field names that `head` shows you are contained in the data frame.

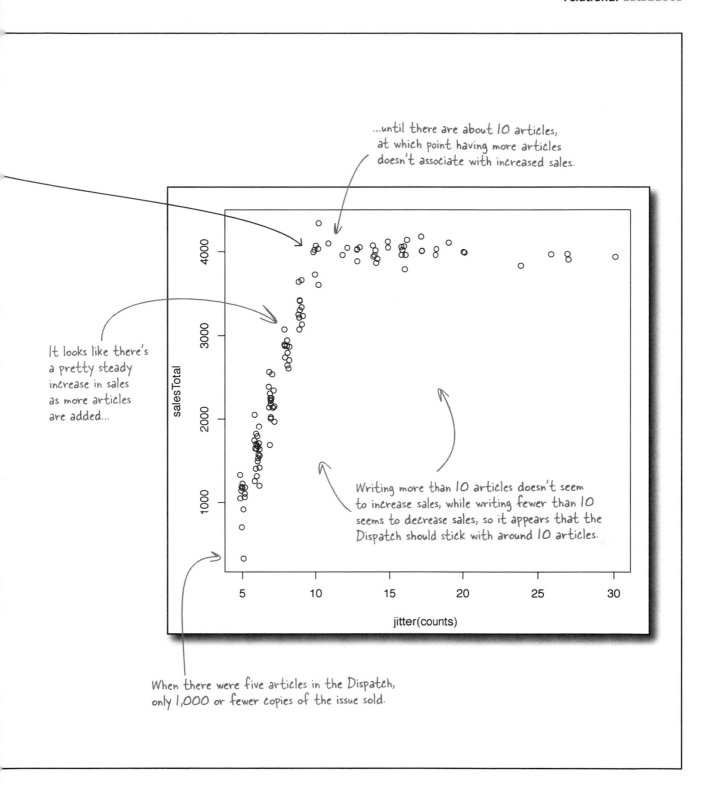

...until there are about 10 articles, at which point having more articles doesn't associate with increased sales.

It looks like there's a pretty steady increase in sales as more articles are added...

Writing more than 10 articles doesn't seem to increase sales, while writing fewer than 10 seems to decrease sales, so it appears that the Dispatch should stick with around 10 articles.

When there were five articles in the Dispatch, only 1,000 or fewer copies of the issue sold.

Looks like your scatterplot is going over really well

From: Dataville Dispatch

Subject: Thank you

Thank you! This is a really big help for us. I'd kind of suspected that a relationship like this was the case, and your analysis demonstrated it dramatically.

And congratulations on a free year of ads! It'll be our pleasure to help spread the word about your amazing skills.

I think I'm going to have a lot more questions for you like this one. Do you think you can handle the work?

— DD

Sounds like more work for you... awesome!

He's downright effusive!

there are no Dumb Questions

Q: Do people actually store data in linked spreadsheets like that?

A: Definitely. Sometimes you'll receive extracts from larger databases, and sometimes you'll get data that people have manually kept linked together like that.

Q: Basically, as long as there are those codes that the formulas can read, linking everything with spreadsheets is tedious but not impossible.

A: Well, you're not always so lucky to recieve data from multiple tables that have neat little codes linking them together. Often, the data comes to you in a messy state, and in order to make the spreadsheets work together with formulas, you need to do some clean-up work on the data. You'll learn more about how to do that in the next chapter.

Q: Is there some better software mechanism for tying data from different tables together?

A: You'd think so, right?

Copying and pasting all that data was a pain

It would suck to go through that process every time someone wanted to **query** (that is, to ask a question of) their data.

Besides, aren't computers supposed to be able to do all that grunt work for you?

Wouldn't it be dreamy if there were a way to maintain data relations in a way that'd make it easier to ask the database questions? But I know it's just a fantasy...

Relational databases manage relations for you

One of the most important and powerful ways of managing data is the RDBMS or **relational database management system**. Relational databases are a huge topic, and the more you understand them, the more use you'll be able to squeeze out of any data you have stored in them.

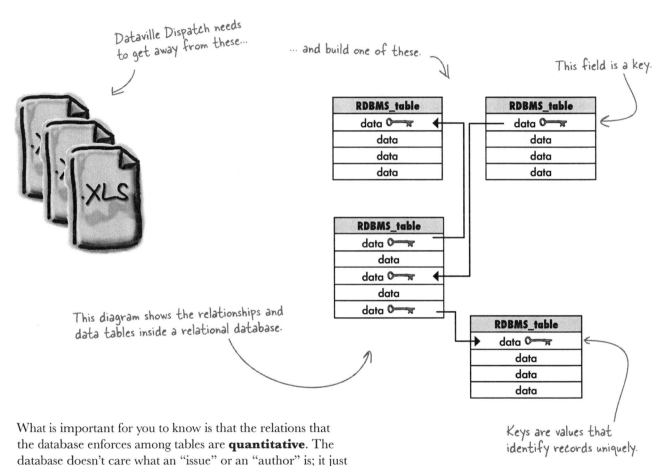

Dataville Dispatch needs to get away from these...

... and build one of these.

This field is a key.

This diagram shows the relationships and data tables inside a relational database.

Keys are values that identify records uniquely.

What is important for you to know is that the relations that the database enforces among tables are **quantitative**. The database doesn't care what an "issue" or an "author" is; it just knows that one issue has multiple authors.

Each row of the RDBMS has a unique key, which you'll often see called IDs, and it it uses the keys to make sure that these quantitative relationships are never violated. Once you have a RDBMS, watch out: well-formed relational data is a treasure trove for data analysts.

If the Dataville Dispatch had a RDBMS, it would be a lot easier to come up with analyses like the one you just did.

Dataville Dispatch built an RDBMS with your relationship diagram

It was about time that the *Dispatch* loaded all those spreadsheets into a real RDBMS. With the diagram you brainstormed, along with the managing editor's explanation of their data, a database architect pulled together this relational database.

> Now that we've found the optimum article count, we should figure out who our most popular authors are so that we can make sure they're always in each issue. You could count the web hits and comments that each article gets for each author.

Sharpen your pencil

Here is the schema for the *Dataville Dispatch*'s database. Circle the tables that you'd need to pull together into a single table in order to show which author has the articles with the most web hits and web comments.

Then draw the table below that would show the fields you'd need in order create those scatterplots.

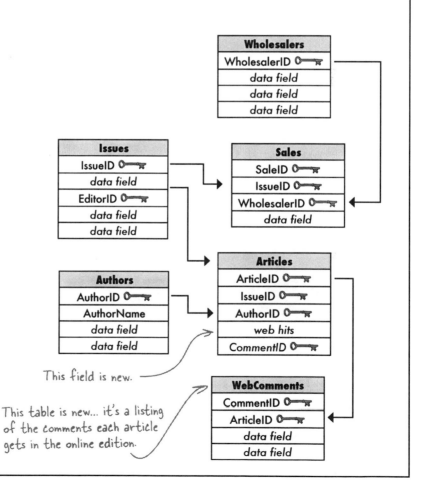

Wholesalers
| WholesalerID 0—⚷ |
| data field |
| data field |
| data field |

Issues
| IssueID 0—⚷ |
| data field |
| EditorID 0—⚷ |
| data field |
| data field |

Sales
| SaleID 0—⚷ |
| IssueID 0—⚷ |
| WholesalerID 0—⚷ |
| data field |

Authors
| AuthorID 0—⚷ |
| AuthorName |
| data field |
| data field |

Articles
| ArticleID 0—⚷ |
| IssueID 0—⚷ |
| AuthorID 0—⚷ |
| web hits |
| CommentID 0—⚷ |

This field is new.

This table is new... it's a listing of the comments each article gets in the online edition.

WebComments
| CommentID 0—⚷ |
| ArticleID 0—⚷ |
| data field |
| data field |

Draw the table you'd need to have here.

Sharpen your pencil
Solution

What tables do you need to join together so that you can evaluate each author's popularity, by counting the web hits and comments that author receives?

You need a table that draws these three tables from the database together.

In the last table you used, each row represented an issue, but now each row represents an article.

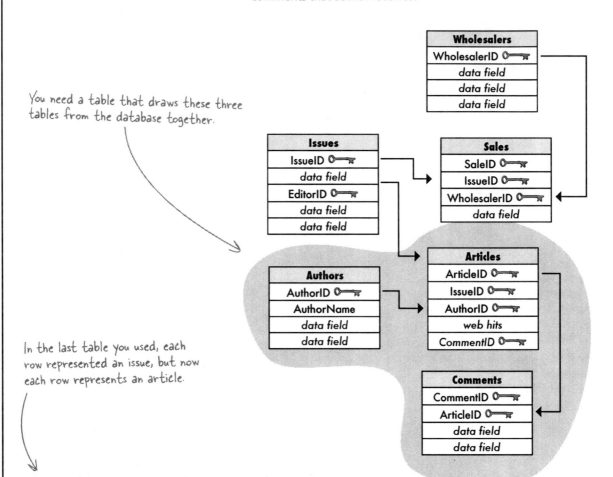

Article	Author	Web Hits	Comment Count
1	Ann	2016	20
2	Ann	2016	15
3	Cathy	2164	40
4	Jeff	749	5
5	George	749	14

Ann is the author of both articles 1 and 2 for this hypothetical table.

Dataville Dispatch extracted your data using the SQL language

SQL, or *Structured Query Language*, is how data is extracted from relational databases. You can get your database to respond to your SQL questions either by tying the code directly or using a graphical interface that will create the SQL code for you.

Here's the output from the query that gets you the table you want.

Load this!

www.headfirstlabs.com/books/hfda/ hfda_ch12_articleHitsComments.csv

Here's a simple SQL query.

```
SELECT AuthorName
     FROM Author WHERE
     AuthorID=1;
```
Example SQL Query

The query that created this data is much more complex than the example on the left.

This query returns the name of the author listed in the Author *table with the* AuthorID *field equal to* 1.

You don't have to learn SQL, but it's a good idea. What's crucial is that you understand **how to ask the right questions** of the database by **understanding the tables** inside the database and the relations among them.

Exercise

1 Use the command below to load the *hfda_ch12_ articleHitsComments.csv* spreadsheet into R, and then take a look at the data with the head command:

Make sure you're connected to the Internet for this command.

```
articleHitsComments <- read.csv(
      "http://www.headfirstlabs.com/books/hfda/
      hfda_ch12_articleHitsComments.csv",header=TRUE)
```

2 We're going to use a more powerful function to create scatterplots this time. Using these commands, load the lattice package and then run the xyplot formula to draw a "lattice" of scatterplots:

```
library(lattice)
xyplot(webHits~commentCount|authorName,data=articleHitsComments)
```

This is a new symbol!

This is the data frame that you loaded.

3 What author or authors perform the best, based on these metrics?

Exercise Solution

What do your scatterplots show? Do certain authors get greater sales?

1   Load the *hfda_ch12_articleHitsComments.csv* spreadsheet into R.

2   We're going to use a more powerful function to create scatterplots this time. Using these commands, load the `lattice` package and then run the `xyplot` formula to draw a "lattice" of scatterplots:

```
library(lattice)
xyplot(webHits~commentCount|authorName,data=articleHitsComments)
```

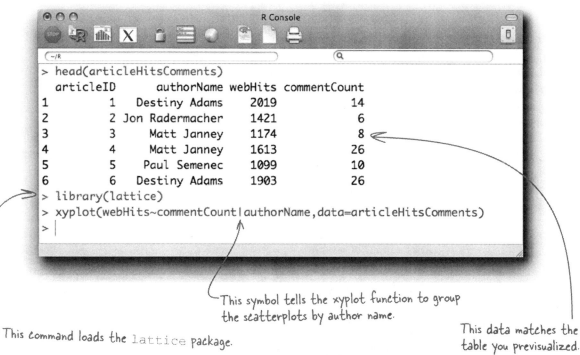

> head(articleHitsComments)
```
   articleID        authorName webHits commentCount
1          1     Destiny Adams    2019           14
2          2 Jon Radermacher    1421            6
3          3      Matt Janney    1174            8
4          4      Matt Janney    1613           26
5          5     Paul Semenec    1099           10
6          6     Destiny Adams    1903           26
```
> library(lattice)
> xyplot(webHits~commentCount|authorName,data=articleHitsComments)
>

This symbol tells the xyplot function to group the scatterplots by author name.

This command loads the `lattice` package.

This data matches the table you previsualized.

Article	Author	Web Hits	Comment Count
1	Ann	2016	20
2	Ann	2016	15
3	Cathy	2164	40
4	Jeff	749	5
5	George	749	14

This array of scatterplots shows web hits and comments for each article, grouped by author.

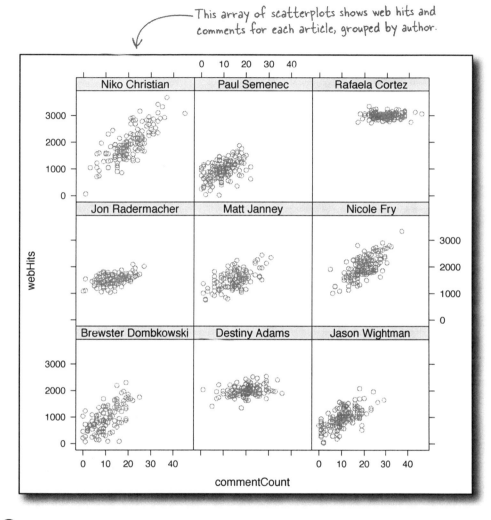

The web stats are all over the map, with authors performing very differently from each other.

3 What author or authors perform the best on these metrics?

It's pretty clear that Rafaela Cortez performs the best. All her articles have 3,000 or more web

hits, and host of them show more than 20 comments. People seem really to like her. As for the

rest of the authors, some (like Destiny and Nicole) tend to do better than the rest. Niko has a

pretty big spread in his performance, while Brewster and Jason tend not to be too popular.

From:Dataville Dispatch

Subject: About our data

Wow, that really surprised me. I'd always suspected that Rafaela and Destiny were our star writers, but this shows that they're way ahead of everyone. Big promotion for them! All this information will make us a much leaner publication while enabling us to better reward our authors' performance. Thank you.

— DD

Here's what the managing editor has to say about your most recent analysis.

Comparison possibilities are endless if your data is in a RDBMS

Think about how far you can reach across this sea of tables to make a brilliant comparison!

The complex visualization you just did with data from the *Dispatch*'s RDMS just scratches the tip of the iceberg. Corporate databases can get big—really, really big. And what that means for you as an analyst is that the range of comparisons relational databases give you the ability to make is just **enormous**.

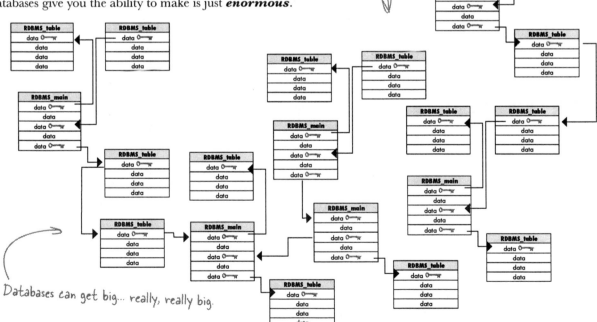

Databases can get big... really, really big.

If you can envision it, a RDBMS can tie data together for powerful comparisons. Relational databases are a dream come true for analysts

The Dataville Dispatch's database structure isn't anywhere near this complex, but databases easily get this large.

You're on the cover

The authors and editors of the *Dataville Dispatch* was so impressed by your work that they decided to feature you in their big data issue! Nice work job. Guess who wrote the big story?

Australian Dog Has His Day
Dingo and Emu have been reunited thanks to HF Physics

Rails Apps In High Places

Abducted Dog Paris Sighting
Who new PHP and MySQL could find pets

DATAVILLE DISPATCH

Analyst Shows Future of Data with RDBMS and Lattice Scatterplot Visualizations

By Rafaela Cortez and Destiny Adams

YoUR face HeRe

> I can't believe we had this data all along but never could figure out how to use it. Thank you so much.

Looks like you made some friends on the writing staff!

13 cleaning data

Impose order

I do my best work when everything's where it's supposed to be.

Your data is useless...

...if it has messy structure. And a lot of people who *collect* data do a crummy job of maintaining a neat structure. If your data's not neat, you can't slice it or dice it, run formulas on it, or even really *see* it. You might as well just ignore it completely, right? Actually, you can do better. With a **clear vision** of how you need it to look and a few **text manipulation tools**, you can take the funkiest, craziest mess of data and **whip** it into something useful.

Just got a client list from a defunct competitor

Your newest client, Head First Head Hunters, just received a **list of job seekers** from a defunct competitor. They had to spend big bucks to get it, but it's hugely valuable. The people on this list are the best of the best, the most employable people around.

This list could be a gold mine…

Load this!

www.headfirstlabs.com/books/hfda/
hfda_ch13_raw_data.csv

Look at all this stuff!

What are you going to do with this data?

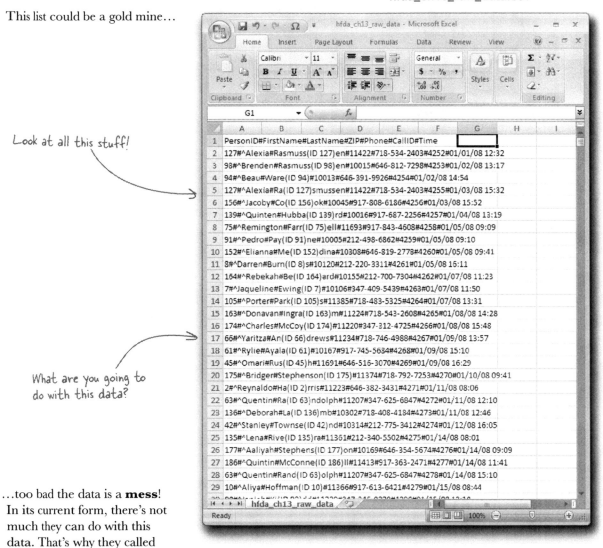

…too bad the data is a **mess**! In its current form, there's not much they can do with this data. That's why they called you. Can you help?

The dirty secret of data analysis

The dirty secret of data analysis is that as analyst you might spend more time *cleaning* data than *analyzing* it. Data often doesn't arrive perfectly organized, so you'll have to do some heavy text manipulation to get it into a useful format for analysis.

This is the fun part of data analysis.

The visionary at work

But your work as a data analyst may actually involve a lot of this...

Sharpen your pencil

What will be your ***first step*** for dealing with this messy data? Take a look at each of these possibilities and write the pros and cons of each.

1 Start retyping it.

....

....

2 Ask the client what she wants to *do* with the data once it's cleaned.

....

....

3 Write a formula to whip the data into shape.

....

....

Sharpen your pencil
Solution

Which of these options did you choose as your first step?

1 Start retyping it.

This sucks. It'll take forever, and there's a good chance I'll transcribe it incorrectly, messing up the data. If this is the only way to fix the data, we'd better be sure before going this route.

2 Ask the client what she wants to *do* with the data once it's cleaned.

This is the way to go. With an idea of what the client wants to do with the data, I can make sure that whatever I do puts the data in exactly the form that they need.

3 Write a formula to whip the data into shape.

A powerful formula or two would definitely help out, once we have an idea of what the data needs to look like from the client. But let's talk to the client first.

Head First Head Hunters wants the list for their sales team

> We need a call list for our sales team to use to contact prospects we don't know. The list is of job seekers who have been placed by our old competitor, and we want to be the ones who put them in their next job.

Even though the raw data is a mess, it looks like they just want to extract names and phone numbers. Shouldn't be too much of a problem. Let's get started...

Sharpen your pencil

The data looks like a list of names, which is what we'd expect from the client's description of it. What you need is a clean layout of those names.

Draw a picture that shows some columns and sample data for what you *want* the messy data to look like.

Looks like these are field headings up top.

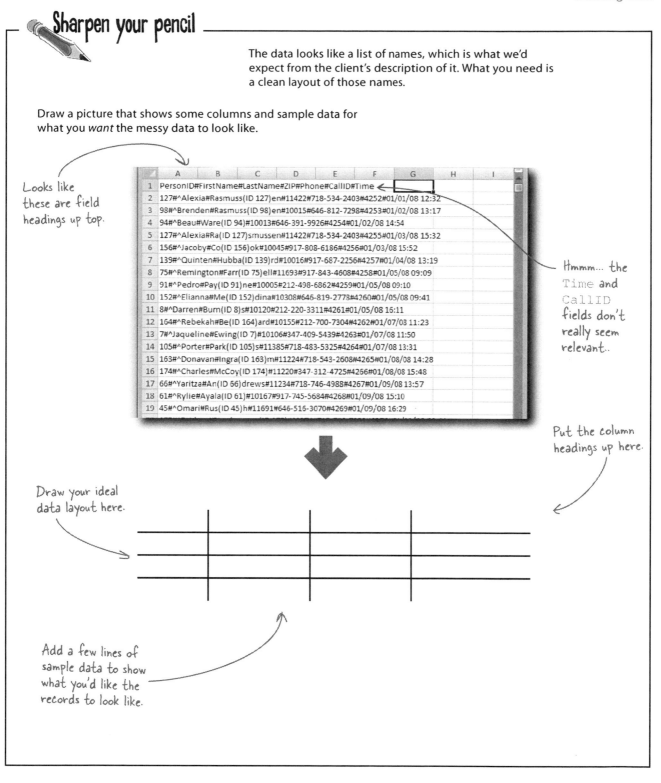

Hmmm... the `Time` and `CallID` fields don't really seem relevant..

Put the column headings up here.

Draw your ideal data layout here.

Add a few lines of sample data to show what you'd like the records to look like.

Sharpen your pencil
Solution

How would you like your data to look once you've cleaned it up?

You can see the information you want that's been all mashed together in Column A...

...what you need is for that information to be split into columns.

	A	B	C	D	E	F	G	H	I
1	PersonID#FirstName#LastName#ZIP#Phone#CallID#Time								
2	127#^Alexia#Rasmuss(ID 127)en#11422#718-534-2403#4252#01/01/08 12:32								
3	98#^Brenden#Rasmuss(ID 98)en#10015#646-812-7298#4253#01/02/08 13:17								
4	94#^Beau#Ware(ID 94)#10013#646-391-9926#4254#01/02/08 14:54								
5	127#^Alexia#Ra(ID 127)smussen#11422#718-534-2403#4255#01/03/08 15:32								
6	156#^Jacoby#Co(ID 156)ok#10045#917-808-6186#4256#01/03/08 15:52								
7	139#^Quinten#Hubba(ID 139)rd#10016#917-687-2256#4257#01/04/08 13:19								
8	75#^Remington#Farr(ID 75)ell#11693#917-843-4608#4258#01/05/08 09:09								
9	91#^Pedro#Pay(ID 91)ne#10005#212-498-6862#4259#01/05/08 09:10								
10	152#^Elianna#Me(ID 152)dina#10308#646-819-2778#4260#01/05/08 09:41								
11	8#^Darren#Burn(ID 8)s#10120#212-220-3311#4261#01/05/08 16:11								
12	164#^Rebekah#Be(ID 164)ard#10155#212-700-7304#4262#01/07/08 11:23								
13	7#^Jaqueline#Ewing(ID 7)#10106#347-409-5439#4263#01/07/08 11:50								
14	105#^Porter#Park(ID 105)s#11385#718-483-5325#4264#01/07/08 13:31								
15	163#^Donavan#Ingra(ID 163)m#11224#718-543-2608#4265#01/08/08 14:28								
16	174#^Charles#McCoy(ID 174)#11220#347-312-4725#4266#01/08/08 15:48								
17	66#^Yaritza#An(ID 66)drews#11234#718-746-4988#4267#01/09/08 13:57								
18	61#^Rylie#Ayala(ID 61)#10167#917-745-5684#4268#01/09/08 15:10								
19	45#^Omari#Rus(ID 45)h#11691#646-516-3070#4269#01/09/08 16:29								

When everything's separate, you can sort the data by field, filter it, or pipe it to a mail merge or web page or whatever else.

Gotta have the phone numbers... that's the most important thing for the sales team!

PersonID	FirstName	LastName	Phone
127	Alexia	Rasmussen	718-534-2403
98	Brenden	Rasmussen	646-812-7298
[Etc...]	[Etc...]	[Etc...]	[Etc...]

You need the name and phone fields separated from each other.

This ID field is useful, since it will let you make sure that the records are unique.

News flash! The data's still a mess. How are we going to fix it?

It's true: thinking about what neat data looks like won't actually make it neat. But we needed to previsualize a solution before getting down into the messy data. Let's take a look at our **general strategy** for fixing messy data and then **start coding it**…

Cleaning messy data is all about preparation

It may go without saying, but cleaning data should begin like any other data project: making sure you have copies of the original data so that you can go back and check your work.

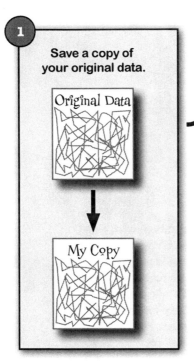

1 Save a copy of your original data.

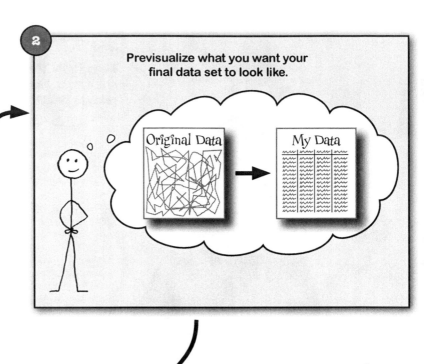

2 Previsualize what you want your final data set to look like.

Already did this!

Once you've figured out what you need your data to look like, you can then proceed to **identify patterns in the messiness**.

The last thing you want to do is go back and change the data line by line—that would take forever—so if you can identify repetition in the messiness you can write formulas and functions that exploit the patterns to make the data neat.

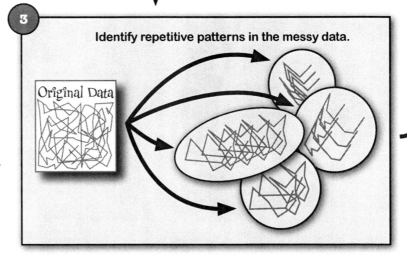

3 Identify repetitive patterns in the messy data.

Once you're organized, you can fix the data itself

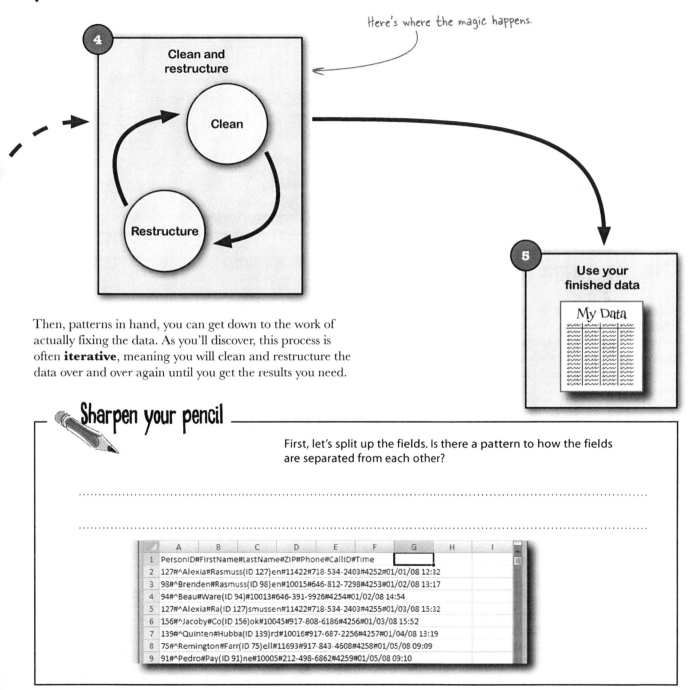

Here's where the magic happens.

4 Clean and restructure

Clean

Restructure

5 Use your finished data

My Data

Then, patterns in hand, you can get down to the work of actually fixing the data. As you'll discover, this process is often **iterative**, meaning you will clean and restructure the data over and over again until you get the results you need.

Sharpen your pencil

First, let's split up the fields. Is there a pattern to how the fields are separated from each other?

....

....

	A	B	C	D	E	F	G	H	I
1	PersonID#FirstName#LastName#ZIP#Phone#CallID#Time								
2	127#^Alexia#Rasmuss(ID 127)en#11422#718-534-2403#4252#01/01/08 12:32								
3	98#^Brenden#Rasmuss(ID 98)en#10015#646-812-7298#4253#01/02/08 13:17								
4	94#^Beau#Ware(ID 94)#10013#646-391-9926#4254#01/02/08 14:54								
5	127#^Alexia#Ra(ID 127)smussen#11422#718-534-2403#4255#01/03/08 15:32								
6	156#^Jacoby#Co(ID 156)ok#10045#917-808-6186#4256#01/03/08 15:52								
7	139#^Quinten#Hubba(ID 139)rd#10016#917-687-2256#4257#01/04/08 13:19								
8	75#^Remington#Farr(ID 75)ell#11693#917-843-4608#4258#01/05/08 09:09								
9	91#^Pedro#Pay(ID 91)ne#10005#212-498-6862#4259#01/05/08 09:10								

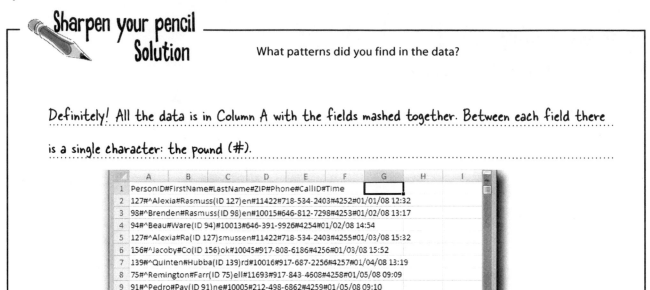

Sharpen your pencil
Solution

What patterns did you find in the data?

Definitely! All the data is in Column A with the fields mashed together. Between each field there is a single character: the pound (#).

Use the # sign as a delimiter

Excel has a handy tool for splitting data into columns when the fields are separated by a **delimiter** (the technical term for a character that makes the space between fields). Select Column A in your data and press the Text to Columns button under the Data tab...

Select Column A and click this button.

Tell Excel you have a delimiter.

Specify the delimiter.

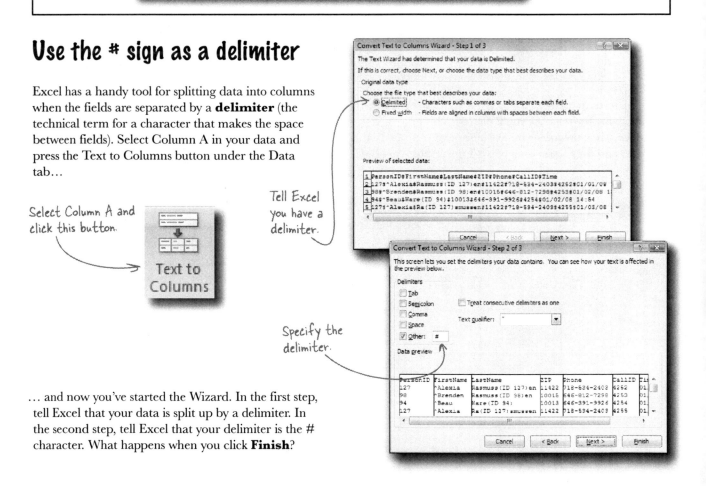

... and now you've started the Wizard. In the first step, tell Excel that your data is split up by a delimiter. In the second step, tell Excel that your delimiter is the # character. What happens when you click **Finish**?

Excel split your data into columns using the delimiter

And it was no big deal. Using Excel's Convert Text to Column Wizard is a great thing to do if you have simple delimiters separating your fields.

But the data still has a few problems. The first and last names, for example, both appear to have junk characters inside the fields. You'll have to come up with a way to get rid of them!

The data is now neatly separated into columns.

Now that the pieces of data are separated, you can manipulate them individually if you want to.

What are you going to do to fix the `FirstName` *field?*

What about the `LastName` *field?*

	A	B	C	D	E	F	G
1	PersonID	FirstName	LastName	ZIP	Phone	CellID	Time
2	127	^Alexia	Rasmuss(ID 127}en	11422	718-534-2403	4252	1/1/2008 12:32
3	98	^Brenden	Rasmuss(ID 98}en	10015	646-312-7298	4253	1/2/2008 13:17
4	94	^Beau	Ware(ID 94)	10013	646-391-9926	4254	1/2/2008 14:54
5	127	^Alexia	Ra{ID 127}smussen	11422	719-534-2403	4255	1/3/2008 15:32
6	156	^Jacoby	Co{ID 156}ok	10045	917-308-6186	4256	1/3/2008 15:52
7	139	^Quinten	Hubba(ID 139}rd	10016	917-687-2256	4257	1/4/2008 13:19
8	75	^Remington	Farri(ID 75}ell	11693	917-843-4609	4258	1/5/2008 9:09
9	91	^Pedro	Pav{ID 91}ne	10005	212-498-6862	4259	1/5/2008 9:10
10	152	^Elianna	Me{ID 152}dina	10803	646-819-2778	4260	1/5/2008 9:41
11	8	^Darren	Burn(ID 8}s	10120	212-220-3311	4261	1/5/2008 16:11
12	164	^Rebekah	Be{ID 164}ard	10155	212-700-7304	4262	1/7/2008 11:23
13	7	^Jaqueline	Ewing(ID 7)	10106	347-409-5439	4263	1/7/2008 11:50
14	105	^Porter	Park{ID 105}s	11355	718-485-5325	4264	1/7/2008 13:31
15	163	^Donavan	Ingra(ID 163}m	11224	718-543-2608	4265	1/8/2008 14:28
16	174	^Charles	McCoy(ID 174}	11220	347-312-4725	4266	1/8/2008 15:48
17	66	^Yantza	An{ID 66}drews	11234	718-746-4988	4267	1/9/2008 13:57
18	61	^Rylie	Ayala(ID 61)	10167	917-745-5684	4268	1/9/2008 15:10
19	45	^Omari	Rus(ID 45}h	11691	646-516-3070	4269	1/9/2008 16:29
20	175	^Bridger	Stephenson{ID 175)	11374	718-792-7253	4270	1/10/2008 9:41
21	2	^Reynaldo	Ha{ID 2)rris	11225	646-382-3431	4271	1/11/2008 8:06
22	63	^Quentin	Ra{ID 63}ndolph	11207	347-625-6847	4272	1/11/2008 12:10
23	136	^Deborah	La(ID 136}mb	10302	718-408-4184	4273	1/11/2008 12:46
24	42	^Stanley	Townse(ID 42}nd	10314	212-775-3412	4274	1/12/2008 16:05
25	135	^Lena	Rive(ID 135}ra	11361	212-340-5502	4275	1/14/2008 8:01
26	177	^Aaliyah	Stephens(ID 177}on	10169	646-354-5674	4276	1/14/2008 9:09
27	186	^Quintin	McConne(ID 186}ll	11413	917-363-2471	4277	1/14/2008 11:41
28	63	^Quentin	Rand(ID 63}olph	11207	347-625-6847	4278	1/14/2008 15:10
29	10	^Aliya	Hoffman(ID 10)	11366	917-913-6421	4279	1/15/2008 8:44
30	90	^Janiah	Ki(ID 90}dd	11220	347-346-5229	4280	1/15/2008 13:10

hfda_ch13_raw_data

Sharpen your pencil

What's the pattern you'd use to fix the `FirstName` column?

....

....

Sharpen your pencil Solution

Is there a pattern to the messiness in the FirstName field?

At the beginning of every name there is a ^ character. We need to get rid of all of them in order to have neat first names.

^FirstName

This character is just in our way.

Here's the useful stuff.

B
FirstName
^Alexia
^Brenden
^Beau
^Alexia
^Jacoby
^Quinten
^Remington
^Pedro
^Elianna
^Darren
^Rebekah
^Jaqueline
^Porter
^Donavan

B
FirstName
Alexia
Brenden
Beau
Alexia
Jacoby
Quinten
Remington
Pedro
Elianna
Darren
Rebekah
Jaqueline
Porter
Donavan

This character is everywhere!

You need some software tool to pull out all the carat characters.

Let's see what Excel has for us…

WHO DOES WHAT?

Match each Excel text formula with its function. Which function do you think you'll need to use the clean up the Name column?

FIND   Tells you the length of a cell.

LEFT   Returns a numerical value for a number stored as text.

RIGHT   Grabs characters on the right side of a cell.

TRIM   Replaces text you don't want in a cell with new text that you specify.

LEN   Tells you where to find a search string within a cell.

CONCATENATE   Takes two values and sticks them together.

VALUE   Grabs characters on the left side of a cell.

SUBSTITUTE   Removes excess blank spaces from a cell.

WHO DOES WHAT? SOLUTION

Match each Excel text formula with its function. Which function do
you think you'll need to use the clean up the Name column?

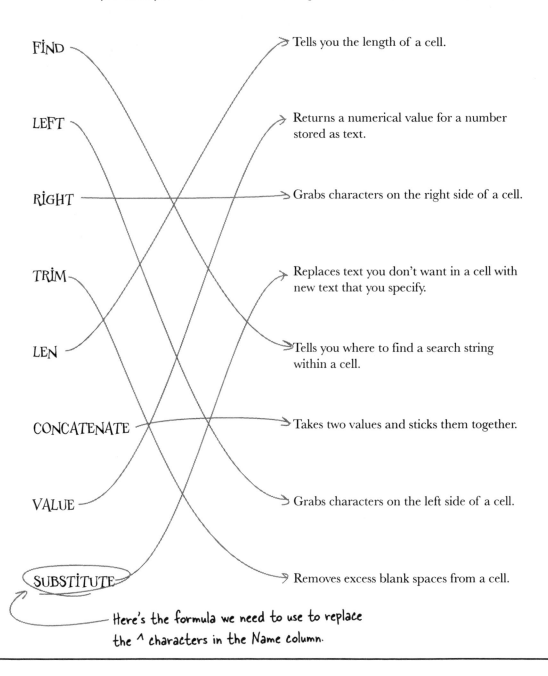

FIND — Tells you the length of a cell.

LEFT — Returns a numerical value for a number stored as text.

RIGHT — Grabs characters on the right side of a cell.

TRIM — Replaces text you don't want in a cell with new text that you specify.

LEN — Tells you where to find a search string within a cell.

CONCATENATE — Takes two values and sticks them together.

VALUE — Grabs characters on the left side of a cell.

SUBSTITUTE — Removes excess blank spaces from a cell.

Here's the formula we need to use to replace
the ^ characters in the Name column.

Use SUBSTITUTE to replace the carat character

Do this!

1 To fix the `FirstName` field, type this formula into cell H2:

`=SUBSTITUTE(B2,"^","")`

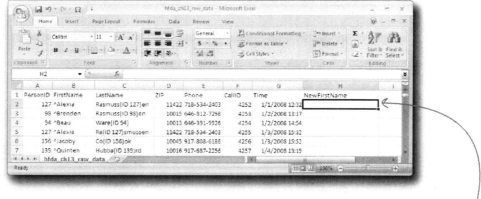

2 Copy this formula and paste it all the way down to the end of the data in Column H. What happens?

Put the formula here.

there are no Dumb Questions

Q: Am I limited to just these formulas? What if I want to take the characters on the left and right of a cell and stick them together? It doesn't look there's a formula that does just that.

A: There isn't, but if you nest the text functions inside of each other you can achieve much more complicated text manipulations. For example, if you wanted to take the first and last characters inside of cell A1 and stick them together, you'd use this formula:

```
CONCATENATE(LEFT(A1,1),
    RIGHT(A1,1))
```

Q: So I can nest a whole bunch of text formulas inside of each other?

A: You can, and it's a powerful way to manipulate text. There's a problem, though: if your data is really messy and you have to nest a whole bunch of formulas inside of each other, your entire formula can be almost impossible to read.

Q: Who cares? As long as it works, I'm not going to be reading it anyway.

A: Well, the more complex your formula, the more likely you'll need to do subtle tweaking of it. And the less readable your formula is, the harder that tweaking will be.

Q: Then how do I get around the problem of formulas that are big and unreadable?

A: Instead of packing all your smaller formulas into one big formula, you can break apart the small formulas into different cells and have a "final" formula that puts them all together. That way, if something is a little off, it'll be easier to find the formula that needs to be tweaked.

Q: You know, I bet R has much more powerful ways of doing text manipulation.

A: It does, but why bother learning them? If Excel's `SUBSTITUTE` formula handles your issue, you can save your self some time by skipping R.

You cleaned up all the first names

Using the SUBSTITUTE formula, you had Excel grab the ^ symbol from each first name and replace it with nothing, which you specified by two quotation marks ("").

Lots of different software lets you get rid of crummy characters by replacing those characters with nothing.

Here are your corrected first names.

Here's your original first name data.

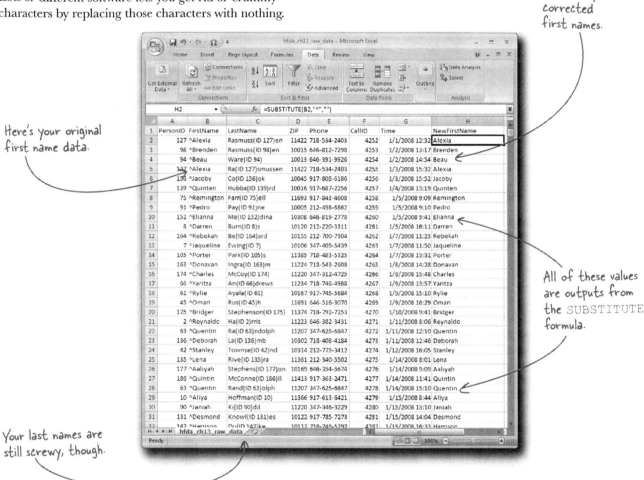

Your last names are still screwy, though.

All of these values are outputs from the SUBSTITUTE formula.

To make the original first name data go away forever copy the H column and then Paste Special > Values to turn these values into actual text rather than formula outputs. After that you can **delete** the FirstName column so that you never have to see those pesky ^ symbols again.

You can delete away... as long as you saved a copy of the original file so you can refer back to it if you made a mistake.

> Hmpf. That first name pattern was easy because it was just a single character at the beginning that had to be removed. But the last name is going to be harder, because it's a tougher pattern.

Exercise

Let's try using SUBSTITUTE again, this time to fix the last names.

C
LastName
Rasmuss(ID 127)en
Rasmuss(ID 98)en
Ware(ID 94)
Ra(ID 127)smussen
Co(ID 156)ok
Hubba(ID 139)rd
Farr(ID 75)ell
Pay(ID 91)ne
Me(ID 152)dina
Burn(ID 8)s
Be(ID 164)ard
Ewing(ID 7)
Park(ID 105)s
Ingra(ID 163)m

First, look for the pattern in this messiness. What would you tell SUBSTITUTE to replace? Here's the syntax again:

```
=SUBSTITUTE(your reference cell,
  the text you want to replace,
  what you want to replace it with)
```

Can you write a formula that works?

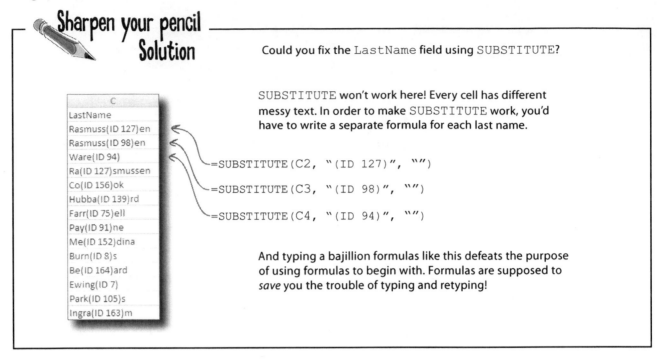

Sharpen your pencil Solution

Could you fix the LastName field using SUBSTITUTE?

SUBSTITUTE won't work here! Every cell has different messy text. In order to make SUBSTITUTE work, you'd have to write a separate formula for each last name.

=SUBSTITUTE(C2, "(ID 127)", "")

=SUBSTITUTE(C3, "(ID 98)", "")

=SUBSTITUTE(C4, "(ID 94)", "")

And typing a bajillion formulas like this defeats the purpose of using formulas to begin with. Formulas are supposed to *save* you the trouble of typing and retyping!

Column C — LastName

LastName
Rasmuss(ID 127)en
Rasmuss(ID 98)en
Ware(ID 94)
Ra(ID 127)smussen
Co(ID 156)ok
Hubba(ID 139)rd
Farr(ID 75)ell
Pay(ID 91)ne
Me(ID 152)dina
Burn(ID 8)s
Be(ID 164)ard
Ewing(ID 7)
Park(ID 105)s
Ingra(ID 163)m

The last name pattern is too complex for SUBSTITUTE

The SUBSTITUTE function looks for a pattern in the form of a single text string to replace. The problem with the last names are that **each has a different text string** to replace.

These text strings are different.

Rasmuss(ID 98)en

Co(ID 156)ok

You can't just type in the value you want replaced, because that value changes from cell to cell.

And that's not all: the pattern of messiness in the LastName field is more complex in that the messy strings show up in **different positions** within each cell and they have **different lengths**.

The messiness here starts on the eighth character of the cell...

...and here it starts on the third character!

Rasmuss(ID 98)en

Co(ID 156)ok

The length of this text is seven characters.

This one is eight characters long.

Handle complex patterns with nested text formulas

Once you get familiar with Excel text formulas, you can **nest** them inside of each other to do complex operations on your messy data. Here's an example:

```
FIND("(",C3)

    LEFT(C3,FIND("(",C3)-1)

    RIGHT(C3,LEN(C3)-FIND(")",C3))

        CONCATENATE(LEFT(C3,FIND("(",C3)-1),
        RIGHT(C3,LEN(C3)-FIND(")",C3)))
```

The FIND formula returns a number that represents the position of the "(".

LEFT grabs the leftmost text

Rasmuss(ID 98)en

Rasmuss(ID 98)en

RIGHT grabs the rightmost text.

Rasmuss(ID 98)**en**

Rasmussen

CONCATENATE puts it all together.

The formula *works*, but there's a **problem**: it's starting to get really hard to read. That's not a problem if you write formulas perfectly the first time, but you'd be better off with a tool that has power *and* simplicity, unlike this nested CONCATENATE formula.

> Wouldn't it be dreamy if there were an easier way to fix complex messes than with long, unreadable formulas like that one. But I know it's just a fantasy...

R can use regular expressions to crunch complex data patterns

Regular expressions are a programming tool that allows you to specify complex patterns to match and replace strings of text, and R has a powerful facility for using them.

Here's a simple regular expression **pattern** that looks for the letter "a". When you give this pattern to R, it'll say whether there's a match.

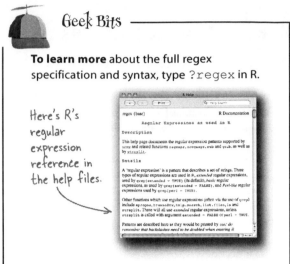

Geek Bits

To learn more about the full regex specification and syntax, type `?regex` in R.

Here's R's regular expression reference in the help files.

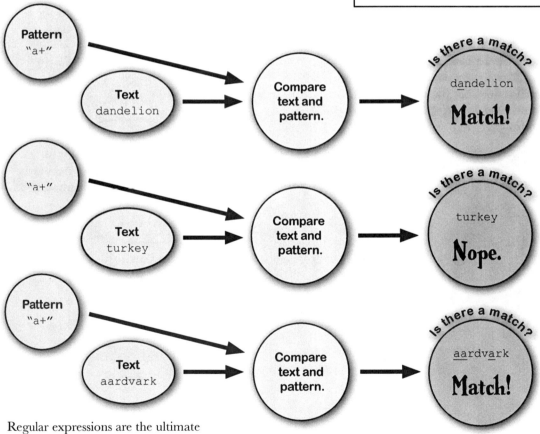

Regular expressions are the ultimate tool for cleaning up messy data. Lots of platforms and languages implement regular expressions, even though Excel doesn't.

From: Head First Head Hunters
To: Analyst
Subject: Need those names NOW

Well get on with it! Those prospects are hot and are only getting colder. I want our sales force to start calling people like yesterday!

Better get moving! Here goes:

Do this!

1 Load your data into R and take a look at what you've got with the head command. You can either save your Excel file as a CSV and load the CSV file into R, or you can use the web link below to get the most recent data.

This command reads the CSV into a table called hfhh.

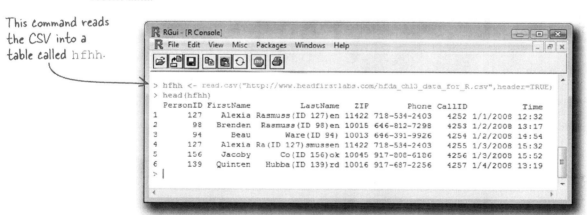

```
> hfhh <- read.csv("http://www.headfirstlabs.com/hfda_ch13_data_for_R.csv",header=TRUE)
> head(hfhh)
  PersonID FirstName          LastName  ZIP        Phone CallID           Time
1      127    Alexia Rasmuss(ID 127)en 11422 718-534-2403   4252 1/1/2008 12:32
2       98   Brenden   Rasmuss(ID 98)en 10015 646-812-7298   4253 1/2/2008 13:17
3       94      Beau        Ware(ID 94) 10013 646-391-9926   4254 1/2/2008 14:54
4      127    Alexia Ra(ID 127)smussen 11422 718-534-2403   4255 1/3/2008 15:32
5      156    Jacoby        Co(ID 156)ok 10045 917-808-6186   4256 1/3/2008 15:52
6      139   Quinten   Hubba(ID 139)rd 10016 917-687-2256   4257 1/4/2008 13:19
> |
```

2 Run this regular expressions command

```
NewLastName <- sub("\\(.*\\)","",hfhh$LastName)
```

3 Then take a look at your work by running the head command to see the first few rows of your table.

```
head(NewLastName)
```

What happens?

The sub command fixed your last names

The sub command used the **pattern** you specified and replaced all instances of it with blank text, effectively deleting every parenthetical text string in the LastName column.

```
> NewLastName <- sub("\\(.*\\)","",hfhh$LastName)
> head(NewLastName)
[1] "Rasmussen" "Rasmussen" "Ware"      "Rasmussen" "Cook"      "Hubbard"
>
```

Let's take a closer look at that syntax:

Here's a new vector for your cleaned last names.

Here's your regular expression pattern.

This is blank text, which replaces text that matches the pattern with nothing.

```
NewLastName <- sub("\\(.*\\)","",hfhh$LastName)
```

If you can find a pattern in the messiness of your data, you can write a regular expression that will neatly exploit it to get you the structure you want.

No need to write some insanely long spreadsheet formula!

Your Regular Expression Up Close

Your regular expression has three parts: the left parenthesis, the right parenthesis, and everything in between.

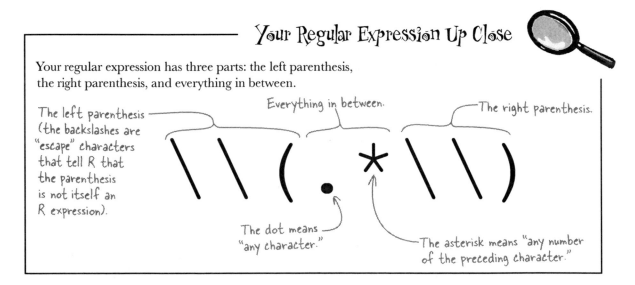

The left parenthesis (the backslashes are "escape" characters that tell R that the parenthesis is not itself an R expression).

Everything in between.

The right parenthesis.

The dot means "any character."

The asterisk means "any number of the preceding character."

Q: Some of those regular expression commands look really hard to read. How hard is it to master regular expressions?

A: They can be hard to read because they're really concise. That economy of syntax can be a real benefit when you have crazy-complex patterns to decode. Regular expressions are easy to get the hang of but (like anything complex) hard to master. Just take your time when you read them, and you'll get the hang of them.

Q: What if data doesn't even come in a spreadsheet? I might have to extract data from a PDF, a web page, or even XML.

A: Those are the sorts of situations where regular expressions really shine. As long as you can get your information into some sort of text file, you can parse it with regular expressions. Web pages in particular are a really common source of information for data analysis, and it's a snap to program HTML tag patterns into your regex statements.

Q: What other specific platforms use regular expressions?

A: Java, Perl, Python, JavaScript... all sorts of different programming languages use them.

Q: If regular expressions are so common in programming languages, why can't Excel do regular expressions?

A: On the Windows platform, you can use Microsoft's Visual Basic for Applications (VBA) programming language inside of Excel to run regular expressions. But most people would sooner just use a more powerful program like R than take the trouble to learn to program Excel. Oh, and since VBA was dropped from the recent release of Excel for Mac, you can't use regex in Excel for Mac, regardless of how badly you might want to.

Now you can ship the data to your client

Better write your new work to a CSV file for your client.

Do this!

Remove old `LastName` vector from the `hfhh` data frame.

Add the new `LastName` vector to `hfhh`.

```
> hfhh$LastName <- NULL
> hfhh["LastName"] <- NewLastName
> write.csv(hfhh, file="hfhh.csv")
> |
```

Write the results to a CSV file.

This file will be found in your R working directory, which R will tell you about with the `getwd()` command.

Regardless of whether your client is using Excel, OpenOffice, or any statistical software package, he'll be able to read CSV files.

hfhh.csv

Maybe you're not quite done yet...

I can't use this! Look at all the duplicate entries!

The client has a bit of a problem with your work.

He's got a point. Take "Alexia Rasmussen," for example. Alexia definitely shows up more than once. It could be that there are two separate people named Alexia Rasmussen, of course. But then again, both records here have `PersonID` equal to 127, which would suggest that they are the same person.

Maybe Alexia is **the only duplicate name** and the client is just reacting to that one mistake. To find out, you'll need to figure out how you can *see* duplicates more easily than just looking at this huge list as it is.

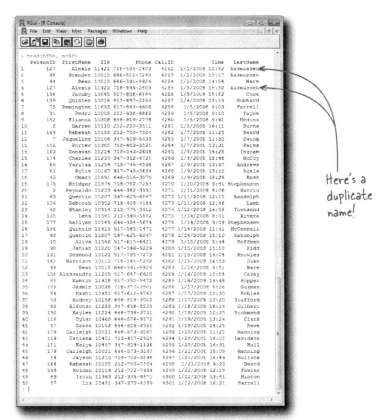

Here's a duplicate name!

Sort your data to show duplicate values together

If you have a lot of data, it can be hard to
see whether values repeat. It's a lot easier
to see that repetition if the lists are sorted.

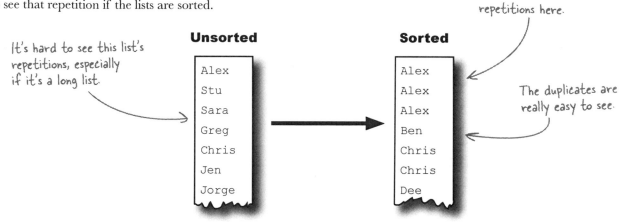

It's hard to see this list's
repetitions, especially
if it's a long list.

Unsorted

```
Alex
Stu
Sara
Greg
Chris
Jen
Jorge
```

Sorted

```
Alex
Alex
Alex
Ben
Chris
Chris
Dee
```

Lots of
repetitions here.

The duplicates are
really easy to see.

Exercise

Let's get a better look at the duplicates in your list by sorting the data.

In R, you sort a data frame by using the order function
inside of the subset brackets. Run this command:

A new, sorted
copy of your list.

```
hfhhSorted <- hfhh[order(hfhh$PersonID), ]
```

Because the PersonID field probably represents a unique number for
each person, that makes it a good field to use it to sort. After all, it's possible
that there's more than one person in the data named "John Smith."

Next, run the head command to see what you've created:

```
head(hfhhSorted, n=50)
```

What does R do?

Did sorting your data frame in R by `PersonID` reveal any duplicates?

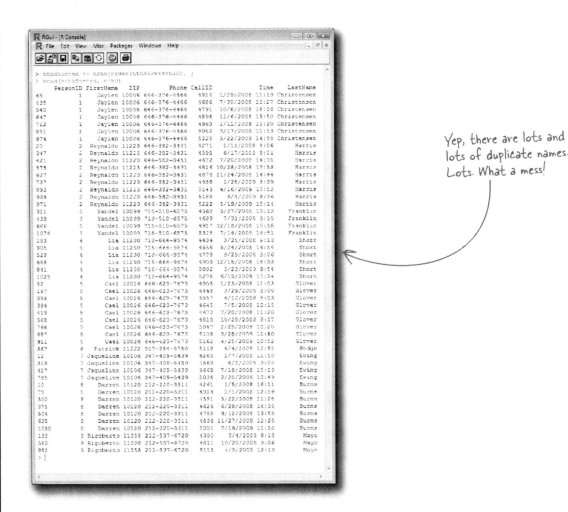

Yep, there are lots and lots of duplicate names. Lots. What a mess!

When you get messy data, you should **sort liberally**. Especially if you have a lot of records. That's because it's often hard to see all the data at once, and sorting the data by different fields lets you visualize groupings in a way that will help you find duplicates or other weirdness.

There's something fishy here. Why would our competitor store duplicate data? Is this some sort of joke?

Sharpen your pencil

Take a close look at the data. Can you say *why* the names might be duplicated?

Write your answer here.

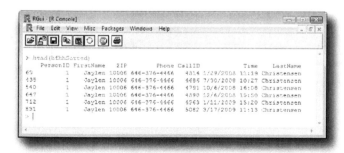

....

....

....

....

....

....

Sharpen your pencil
Solution

Why do you think the same names show up repeatedly?

If you look at the far right column, you can see that there is a data point unique to each record: a time stamp of a phone call. That probably means that each of the lines in this database represents a phone call, so the names repeat because there are multiple calls to the same people.

The data is probably from a relational database

If elements of your messy list repeat, then the data probably come from a relational database. In this case, your data is the output of a query that consolidated two tables.

Because you understand RDBMS architecture, you know that repetition like what we see here stems from **how queries return data** rather than from **poor data quality**. So you can now remove duplicate names without worrying that something's fundamentally wrong with your data.

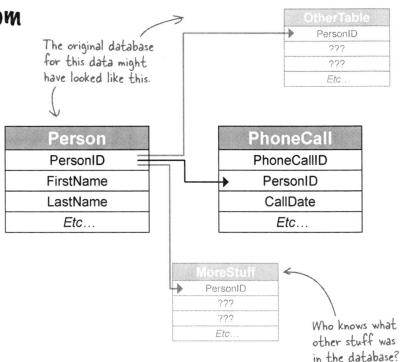

The original database for this data might have looked like this.

OtherTable
| PersonID |
| ??? |
| ??? |
| *Etc...* |

Person
| PersonID |
| FirstName |
| LastName |
| *Etc...* |

PhoneCall
| PhoneCallID |
| PersonID |
| CallDate |
| *Etc...* |

MoreStuff
| PersonID |
| ??? |
| ??? |
| *Etc...* |

Who knows what other stuff was in the database?

Remove duplicate names

Now that you know *why* there are duplicate names, you can start **removing** them. Both R and Excel have quick and straightforward functions for removing duplicates.

Removing duplicates in R is simple:

The `unique` function returns a vector or data frame like the one you specify, except that the duplicates are removed.

`unique(mydata)`

That's it! Be sure you assign the resulting value to a new name so that you can use the data `unique` returns.

In R, the `unique` function is what you need.

To remove duplicates in Excel, use this button.

Removing duplicates in Excel is a snap:

Make sure your cursor is placed in your data and click this button:

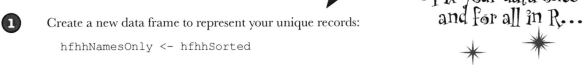

Excel will ask you to specify which columns contain the duplicate values, and data from other columns that isn't duplicated will be deleted.

So now that you have the tool you need to get rid of those pesky duplicate names, let's clean up your list and give it back to the client.

Fix your data once and for all in R...

1 Create a new data frame to represent your unique records:

```
hfhhNamesOnly <- hfhhSorted
```

2 Remove the `CallID` and `Time` fields, which the client doesn't need and which are the cause of your duplicate names:

```
hfhhNamesOnly$CallID <- NULL
hfhhNamesOnly$Time <- NULL
```

Here's `unique` in action!

3 Use the `unique` function to remove duplicate names:

```
hfhhNamesOnly <- unique(hfhhNamesOnly)
```

4 Take a look at your results and write them to a new CSV:

```
head(hfhhNamesOnly, n=50)
write.csv(hfhhNamesOnly, file="hfhhNamesOnly.csv")
```

You created nice, clean, unique records

This data looks totally solid.

No columns mashed together, no funny characters, no duplicates. All from following the basic steps of cleaning a messy data set:

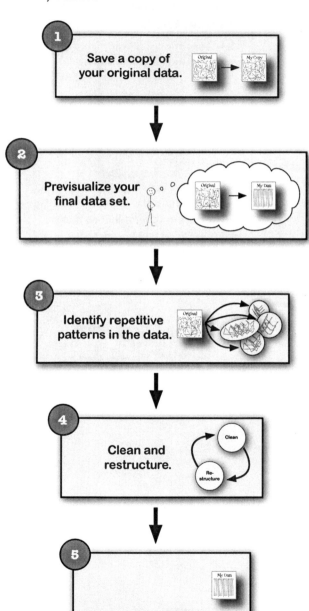

1 Save a copy of your original data.

2 Previsualize your final data set.

3 Identify repetitive patterns in the data.

4 Clean and restructure.

5

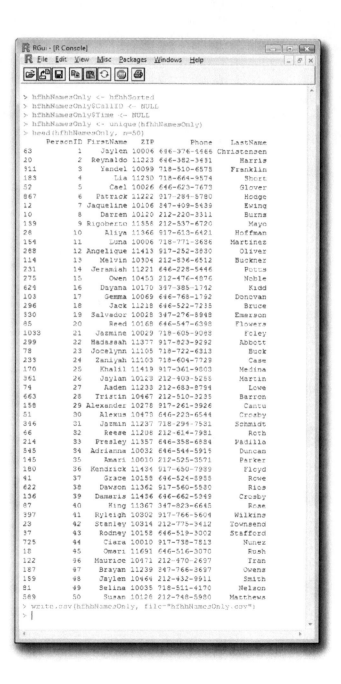

```
R RGui - [R Console]
R File  Edit  View  Misc  Packages  Windows  Help

> hfhhNamesOnly <- hfhhSorted
> hfhhNamesOnly$CallID <- NULL
> hfhhNamesOnly$Time <- NULL
> hfhhNamesOnly <- unique(hfhhNamesOnly)
> head(hfhhNamesOnly, n=50)
     PersonID FirstName   ZIP      Phone      LastName
63          1    Jaylen 10006 646-376-4466 Christensen
20          2  Reynaldo 11223 646-382-3431      Harris
911         3    Yandel 10099 718-510-6575    Franklin
183         4       Lia 11230 718-664-9574       Short
52          5      Cael 10026 646-623-7673      Glover
867         6   Patrick 11222 917-284-5780       Hodge
12          7 Jaqueline 10106 347-409-5439       Ewing
10          8    Darren 10120 212-220-3311       Burns
139         9 Rigoberto 11358 212-537-6720        Mayo
28         10     Aliya 11366 917-613-6421     Hoffman
164        11      Luna 10006 718-771-3686    Martinez
288        12 Angelique 11413 917-252-3830      Oliver
114        13    Melvin 10304 212-836-6512     Buckner
231        14  Jeramiah 11221 646-228-5446       Potts
275        15      Owen 10453 212-476-4876       Noble
624        16    Dayana 10170 347-385-1742        Kidd
103        17     Gemma 10069 646-768-1792     Donovan
296        18      Jack 11218 646-522-7235       Bruce
930        19  Salvador 10028 347-276-8948     Emerson
85         20      Reed 10168 646-547-6398     Flowers
1033       21   Jazmine 10029 718-605-9088       Foley
299        22  Hadassah 11377 917-823-9292      Abbott
78         23  Jocelynn 11105 718-722-6313        Buck
233        24   Zaniyah 11103 718-604-7729        Case
170        25    Khalil 11419 917-361-9803      Medina
361        26    Jaylan 10123 212-403-5255      Martin
74         27     Aaden 11233 212-683-8794        Lowe
663        28   Tristin 10467 212-510-3235      Barron
158        29 Alexander 10278 917-261-3926       Cantu
51         30    Alexus 10473 646-223-6544      Crosby
346        31    Jazmin 11237 718-294-7531     Schmidt
66         32     Reese 11208 212-614-7981        Roth
214        33   Presley 11357 646-358-6884     Padilla
545        34  Adrianna 10032 646-544-5915      Duncan
145        35     Amari 10010 212-525-3571      Parker
180        36  Kendrick 11434 917-650-7939       Floyd
41         37     Grace 10158 646-524-5955        Rowe
622        38    Dawson 11362 917-560-5530        Rios
136        39   Damaris 11456 646-662-5349      Crosby
87         40      King 11367 347-823-6645        Rose
397        41   Ryleigh 10302 917-766-5604     Wilkins
23         42   Stanley 10314 212-775-3412    Townsend
37         43    Rodney 10158 646-519-3002    Stafford
725        44     Ciara 10010 917-738-7813       Nunez
18         45     Omari 11691 646-516-3070        Rush
122        46   Maurice 10471 212-470-2697        Tran
187        47    Brayan 11239 347-766-3697       Owens
159        48    Jaylen 10464 212-432-9911       Smith
81         49    Selina 10035 718-511-4170      Nelson
589        50     Susan 10128 212-748-5980    Matthews
> write.csv(hfhhNamesOnly, file="hfhhNamesOnly.csv")
> |
```

Head First Head Hunters is recruiting like gangbusters!

Your list has proven to be incredibly powerful. With a clean data set of live prospects, HFHH is picking up more clients than ever, and they'd never have been able to do it without your data cleaning skills. Nice work!

This is great! We've got more new clients than ever!

Leaving town...

It's been great having you here in Dataville!

We're sad to see you leave, but there's nothing like taking what you've learned and putting it to use. You're just beginning your data analysis journey, and we've put you in the driver's seat. We're dying to hear how things go, so ***drop us a line*** at the Head First Labs website, ***www.headfirstlabs.com***, and let us know how data analysis is paying off for **YOU!**

appendix i: leftovers

The Top Ten Things (we didn't cover)

You're not finished yet, are you? But there is so much left!

You've come a long way.

But data analysis is a vast and constantly evolving field, and there's so much left to learn. In this appendix, we'll go over ten items that there wasn't enough room to cover in this book but should be high on your list of topics to learn about next.

#1: Everything else in statistics

Statistics is a field that has a **huge array of tools and technologies** for data analysis. It's so important for data analysis, in fact, that many books about "data analysis" are really statistics books.

Here is an incomplete list of the tools of statistics not covered in *Head First Data Analysis*.

It's a great idea to learn about all of these topics if you're a data analyst.

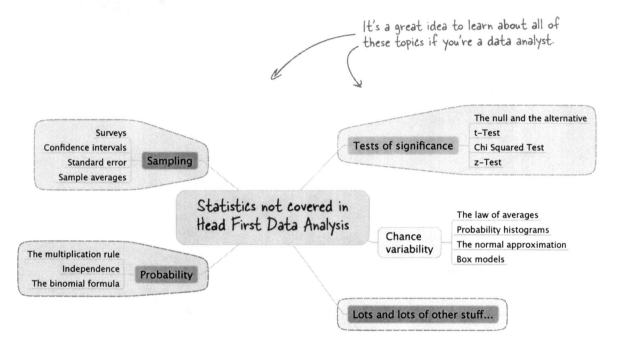

Much of what you *have* learned in this book, however, has raised your awareness of deep issues involving assumptions and model-building, preparing you not only to use the tools of statistics but also to understand their **limitations**.

The better you know statistics, the more likely you are to do great analytical work.

#2: Excel skills

This book has assumed that you have basic spreadsheet skills, but skilled data analysts tend to be spreadsheet *ninjas*.

Compared to programs like R and subjects like regression, it's not terribly hard to master Excel. And you should!

A	B	C	D	E	F	G	H	I	J	K	L	M	N	O	
Analyst	1	2	3	4	5	6	7	8	9	10	11	12	13	14	15	16
Statement1	87%	88%	89%	91%	91%	92%	87%	92%	88%	92%	88%	89%	92%	88%	89%	90%
Statement2	68%	40%	47%	88%	37%	60%	47%	46%	59%	23%	34%	78%	70%	80%	54%	67%
Statement3	37%	11%	67%	7%	8%	30%	66%	41%	83%	9%	0%	46%	45%	35%	15%	63%
Statement4	39%	56%	33%	38%	19%	19%	27%	33%	14%	30%	58%	28%	33%	35%	16%	19%
Statement5	5%	28%	0%	24%	0%	18%	5%	3%	12%	9%	2%	5%	1%	13%	5%	3%
Statement6	77%	81%	85%	78%	72%	84%	88%	69%	74%	91%	92%	70%	3%	81%	87%	70%

hfda_ch07_data.csv

The best data analysts can do spreadsheets in their sleep.

#3: Edward Tufte and his principles of visualization

Good data analysts spend a lot of time reading and rereading the work of great data analysts, and Edward Tufte is unique not only in the quality of his own work but in the quality of the work of other analysts that he collects and displays in his books. **Here are his fundamental principles of analytical design**:

"Show comparisons, contrasts, differences."

"Show causality, mechanism, explanations, systematic structure."

"Show multivariate data; that is, show more than 1 or 2 variables."

"Completely integrate words, numbers, images, diagrams."

"Thoroughly describe the evidence."

"Analytical presentations ultimately stand or fall depending on the quality, relevance, and integrity of their content."

—Edward Tufte

These words of wisdom, along with much else, are from pages 127, 128, 130, 131, 133, and 136 of his book *Beautiful Evidence*. His books are a gallery of the very best in the visualization of data.

What's more, his book *Data Analysis for Public Policy* is about as good a book on regression as you'll ever find, and you can download it for free at this website: *http://www.edwardtufte.com/tufte/dapp/*.

#4: PivotTables

Pivot tables are one of the more powerful data analysis tools built into spreadsheets and statistical software. They're fantastic for **exploratory data analysis** and for summarizing data extracted from **relational databases**.

From this raw data, you can create a bunch of different pivot table summaries.

Here are two really simple pivot tables.

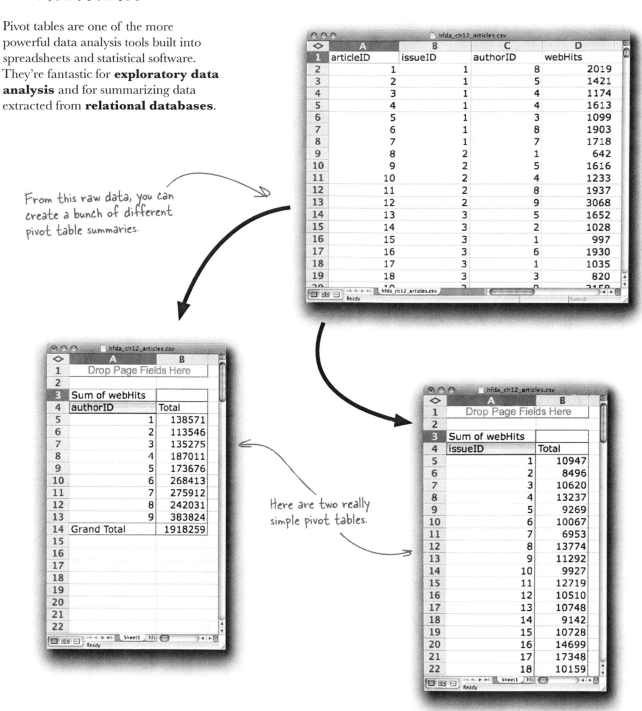

#5: The R community

R isn't just a great software program, it's a
great software **platform**. Much of its power
comes from a global community of users and
contributors who contribute free **packages** with
functions you can use for your analytic domain.

You got a taste of this community when you ran
the xyplot function from the **lattice**, a
legendary package for data visualization.

Your installation of R can have
any combination of packages
that suits your needs.

Economists

The R Team

Designers

Contributed
Package

Contributed
Package

Contributed
Package

R Core
Package

Biologists

Contributed
Package

Contributed
Package

Your installation of R

Finance people

Statisticians

#6: Nonlinear and multiple regression

Even if your data do not exhibit a linear pattern, under some circumstances, you can make predictions using regression. One approach would be to apply a numerical **transformation** on the data that effectively makes it linear, and another way would be to draw a **polynomial rather** than linear regression line through the dots.

Also, you don't have to limit yourself to predicting a dependent variable from a single independent variable. Sometimes there are **multiple** factors that affect the variable, so in order to make a good prediction, you can use the technique of **multiple regression**.

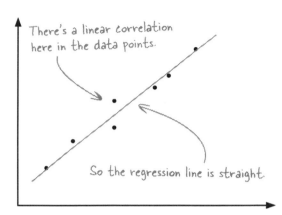

There's a linear correlation here in the data points.

So the regression line is straight.

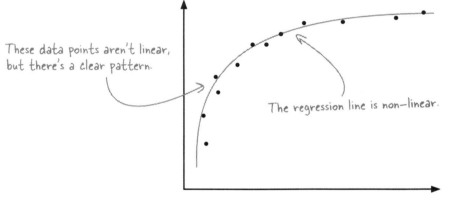

These data points aren't linear, but there's a clear pattern.

The regression line is non-linear.

y = a + bx

You use this equation to predict a dependent variable from a single independent variable.

But you can also write an equation that predicts a dependent variable from multiple independent variables.

y = a + bx₁ + cx₂ + dx₃ + ...

This equation is for multiple regression.

#7: Null-alternative hypothesis testing

While the hypothesis testing technique you learned in Chapter 5 is very general and can accommodate a variety of analytical problems, **null-alternative testing** is the statistical technique many (especially in academia and science) have in mind when they hear the expression "hypothesis testing."

This tool is used more often than it's understood, and *Head First Statistics* is a great place to start if you'd like to learn it.

> Given my data, what is the viability of the null hypothesis?

#8: Randomness

Randomness is a big issue for data analysis.

That's because **randomness is hard to see**. When people are trying to explain events, they do a great job at fitting models to evidence. But they do a terrible job at deciding against using explanatory models at all.

If your client asks you why a specific event happened, the honest answer based on the best analysis will often be, "the event can be explained by random variations in outcomes."

> Wanna go to the park?

> I never know what this guy has in store for me. He breaks every model I try to fit to his behavior. I wish I spoke English...

#9: Google Docs

We've talked about Excel, OpenOffice, and R, but Google
Docs definitely deserves an honorable mention. Not
only does **Google Docs** offer a fully functioning online
spreadsheet, it has a **Gadget** feature that offers a large
array of visualizations.

*You can make a lot of different visualizations
using the Gadget feature in Google Docs.*

*It's fun to explore
the different charts
that you can do
with Google Docs.*

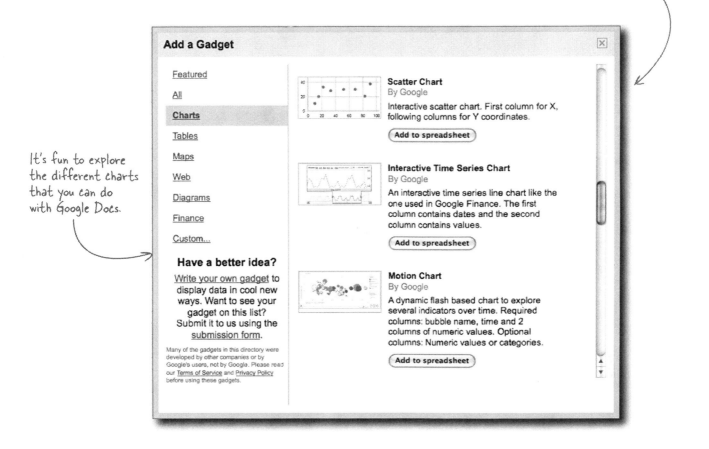

What's more, Google Docs has a variety of functions that
offer access to **real-time online data sources**. It is free
software that's definitely worth checking out.

#10: Your expertise

You've learned many tools in this book, but what's more exciting than any of them is that you will combine your expertise in **your domain of knowledge** with those tools to understand and improve the world. Good luck.

Your expertise and new analytical tools are a force to be reckoned with!

You!

appendix ii: install r

Start R up!

> Yes, I'd like to order up a world-class statistical software package that will unleash my analytic potential and, uh, no hassles with that, please.

Behind all that data-crunching power is enormous complexity.

But fortunately, getting R installed and *started* is something you can accomplish in just a few minutes, and this appendix is about to show you how to pull off your R install without a hitch.

Get started with R

Installing the powerful, free, open source statistical software R can be done in these four quick and easy steps.

1. **Head on over** to *www.r-project.org* to download R. You should have no problem finding a mirror near you that serves R for Windows, Mac, and Linux.

Click this download link.

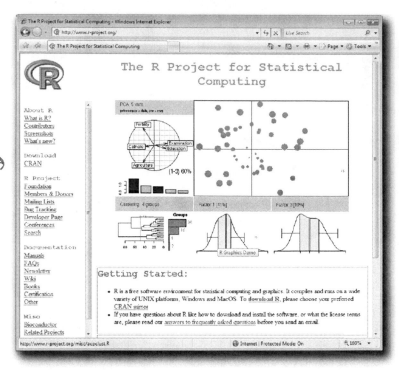

2. Once you've downloaded the program file for R, **double-click** on it to start the R installer.

Here's the R installer window.

This is the R program file.

Click here.

3 Accept all the default options for loading R by clicking **Next** through these windows, and let the installer do its work.

Just accept all the default configurations for R by clicking Next.

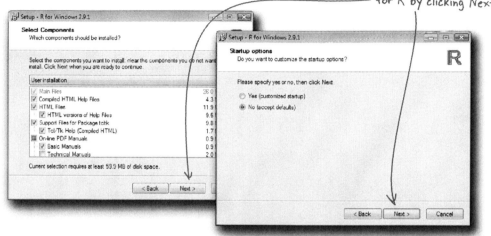

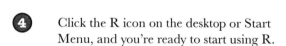

Waiting is the hardest part.

4 Click the R icon on the desktop or Start Menu, and you're ready to start using R.

Here's what the R window looks like when you start it for the first time.

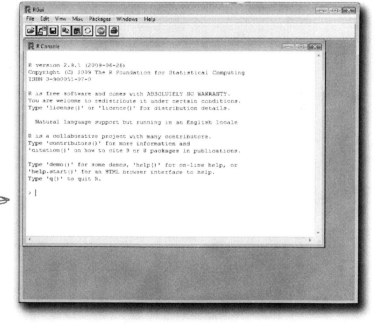

appendix iii: install excel analysis tools

The ToolPak

> I want to optimize now! I don't want to have to install some add-in...

Some of the best features of Excel aren't installed by default.

That's right, in order to run the optimization from Chapter 3 and the histograms from Chapter 9, you need to activate the **Solver** and the **Analysis ToolPak**, two extensions that are included in Excel by default but not activated without your initiative.

Install the data analysis tools in Excel

Installing the Analysis ToolPak and Solver in Excel is no problem if you follow these simple steps.

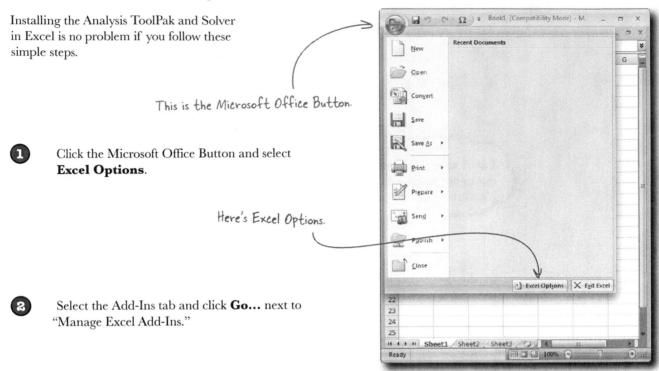

This is the Microsoft Office Button.

1 Click the Microsoft Office Button and select **Excel Options**.

Here's Excel Options.

2 Select the Add-Ins tab and click **Go...** next to "Manage Excel Add-Ins."

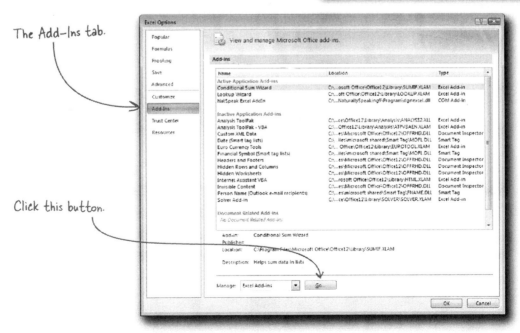

The Add-Ins tab.

Click this button.

3 Make sure that the Analysis ToolPak and the Solver Add-in boxes are checked, and then press **OK**.

Make sure that these two boxes are checked.

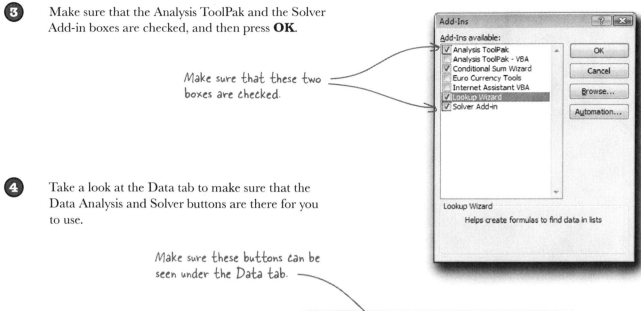

4 Take a look at the Data tab to make sure that the Data Analysis and Solver buttons are there for you to use.

Make sure these buttons can be seen under the Data tab.

That's it!

Now you're ready to start running optimizations, histograms, and much more.

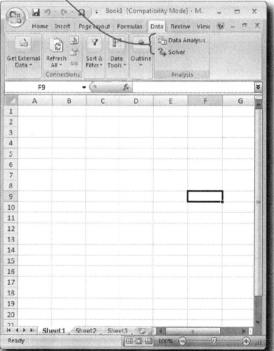

Index

Numbers

3D scatterplots, 291

Symbols

~ not (probability), 176

<- assign (R), 413

\ escape character, 406

| given (probability), 176

| output (R), 380

* regular expressions wildcard, 406

. regular expressions wildcard, 406

? topic information (R), 404

A

accuracy analysis, 172–174, 185–188, 214, 248, 300, 350

Adobe Illustrator, 129

algorithm, 284

alternative causal models, 131

analysis
  accuracy, 172–174, 185–188, 214, 248, 300, 350
  definitions of, 4, 7, 286
  exploratory data, 7, 124, 421
  process steps, 4, 35
    step 1: define, 5–8
    step 2: disassemble, 9–12, 256–258
    step 3: evaluate, 13–14
    step 4: decide, 15–17
  purpose of, 4
Analysis ToolPak (Excel), 431–433

"anti-resume," 25

arrays (lattices) of scatterplots, 126, 291, 379–381

association
  vs. causation, 291
  linear, 291–302

assumptions
  based on changing reality, 109
  baseline set of, 11, 14
  cataloguing, 99
  evaluating and calibrating, 98–100
  and extrapolation, 321–324
  impact of incorrect, 20–21, 34, 100, 323
  inserting your own, 14
  making them explicit, 14, 16, 27, 99, 321–324
  predictions using, 322–323
  reasonableness of, 323–324
  reassessing, 24
  regarding variable independence, 103

asterisk (*), 406

averages, types of, 297

=AVG() in Excel/OpenOffice, 121

B

backslash (\), 406

baseline expectations, 254
  (see also assumptions)

baseline (null) hypothesis, 155

base rate fallacy, 178

base rates (prior probabilities), 178–189
  Bayes' rule and, 182–189, 218
  defined, 178
  how new information affects, 185–188

R

CPSIA information can be obtained at www.ICGtesting.com
Printed in the USA
LVOW020336051211

257724LV00002B/3/P